SUPERNATURAL CALIFORNIA

A Golden State Guide to UFOs, Extraterrestrials, Ghosts, Hauntings, Cryptozoological Creatures, Psychics, Mediums, Miracles, Mystical Spots, Buried Treasures, Gravity Hills, Local Legends, Ancient Civilizations, and Other Strange Mysteries

Preston Dennett

Artwork by Kesara

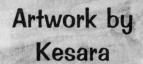

4880 Lower Valley Road, Atglen, PA 19310 USA

Photo Credits: all photographs by Preston Dennett unless otherwise credited.

Artwork by Christine Kesara Dennett.

Library of Congress Cataloging-in-Publication Data

Dennett, Preston E., 1965-
  Supernatural California : a Golden State guide to UFOs, extraterrestrials, ghosts, hauntings, cryptozoological creatures, psychics, mediums, miracles, mystical spots, buried treasures, gravity hills, local legends, ancient civilizations, and other strange mysteries / Preston Dennett ; artwork by Kesara.
     p. cm.
  ISBN 0-7643-2401-2 (pbk.)
1. Occultism—California. 2. Supernatural—California. 3. Parapsychology—California. I. Title.

BF1434.U6D46 2006
130.9794—dc22
                              2005031361

Designed by Mark David Bowyer
Type set in Impress BT / Lydian BT

ISBN: 0-7643-2401-2
Printed in China

Published by Schiffer Publishing Ltd.
4880 Lower Valley Road
Atglen, PA 19310
Phone: (610) 593-1777; Fax: (610) 593-2002
E-mail: Info@schifferbooks.com

For the largest selection of fine reference books on this and related subjects, please visit our web site at www.schifferbooks.com
We are always looking for people to write books on new and related subjects. If you have an idea for a book please contact us at the above address.

This book may be purchased from the publisher.
Include $3.95 for shipping.
Please try your bookstore first.
You may write for a free catalog.

In Europe, Schiffer books are distributed by
Bushwood Books
6 Marksbury Ave.
Kew Gardens
Surrey TW9 4JF England
Phone: 44 (0) 20 8392-8585; Fax: 44 (0) 20 8392-9876
E-mail: info@bushwoodbooks.co.uk
Free postage in the U.K., Europe; air mail at cost.

Contents

Preface

You hold in your hands a unique and comprehensive guidebook to more than 200 locations in California you can visit — all involving the supernatural, the paranormal, and the "Unknown." Many incredible and weird adventures are literally at your fingertips! If you want to see a UFO, it turns out that the Golden State is the leading producer of UFO reports in the United States. If Bigfoot is your interest, California contains the nation's largest population concentration of the mysterious hairy creature. If sea serpents or lake monsters are your preference, California again leads the nation with hundreds of reports.

And this is just the beginning of the weirdness. Gravity hills, earth lights, religious miracles, lost treasures, underground cities, ancient ruins, mystic sites, and more than 100 authentic haunted public places — all are here and all are absolutely true. Inside this book you will find:

—the top five California UFO hotspots
—a statewide history of local Bigfoot encounters
—four lakes with unknown lake monsters, and numerous coastal sea serpents
—the locations of several little known gravity hills and mystery spots
—a study of ancient stone walls and other mysterious ruins found throughout California
—rare chupacabra sightings and other cryptozoological creatures
—Virgin Mary trees and other religious miracles
—legends of lost treasures still waiting to be found
—the story of the Oriflamme Mountain and Mount San Gorgonio earth lights
—haunted hotels, parks, museums, theaters, businesses, roadways, and more
—and numerous other uniquely Californian people, places, mysteries, and legends.

This unusual volume is more than just a guidebook to the weirdness of California; it also tells the fascinating history behind all these locations and events, complete with new interviews from firsthand witnesses, and more than sixty illustrations and photographs. Directions and locations are provided. A fantastic journey into the heart of *Supernatural California* is waiting for you. Are you ready?

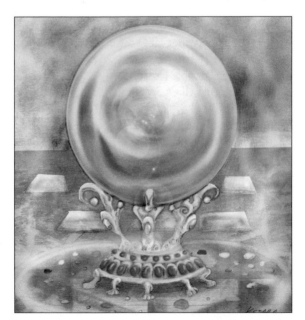

> **The world is a very strange place, and one of the strangest places in the world is undoubtedly the state of California.**

Introduction

The world is a very strange place, and one of the strangest places in the world is undoubtedly the state of California. An incredibly large number and wide variety of supernatural events occur here. If you want to see a UFO, it turns out that California is the leading producer of reports in the United States. If Bigfoot is your interest, California contains one of the highest population concentrations of the hairy creature, with cases coming from every corner of the state. And this is just the beginning of the weirdness.

For some unknown reason, California is a powerful magnet for the strange and unusual. It has *always* been a leading influence in the New Age movement, attracting all kinds of psychics, healers, and people with "alternative" professions. This was true even back in the 1930s and 1940s.

In 1931, author and researcher Wishar Cerve pioneered some of the first investigations into California mysteries, in particular into the Mount Shasta area. Writes Cerve, "I am aware of the fact that no Chamber of Commerce in any of the very progressive cities of California would think of writing a book about the local allurements of each community by giving any emphasis to the weird sights, strange sounds or peculiar mysteries within its own borders…But to the lover of mystery, the student of the sciences, the research worker, the thinker, and those intellectually inclined, the mysteries of California are not only appealing but never completely solved and never forgotten." (Cerve, 250-252)

Cerve was apparently gifted with prophecy. A little more than ten years later, in 1944, Section 43.30 of the Los Angeles Municipal Code was passed in order to control what city officials believed was a dangerous situation — fortune telling.

Reads Section 43.30: FORTUNE TELLING: No person shall advertise by sign, circular, handbill, or in any newspaper, periodical or magazine, or other publication or publications, or by any other means, to tell fortunes, to find or restore lost or stolen property, to locate oil wells, gold or silver or other ore or metal or natural product, to restore lost love or friendship or affection, to unite or procure lovers, for or without pay, by means of occult or psychic powers, faculties or forces, clairvoyance, psychology, psychometry, spirits, mediumship, seership, prophecy, astrology, palmistry, necromancy, or other craft, science, cards, talismen, charms, potions, magnetism or magnetized articles or substances, Oriental mysteries or magic of any kind or nature, or numerology, or to engage in or carry on any business the advertisement of which is prohibited by this section." (Hearn, 151-152)

Despite the code (which no longer stands), the New Age Movement took hold, and California became The Place to have virtually any type of psychic experience. Researcher David St. Clair writes, "California [is] America's most psychic, occult and mystic state…the strangest state in the nation. No one disputes it. The forces of good and evil are at work in California. This is nothing new. The occult has been a way of life there since time immemorial." (St. Clair, 1)

Another prominent investigator into California mysteries is author, Mike Marinacci. Like other researchers, Marinacci became fascinated by the powerful effect California had on the population, particularly in its early history. Writes Marinacci, "As American civilization settled over the Golden State near the end of the nineteenth century, a new kind of dreamer began to migrate West. These were not pioneers out to tame the land for mining and farming, but visionaries seeking freedom and enlightenment. Victimized by uptight, Victorian mainstream America, they saw California as a new wide-open world. If they wanted to eat only vegetables, walk around nude, meditate or communicate with Enlightened Masters or Space Brothers, there was plenty of beautiful open land for doing so. And in a state already filled with mavericks and individualists, they would fit right in…Hundreds of new religions, sects, cults, and ashrams sprung up in California, either imported or grown out of the fertile environment of social eccentricity and tolerance…Countless freelove, communalistic, and renegade Christian sects have also lived and died here, from the mid-1850s all the way up the approaching Millennium." (Marinacci, 10-11)

For whatever reason, no other state in the union has this reputation for pushing the edge of reality. California remains a stronghold for the strange and unusual. So whether you want to hunt for ghosts, explore ruins of ancient civilizations, search for cryptozoological creatures, or try to call down an extraterrestrial spacecraft, California is definitely the place to be.

Looking for the Strange?
It's Found in California!

Your choices are incredibly wide and varied. How about visiting the oldest living creature on Earth? How about a mind-bending climb up Confusion Hill or a mystifying trip to Santa Cruz's Mystery Spot? How about searching for one of many mysterious lake monsters lurking in the depths of Lake Elsinore, Lake Tahoe or several other lakes? Not surprisingly, California has more lake monsters than any other state. Or maybe a creepy visit to a haunted hotel, museum or graveyard? Or perhaps you'd like to study the mysterious sliding rocks of Death Valley or test one of California's little-known Gravity Hills? Sites of religious miracles, chupacabra haunts, UFO hotspots, ancient civilizations, lost treasures, local legends, and a comprehensive list of authenticated public California hauntings — they're all here and they're all absolutely true.

These are just a few of the more than 200 weird and unusual places in this book that you can visit – places you won't find in ordinary guidebooks. If it's strange, odd, weird, unexplained, unknown, paranormal, supernatural, mysterious…it can be found in California. More than just a guidebook, the incredible and bizarre histories behind all these mysterious sites and local legends are also revealed. Even more exciting, exact locations and detailed directions are given on how to get there. Beyond that, it is up to you!

Venture into Weirdness

My own introduction into the weirdness of California began in 1971, shortly after I moved here as a child with my family. By chance, we moved into a little community outside Los Angeles known as Topanga Canyon. Located in the Santa Monica Mountains along the coast west of Los Angeles, we soon realized that Topanga had a reputation for being a little off the beaten path. It was the site for one of California's first nudist colonies. It contained a number of different spiritual groups. It attracted all kinds of alternative lifestyles from hippies and musicians to New Age-crystal types. It also had a reputation for being haunted by ghosts and visited by UFOs.

As kids, we spent hours exploring the caves that used to be inhabited by the Chumash and Gabrielano Native Americans. Numerous artifacts have been recovered from the vicinity, which was used as a meeting ground for various tribes and considered sacred.

One of my favorite spots was Eagle Rock, a large spur of sandstone bedrock jutting out of the mountainside in Topanga State Park. It contains numerous caves and a sheer cliff dropping more than 150 feet straight down. One interesting cave we called the "Ohm Cave." If you sit in the back of the cave and chant "ohm", the sound echoes around you in a way that overwhelms all other sounds. It was one of the many strange, little-known local spots I would eventually explore.

In 1984, following the death of my mother, I saw her ghost. Having been alerted to the fact that ghosts might be real, I began to ask around and learned that several locations in Topanga Canyon were actually haunted. I also learned that sometime in the 1700s-1800s, Spanish pirates supposedly came into the nearby mountains and buried caches of treasure. Then I began to get reports of UFO encounters. My interest in UFOs and the paranormal grew. I soon became a field investigator for the Mutual UFO Network (MUFON.) I eventually interviewed hundreds of witnesses of all kinds of paranormal events, from ghost, UFO, and Bigfoot encounters to near-death experiences, religious miracles, premonitions, levitation…anything and everything weird or supernatural. I began speaking at conventions, writing articles and books, and appearing on radio and television. This entailed more travels across California, where I got to see more strange and mystical sites.

Before long I had a network of contacts, and people began to come to me with their stories. Today, after more than twenty years of investigation, I have uncovered supernatural events and mystical sites from virtually every corner of California. I have not only read about these places and talked to firsthand witnesses, I have visited many of the locations myself. To my utter amazement, I have been able to make contact with UFOs. I've talked to psychics and mediums who have given me amazing and accurate predictions. I've walked through haunted places and felt the ghosts. I've wandered through possible ancient ruins, explored sites of lost treasures, and walked among Death Valley's mysterious sliding stones. I've driven on the gravity hills to see for myself if they are real. I even had my very own Bigfoot encounter! It has been an exciting adventure that shows no signs of ending.

There is much more weirdness in the Golden State than most people would ever believe. And as strange as all these places and events are, again they are all absolutely true and just waiting to be explored.

The world is a much stranger place than most people can imagine. Mystic sites like the Great Pyramids of Egypt, Stonehenge, Easter Island, and others have fascinated humans for centuries. While these are among the most famous of the world's mystic spots, many other lesser-known spots exist. True to its nature, California has numerous mystic locations – places where magic and mystery reign supreme over logic and science.

Below are more than twenty California locations which have baffled people for generations. Maybe you can figure out the mystery!

1. The Santa Cruz Mystery Spot

Gravity is one of the least understood forces in our universe. Scientists have yet to discover the exact mechanics behind the phenomenon. This becomes even clearer when one begins to count the number of so-called "mystery spots," places where the normal rules of gravity and physics don't seem to apply. There are literally hundreds of such spots across the United States. However, California, not surprisingly, is near the top of the list with at least two well-known spots and several other lesser-known areas.

By far, the most famous California mystery spot is known appropriately as ... "The Mystery Spot." For some unknown reason, this 150-foot diameter section of Redwood forest appears to defy or distort the laws of

physics. Receiving upwards of 100,000 visitors a year, nobody has been able to fully explain the bizarre influence the Mystery Spot has on its surrounding environment. The area reportedly deflects a compass needle. Trees grow at strange angles. Visitors regularly become dizzy and disoriented as soon as they enter the spot. Some feel a strange force. Others shake their heads skeptically and say its all an optical illusion.

The mysterious properties of this location weren't discovered until the 1930s. As the story goes, the owner of the land was surveying the hillside when he felt a strange force dragging him downwards. He sold the property to Mr. and Mrs. Prather in 1939. It was opened to the public one year later in 1940. The area now attracts up to a thousand people a day in the summer months.

The Santa Cruz Mystery Spot. Does this location defy the laws of physics?

Mr. Prather reveals how he discovered the unusual influences of his property. As he says, "Originally, we wanted to get the level ground below here for a summer house or mountain cabin, but the gentleman we were buying it from would not sell the level ground unless we purchased a strip across the entire south end of his property, including this hillside." (www.mysteryspot.com)

The Prathers were reluctant to purchase the extra piece of land because it obviously had problems. Says Prather, "Finally, we bought the entire piece, mainly to get the level ground." Little did they know what they were in for.

As soon as they started surveying the land, the Prathers ran into strange problems. Says Prather, "As we were helping the surveyor along the north line, we noted the compass to vary a small amount on the transit and spoke to him about it at that time. He said we might get that variation along a barbed wire fence or some mineral in the ground and let it pass at that. On thinking it over later, there was no barbed wire fence near where we were at the time, and as far as we knew, no excessive mineral in this ground."

This began a long and involved investigation. The Prathers quickly realized a number of unusual things about their property. Says Prather, "We took our own small hand compass and went up over the north line to try and check on it. The variation there was not great enough that we could tell anything about it with the point of the hill and through the brush. On returning, we came down the little canyon or draw above here. In doing so, [we] felt very light headed or top heavy, felt like something trying to force us right off the hill. We sat down for a while to try and overcome that feeling. While sitting there we happened to look at the compass again. There the compass had varied enough that we needed nothing to compare it with to see that it was not correct."

This puzzling effect inspired the Prathers to continue their investigation. "We began to check from that, and we found the more we checked, the more we found,

until we found we had this spot of ground here. About 150 feet in diameter, that so far, we have not found any instrument absolutely correct over. A portable radio will play any place over it, but with very little variation, being the nearest correct that we have found." (www.mysteryspot.com)

The Prathers knew a good thing when they saw it. They opened up their unique piece of land as a tourist attraction.

Jeff Sens was one of the thousands of yearly visitors. Says Sens, "Lots of odd stuff strikes you as you stroll up the hill. The slope doesn't get steeper, but your legs grow heavy. Each step is harder than the one before." (Sens, 1-10)

Goofy Gravity,

Shrinking Tourists

Inside a structure on The Mystery Spot, however, is where things go from weird to bizarre. Says Sens, "Stand on a plank – it's perfectly level. Put a cue ball down and it won't roll away. Now walk the plank. Your friends will swear you're shrinking. Walk the other way, and they will insist you've grown. At other spots, try to stand up straight and you'll be leaning backward. You can't help it. Gravity is goofy here." (Sens, 1-10)

Another visitor is James Young. As he says, "You walk into a cabin that's built with a floor tilted about 30 degrees off the ground. It's weird walking inside. Notice that there is a mysterious force pulling you to one side of the cabin. I think it's called gravity."

Young wasn't completely skeptical. As he says, "There is a pendulum hanging from the roof of the lopsided cabin. Notice that it is easier to push the pendulum to one side of the cabin than to the other. I thought this one was pretty neat."

Young also tried the "level beam demonstrations." As he says, "Two people stand at opposite ends of a beam. One appears taller than the other. Then the taller-looking person walks toward the shorter person at the other end of the beam. The taller-looking person was actually shorter!!! Another level beam demo. But this time we are only a few feet from the center of the Mystery Spot so the effect is more pronounced. One person walks from one side of a concrete slab to another. His/her height appears to change!" (Young, 1-2)

Spiraling

Trees

The guide expounds on the strangeness of the mystery spot as he appears to stand at an angle, hanging out in space. The group then exits the structure where the guide then repeats the level beam demonstration outside of the mystery spot, showing that there is no change in height. Optical illusion? Perhaps...but then how do you explain the trees?

> "Lots of odd stuff strikes you as you stroll up the hill. The slope doesn't get steeper, but your legs grow heavy. Each step is harder than the one before."

Writes Young, "The guide directs your attention to the Eucalyptus tree towering above your head. Notice how the tree grows in a mysterious spiral! The guide had mentioned at the beginning of the tour how the limbs of the trees in the Mystery Spot grow in a manner akin to that of trees in zero gravity. The trees are also tilted a few degrees from vertical. Perplexing!"

Young came away, if not convinced, at least intrigued. As he writes, "The Verdict: The Mystery Spot is a great place to go for anyone interested in science and nature. To make it as interesting as possible, be sure to bring your own tape measures, levels, compasses and force meters. Also be sure to ask the guide a lot of questions. Whether you believe the Spot is 'mysterious' or not, I think it is definitely a worthwhile place to visit…There is really no other place like it on earth." (Young, 1-2)

Theories Abound!

The theories to explain the Mystery Spot range from the bizarre to the ludicrous. Some have speculated that the effects are caused by UFOs. Others say they are caused by carbon dioxide seeping from the earth, or "dielectric biocosmic radiation." Others say it is a natural defect in the gravitational/magnetic field of the earth. Travel writer Rachel Anne Goodman thought at first that it was just a "brilliant optical illusion." However, that raises the question, as she asks, "But what explains the other phenomena here, like spinning compasses and trees that lean towards the center of the Mystery Spot? Theories range from alien space ships to buried asteroids, but nobody really knows." (Goodman, 1-3) Whatever the case, the Mystery Spot continues to be a leading mysterious attraction in California.

See for Yourself

For those who want to bend their senses, the Mystery Spot is not hard to find. It is located at 465 Mystery Spot Rd, 2 1/2 miles north of Highway One in Santa Cruz. Their phone number is 831-423-8897.

Website: www.mysteryspot.com. Guided tours are available on a daily basis from 9:30 to 5:00 pm. Admission is $4.00 for adults, $2.00 for children under 12.

2. Confusion Hill

Confusion Hill. Another strange geographic spot that exhibits mysterious gravitational effects.

Wobbling Weebles

Another apparent gravity defying spot is located in the small town of Piercy, off Highway 101. If you're looking for a unique experience in a "confused gravitational field" then you absolutely must put Confusion Hill on your list of places to visit. Josh Sens writes, "Try walking up it and you wobble like a Weeble. Maybe the place was once a landing site for aliens. People have come up with all kinds of ideas."

Another visitor speculated, "Gravity appears to have gone just a little crazy. Meteorite? Metal deposits deep in the earth? Supernatural? Who knows???"

The history is revealed by the current owners, the Campbells, whose motto is, "Seeing is Believing."

Gravity House

Says Mr. Doug Campell, "My wife Carol and I along with my brother Don Campbell bought it in 1999. It's now called Campbell's Brothers Confusion Hill. It was built [a Gravity House] by George Hudson in 1949. After WW II he started a search for a spot similar to the Oregon Vortex and the Santa Cruz Mystery Spot. He was intrigued with the idea of finding his own 'special' place. He believed that there were more than just a few places in NATURE that defied its own LAWS. For centuries people have called such things as magnetism and Gravity Laws of Nature. He felt that at specific locations these two forces can combine in a way that alters our perception of the world around us. By building the Gravity House and the other exhibits, he structurally enhanced this phenomenon. No one has ever spent the money it would take to do a truly scientific study but people have come up with a variety of theories over the years."

What happens inside the structure? Says the owners, "There are height variations where you seem to shrink at one end and then grow taller at the other end! There is a small trough with water in it that sure seems to be flowing uphill. You can roll golf balls out the window and they come back to you. Have fun standing on the walls trying to get out of the Gravity Chair."

According to the Campbells, people react to Confusion Hill in different ways. "Many people feel an unexplainable force pulling them downhill. Others come back from the Gravity House complaining that it made them feel sick! Well everyone is different but once you have experienced it you won't soon forget it."

When asked straight out if the strange effects are due to complex optical illusions, the Campbells reply that visitors will have to make up their own minds. As they say, "There is no right or wrong answer on Confusion Hill." (Campbell, 1-18)

Confusing Chipalope

Incidentally, the Campbells also display the world's tallest free-standing chainsaw-carved totem pole, standing over 40 feet tall and carved from a redwood stump. And if you've ever heard of a jackalope (half jackrabbit, half antelope) you might also be interested in the photo of a Chipalope, (half chipmunk, half antelope), apparently a rare relative of the jackalope.

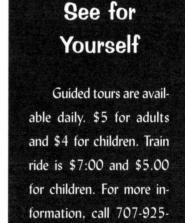

See for Yourself

Guided tours are available daily. $5 for adults and $4 for children. Train ride is $7:00 and $5.00 for children. For more information, call 707-925-6456.

Email at skibar@asis.com.

3. The Gravity Hills of California

Among the strangest of the many unexplained mysteries on our planet are a phenomenon known as *gravity hills*. Also called *magnetic hills*, *anti-gravity hills* or *spook hills*, these locations can be found across the planet.

Inclined to Roll

Gravity hills can be defined as particular areas in which the laws of gravity don't seem to apply. In virtually every case, a gravity hill involves a short section of road, usually no more than a few hundred yards long, which appears to go uphill, but does it really? A true gravity hill *appears* to go uphill, but when you park your car at the base of the apparent incline, put the transmission in neutral and remove the brake, you will find that the car rolls up the apparent hill!

There are at least four main theories to account for this strange effect. The most popular theory is a gravitational anomaly caused perhaps by unusual mineral or stone deposits beneath the hill. The second theory is that there exists a geo-magnetic anomaly, which pulls cars uphill. The third theory is that spirits or ghosts are responsible. A few of the locations are reportedly the sites of fatal automobile accidents and/or are near cemeteries. In a few cases, people report having seen handprints on the back hood of their car following the unexplained ascension up a gravity hill. A final theory is that the effects are actually caused by impressive and convincing optical illusions.

Whether they are caused by spirits, optical illusions or actual gravitational/magnetic anomalies, gravity hills are relatively rare and most are exceedingly hard to find. You won't find them on any maps and they are usually known only to the locals.

Not surprisingly, California is filled with them. As one researcher, Marina X., writes, "I never realized how many Gravity Hills there were in California alone. I wonder if it has something to do with the two plates (Pacific and North American) colliding and subducting and whatever else it is they are doing?" (www.pierceclemmer.us/marina/archives/000165.html, Nov. 8, 2003)

Despite the fact that these mysterious locations are rarely advertised, the spots are so unusual that they are becoming increasingly popular. A typical spot is the Gravity Hill of La Jolla.

The Gravity Hill of La Jolla

In 2001, local resident Greg Brown made a trip to the La Jolla hill. He had been to other gravity hills and was curious to see if the La Jolla hill was valid. To his delight, it was.

Says Greg Brown, "The first thing that makes this hill interesting is that you roll forwards up the hill, not backwards like all the other hills I've tested. It looks like a dud at first glance compared to some other hills, but your vehicle will crest the hill you are rolling 'up' then proceed on a long downhill stretch where you will eventually have to stop your vehicle."

According to Brown, the force is actually one of the stronger ones he's tested. As he says, "[It is] worth the trip if you are in the area."

Another visitor was Willie Robinson who was able to shock his friends by pretending to push his car uphill with just a finger. Says Robinson, "Yeah, Gravity Hill was always a source of amazement for those who were new to the experience. One of the best was to finger your car up the hill, that really got 'em going." (www.sniff.org/ojhsmb/messages/111&117)

Revealing Transit

Yet another visitor, Wayne Perry, writes, "Ah, yes, the gravity hill. It amazed many. After graduating, I became an apprentice carpenter and helped build those houses on the south side of Muirlands Drive. Using a transit level and sighting across the road, a person could see the drop in the roadway. I can remember my Dad and uncle talking about that spot when they used the road in 1937."

See for Yourself
Finding the Hill, Rolling On

This particular gravity hill is located on West Muirlands Drive between Nautilus Street and Fay Street, just past the last house, at the telephone poles, across from the golf course, in the city of La Jolla. Says Brown, "Once you are on West Muirlands, line up your right rear tire with the telephone pole on the side of the street with the fairway (it has three yellow stripes). Put the vehicle in neutral and roll on!" (Brown, 1)

The Gravity Hill of Sonoma

The Gravity Hill of Sonoma. Cars will reportedly roll uphill in this location. *Photo credit: Sheila Giovan.*

ever, this is a for real Gravity Hill, not an optical illusion. If you stand near the top of the road, you will find yourself looking down on top of the car. This would not be so if it were an optical illusion, unless somehow light is being bent in funny ways, in which case there is still a mystery here."

Driving Instructions

Marina gives instructions on how to proceed. "Drive down to the bottom of the trough you see in the road. If you start climbing up again, you've gone too far. What I do when I reach this point: I stop my car, but leave the engine running and the car in neutral. I keep my foot off (but near) the brake pedal. My car is facing east. At this point, it starts to roll all the way back up the hill toward the [Gracias Santiago] gate. Of course, I am careful to look in the direction in which the car is rolling, keeping a look-out for other cars, as this is a narrow road."

Another hidden gravity hill lies in the outskirts of Sonoma County, not far from Sonoma State University, along Lichau Road. Like most gravity hills, there are no signs or directions, making it difficult to locate. And again, like most gravity hills, only the locals know about it.

One person who did find it was local resident, Marina X. (Please note I have replaced last names with the initial X to protect the anonymity of the witnesses.) Writes Marina, "There are no signs to it, and no way of knowing you are there if you don't already know that

you are there. Basically, it is a road that follows around on the side of a hill, where the road dips down into a trough, then climbs back up. If you drive to the bottom of the trough in the road and put your car in neutral, the car backs rapidly up the hill. It is a bit eerie and kind of cool.

"Briefly, what happens here," Marina continues, "is that cars placed in neutral in a trough in a road back rapidly up a hill. This is not a unique phenomenon; such are reported all over the world. Some people say that all such phenomena are optical illusions. In this case, how-

Test of an Open Mind

Marina has taken other people there, some who find it very convincing, others who do not. Says Marina, "I have taken a few people there, and it has become sort of a test of a person's ability to hold an open mind and allow for something of wonder in the world. It has been revealing. Two people of whom I expected better instantly tried to explain it away 'rationally,' as though there isn't and couldn't be an as-yet-unknown rational explanation for it being a genuine effect. One friend said it must be an optical illusion, and that the trough must actually be a hill. Even when I had him get out of the car half-way up one slope, and I stood on the opposite slope, to triangulate and show that we were looking DOWN on the roof of the car, he insisted that we must just be being deceived by our eyes. There are none so blind as who will not see. I was extremely disappointed in this friend, who remains a friend and so will remain nameless." (www.pierceclemmer.us/marina/archives/000165.html, Nov. 8, 2003)

Way back in the mid-1970s, Kelly Samson, her brother, and a friend visited this Gravity Hill. Says Samson, "It was an incredible feeling as the car traveled uphill. I have not forgotten it to this day. Now that I have children, I would like to share it with them, but needless to say, I do not remember the way."

"Throw It In Neutral and Say Your Prayers"

Another visitor, local real-estate salesperson Sheila Giovan, writes, "When you cross the cattleguard, look down a sloping grade that clearly appears to run downhill. Go about 10-15 yards, stop, throw it in neutral and say your prayers as the car rolls uphill towards the cattleguard."

Yet another anonymous visitor writes, "There is some debate over whether this area of Lichau Road east of Rohnert Park is simply an optical illusion or a true anomaly in the laws of physics. Its main attraction is to those who drive their cars around the sharp bend in the road and halfway down the hill, then throw their engines into neutral and let go of the brake. Cars will roll backwards, up the hill."

Fenwick Rysen studied the hill with an engineer's compass, a level, and a pendulum. His measurements revealed that the gravity of the hill appears to be misaligned by approximately 12 degrees in the direction

14 degrees south of due west (256 degrees.) As he says, "The stretch [of road] that fools with gravity...seems to be an energy line that the road just happened to cross for that small portion." (www.sacredsonoma.com/gravity.html)

See for Yourself

To visit the Gravity Hill of Sonoma, take Highway 101 to Rohnert Park, just south of Santa Rosa. Take Petaluma Hill south to Roberts Road. Take Roberts Road east to Lichau Road. Drive east down Lichau Road for a short distance until you pass Cannon Road on your left. You are almost there. When you reach the crest of a hill where there is a cattleguard, and/or an iron gate with the ranch name Gracias Santiago, you are there. According to Marina, this is the start of the Gravity Hill section, which stretches down to the bottom of the hill. Don't go up the hill or you've gone too far. (personal files)

Gravity Hill of Kagel Canyon

Says Heather X, "My friend who had already been there said it worked really well for her and it scared her to the point of crying."

Gwen X says, "Okay, first of all I have been to numerous so called 'Gravity Hills' throughout California. I can only confirm that one of them worked...I was a non-believer until I experienced this."

The Dead Push

The effects of some of these Gravity Hills are said by some people to be caused by spirits of people who died at that location. Gwen is convinced that this is the explanation.

Kagel Canyon Expedition

I heard a lot of rumors and conflicting stories concerning the location of the Kagel Canyon Gravity Hill. However, the spot is apparently well known among locals. After asking many people, I found three firsthand witnesses who had been there. Unfortunately, it was many years earlier and all of them were teenagers at the time. Finally, I gathered what information I could and set off to find it.

The Gravity Hill of Kagel Canyon. Like several gravity hills, this one is located next to a graveyard.

With me was my friend, David Fleetwood. He remembered visiting the site as a young kid and being impressed by it. But twenty years had passed and much of the information we had was sketchy. But we knew the approximate location and that it was next to a cemetery.

As we drove up the canyon, David remarked that the area was bringing back memories. The first thing we noticed was the Sholom Memorial cemetery. David said, "This area looks familiar." One of the many conflicting directions I had gotten had mentioned this particular cemetery. That was a good sign. Still, it appeared that finding the location was going to be an uphill battle.

We drove on until we hit Lopez Canyon and turned left. We drove past the Haverhill Cemetery. This certainly seemed to be the right area, but where was the hill? We turned around and began driving back and forth, looking for it. The first few times, we drove right over it.

I noticed it first, an odd-looking dip in the road. "Stop here!" I shouted, after we had turned around a third time to look for it. "I think this might be it."

David looked around and nodded. "I think you might be right." He stopped the car at the bottom of the hill, put it in neutral and slowly took his foot off the brake. We held our breath for a second when suddenly the car lurched forward and began to move apparently up the hill! Mind you, it wasn't a big hill. But the car was definitely moving.

I thought it probably was an optical illusion. But when we reached the top, we turned around and looked down. It certainly *looked* like we were looking downhill.

We did it several times, in both directions, until we were convinced that this was the actual Gravity Hill of the San Fernando Valley.

I returned again later to take some photos and try it out with my own car. Sure enough, it worked. I can see why some people might find the experience frightening. But it was also kind of interesting. Even after visiting other gravity hills, I'm still not sure what to think about these locations. Like all things supernatural, they are best experienced firsthand.

See for Yourself

Location: Immediately south of the entrance of the Sholom Memorial Cemetery on Kagel Canyon Road. Directions: Take 210 freeway. Exit at Osbourne and head north. You will turn right onto Foothill for about a mile and turn left back onto Osbourne, which continues north. Turn left on Garrick until you reach Kagel Canyon. Turn right on Kagel Canyon and drive about five miles north. When you pass Dexter Street on your right, you are almost there. Look for the first cemetery on the left, Sholom Memorial. This is it! If you pass Lopez Canyon on your left, you've gone too far. The actual gravity hill is just a few hundred yards south of the intersection of Lopez Canyon and Kagel Canyon. Or you can take Paxton north up to Lopez Canyon and turn right on Kagel Canyon.

This hill is about 100 yards long and works in both directions. Just pull over onto the shoulder of the road at the bottom of the hill, put your car in neutral and release the brake. If you are facing north, your car will roll backwards. If you are facing south, it will roll forwards.

Rubio Canyon Gravity Hill

The Gravity Hill of Altadena. Perhaps southern California's best-known gravity hill.

While doing research for the Kagel Canyon gravity hill, I started to get reports of another gravity hill located in nearby Altadena. At first I assumed that the two sites were being confused, and that there was actually only one site. But the reports mounted until it became clear that there were, in fact, two gravity hills. The only problem was, nobody seemed to know where the Altadena location was!

Then, after much searching, I finally found a first-hand witness. Elise had been a Pasadena resident for many years. When she was a teenager, she and her friends visited the Altadena gravity hill on at least a couple of occasions. Unfortunately, it was many years ago and Elise was unable to recall the exact location. All she could remember is that she and her friends had great fun parking their car at the bottom and watching it roll uphill, seemingly by itself. Further enquiries with Elise's friends failed to yield any additional information.

While Altadena is not a very large city, without more precise directions, the hill would be virtually impossible to find. Then came a break in the case. I had sent out numerous email requests asking if anybody had heard of the Altadena gravity hill or knew its exact location. A few days later, I received an email from a gentleman named Rumi. Like many local residents, Rumi had visited the location as a teenager and had been very impressed. While he didn't remember the exact location, his friend John did. John not only gave precise directions, he included a map of the area.

Rumi assured me that the hill was pretty obvious and not difficult to locate. I couldn't have been more delighted. I had just about given up on ever finding it. Now I had been informed almost exactly where it was.

Fighting Gravity

I jumped into my Toyota pick-up and began my adventure. Altadena is located north of the 210 Freeway in southern California. As I headed into the city, I was first struck by how the city of Altadena was built. While most southern California cities are built in the valleys, much of Altadena is carved into the foothills of the rugged San Gabriel Mountains. Because of this, many of the streets are steep and winding. Already, I was fighting gravity as I climbed higher and higher in elevation towards my destination.

The directions I had been given were perfect, and as Rumi said, I had no trouble recognizing the gravity hill as soon as it came into view. Like the Kagel Canyon site, the hill was a small stretch of road about a hundred yards long. It started just south of a large stone bridge, near a small white house.

I pulled a quick U-turn and parked at the bottom of the small hill. I looked behind me. Yes, it definitely looked like an uphill grade behind me. There was no way this was going to work.

Neutral Results

I popped the car into neutral and slowly removed my foot from the brake. Almost immediately the car gave a small lurch backwards and started to roll uphill! I couldn't believe it. I was moving only a few miles per hour, but I was definitely moving. And no doubt about it, it *looked* like I was going uphill. A few seconds later, the car eased up to the crest of the hill. I put on the brake, pulled forward and did it again. Just like before, the car rolled easily backwards.

Just to be sure, I did it a third time and pulled farther forward until I found the exact beginning of the strange effect. It worked like a charm. Then I turned the car around and tried it on the west lane of the road.

Just like before, I parked my car at what looked like the bottom of the small incline, placed the transmission in neutral, and removed the brake.

This side of the road didn't work as well. I had to pull the car a little more forward. But as soon as I did, the gravity effect took hold and the car rolled upwards, or at least it seemed to.

I then pulled over and walked up and down the stretch of the road, trying to get a feel for it. Was it an optical illusion or an actual gravitational anomaly? I honestly wasn't sure.

I took several photos and surveyed the surrounding area. The site had many things in common with the Kagel Canyon site. Both were located at the foothills of very large, steep mountains. Both stretches of road went steeply downhill and were interrupted by the same type of minor dip or trough in the road, where it appeared to level out and travel upwards for a short distance, then continue downwards.

Every couple of minutes, cars would drive by, seemingly in total ignorance of the site. As two ladies walked by with their dogs, I asked, "Have either of you heard of the gravity hill in this location?"

They looked at me like I was crazy. "You know, a place where cars appear to roll uphill?"

They shook their heads and quickly walked away. Then another car approached and stopped. It was a lady in a white van. She stopped exactly at the location. At first I thought she was a concerned neighbor who was wondering why I was taking pictures of the area. Then I watched as her van began to inch slowly backwards. As her car moved backwards, she looked at me to see my reaction. She obviously knew about the hill!

I wanted to ask her what she thought when she suddenly raced off. Then a few minutes later, another car pulled up. It was a young man in a black sports car. He pulled over at the bottom of the hill, but he went too far forward and his car failed to roll backwards. It took him a few tries to find the right location. Like me, he also tried the other side, which didn't appear to work as well.

I had been there only about twenty minutes and already two other people had visited the area and tested the apparent anomaly. Like other gravity hills, the location is apparently well known only to the locals. I could only wonder if the owners of the small white house at the base of the hill knew why so many people stopped before their home and rolled their cars backwards.

Will your car really roll uphill? You'll have to try it out for yourself and see.

See for Yourself

Location: In Pasadena, take the 210 Freeway. Exit on Lake and go north to East Palm Drive. Turn right (east) on Palm and go straight until you reach Rubio Canyon Road. Take Rubio Canyon Road up to the Rubio Canyon Wash Basin. The site is immediately adjacent to the Rubio Canyon Wash Basin and begins a few hundred yards south of a large cement bridge. The bottom of the incline begins just south of a small white house. Park your car heading north along the shoulder immediately south of the driveway. You will know it when you find the right spot.

Says one anonymous witness. "That's where you put your car in neutral, and…you get pushed up. I was a real skeptic about this…and right after my car started moving up the hill in neutral, me and my friends all pussied out and just drove the hell back home." (www.ghosttowns.com/wwwboard/messages/5871)

Gravity Hill of Antioch

Outside the San Francisco Bay area of Antioch, again only known by the locals, lies a small stretch of gravity defying road. It is located at the end of a little used road called Empire Mine Road. Also located here is the truly spooky, "Hell's Gate and the Slaughter House" (see the later section on ghosts.)

Beware!

On the evening of August 28, 2003, Monica X. and her friends visited the hill to test it out. Monica came away from the experience totally convinced that the gravity hill is real. As she says, "I went to Gravity Hill in Antioch two nights ago, and I was scared out of my mind! Our car was moved at least 25 feet uphill. Right when we turned the headlights on, the car came to an immediate halt."

On the evening of September 18, 2003, local resident Jessica X. drove alone to see if the stories were true. As she says, "Your car does move, so it does work. But yeah, there are cults around there, for I had a truck come out of nowhere and chase me. So don't go alone and be careful...it's a really creepy place, just so you're warned, and you will get VERY weird vibes there."

Another convinced visitor is Rosie X. As she says, "My friend and I went to Gravity Hill and it does work...The car does move! A good couple of feet! It's awesome but really freaky at the same time."

Resident Angela X. agrees that the gravity hill exists, but believes it has a prosaic explanation. As she says, "It is just a place in the world with an extreme gravitational pull. Don't get me wrong, it's definitely cool and an amazing feeling. It's pretty creepy at night. The cool thing to do is to get out and put a ball on the ground or get on a skateboard. Now that is awesome!" (www.pierceclemmer.us/marina/archives/000165.html)

See for Yourself

The Gravity Hill of Antioch is located on Empire Mine Road in Antioch, outside of Stockton. To get there, take Highway 4 and exit on Lone Tree Road. Turn right on Lone Tree Road to Deer Valley Road. Turn right on Deer Valley Road, past Deer Valley School and Kaiser Hospital. Then turn right on Empire Mine Road. According to one report, there are two large rocks on either side of the road to indicate where the actual Gravity Hill begins.

On the evening of September 18, 2003, local resident Jessica X. drove alone to see if the stories were true. As she says, "Your car does move, so it does work. But yeah, there are cults around there, for I had a truck come out of nowhere and chase me. So don't go alone and be careful...it's a really creepy place, just so you're warned, and you will get VERY weird vibes there."

La Mesa Gravity Hill

The location of this gravity hill comes from Kenny X, who writes, "There's also a Gravity Hill here in San Diego (La Mesa), for all you people coming from Los Angeles. Coming from the 805 heading southbound, exit Mira Mesa Boulevard/Sorrento Valley Road. At the bottom of the exit, there is a stoplight. When you reach the stoplight, check your rear view mirror and put your car in neutral. You should start to roll backwards up the hill."

Another testimony comes from Jeremy X. who visited the area on October 6, 2003. He writes that it is just "an illusion," but admits that "cars roll backward and it trips people out." (www.sd.paranormal.com/articles/article/764209/5942)

The Gravity Hill of Hacienda Heights-Whittier

Located on Turnbull Road in Hacienda Heights, which turns into Beverly Boulevard on the Whittier side, this area has been the location of racial murders and questionable cult-like activity. The gravity hill is reportedly located near the Rose Hills Cemetery rose gardens.

Rumors abound of numerous other California Gravity Hills including locations in Corona, San Bernardino, and Duarte. Yet another reportedly exists on Patterson Road between Tracy and Livermore.

Scare Your Friends ... But Be Careful Out There!

Whether you believe gravity hills are optical illusions or something more mysterious, they are fun places to visit, especially on dark and stormy nights when you want to scare or amaze your friends!

A final warning. One should always use extreme caution when operating a motor vehicle, and this is *especially* true on a gravity hill. I have received a few reports of automobile accidents, some severe. So be careful! Otherwise, good luck and have fun.

At the bottom of the exit, there is a stoplight. When you reach the stoplight, check your rear view mirror and put your car in neutral. You should start to roll backwards up the hill."

4. The Mysterious Sliding Stones of Death Valley

Tea Kettle Junction. Once you reach this location, you know you're finally getting close to the Racetrack Playa.

The Mysterious Sliding Stones of Death Valley. While numerous theories have been raised to explain the movement of these stones, nobody has ever seen them move.

The Racetrack Playa. In the background to the right, you can see the Grandstand, a large crystallized dolomite outcropping which sits alone near the center of the lakebed.

The phenomenon of convergence. While most of the sliding stones move in the same direction, some move sideways or even in opposite directions to each other.

Death Valley is the lowest, hottest, and driest location in the United States. During summer, soil tempatures can reach upwards of 190 degrees! Because the landscape is so harsh, the environment has remained largely untouched. Death Valley actually contains at least twenty-one species of plants that are unique to the valley and found nowhere else in the world, including the Panamint daisy, the Death Valley Sage, and the Death Valley sandpaper plant.

Elusive

Boulder Races

Death Valley is also the location of a bizarre enigma: the mysterious sliding stones. They are found only one place on earth: a small portion of the vast Death Valley National Park known as Racetrack Playa. It is a three-mile-long dry lakebed sandwiched between two mountain ranges.

What makes this remote desert place such a mystery are the hundreds of black, dolomite stones, some originally weighing up to 700 pounds, which move by themselves. Yes, that's right, by *themselves*. At least they seem to do so.

Visitors can easily see the long tracks, about one inch deep, that they make on the dry lakebed. Some of the tracks are straight. Others curve in strange patterns. They seem to be going in all different directions. The tracks of the larger boulders have been measured at about 200 feet. The tracks of the smaller stones exceed 600 feet.

The only problem is, nobody has ever seen them move, and nobody knows exactly how it happens.

One visitor was travel writer Josh Sens. As he says, "Racetrack Playa isn't really a racetrack. It's a dried-out lakebed, nearly two miles long. They just call it that because of the stones. I could see them in the distance as I rolled around a bend and rumbled toward the playa. They were like a flock of ducks sitting on a placid pond. I parked the truck and walked half a mile across the cracked-dry lakebed, just barely keeping my balance in the gale-force winds.

"At last I stood among the sliding stones. There were dozens of them, some barely larger than pebbles, others twice the size of basketballs. I couldn't see them sliding. No one ever has. But I could tell that they'd been on the move. Across the vast expanse of Racetrack Playa, the stones had left snail trails, long snaking furrows in the silt clay. Some of the trails were several hundred feet long."

Logical Explanations?

Like most people who see the stones, Sens was unable to find a logical explanation. As he says, "What makes the stones slide remains a question. As always, some people suspect aliens. If that's the case, ET is stronger than a team of oxen. Remember, some of the stones weigh 700 pounds. Other theories have emerged. Maybe it's the high wind, though wind alone couldn't budge these babies. Maybe it's the rain, which freezes over in cold weather, forming a thin icy film over which the stones could slide. Maybe it's a combination of the two." (Sens, 1-10)

Against the Wind

Numerous scientists and enthusiasts have studied the area in depth. Scientist Dr. Robert P. Sharp conducted a thorough study of the phenomenon. He tagged the position of thirty stones and recorded their positions over the period of one year. He recorded the movements of several stones, one of which moved 860 feet in a series of moves. While most of the stones moved in the direction of the prevailing winds, two it appeared did not.

Geologist John Reid explored the site with his students right after melting snows had left several inches of water standing on the absolutely flat and level lakebed. Reid and his students did find that the surface of the lake was slippery, but when they tried to move the bigger boulders, they were unable to do so.

Glen Turner visited the area with a friend. They camped out on the racetrack next to a large boulder. When they woke the next morning, they claimed that boulder had allegedly moved about sixty feet. If true, this is the closest anyone has come to seeing one of the rocks move, and it certainly seems to disprove the wind theory.

Another group of researchers discovered one instance where it seemed that wind could not have been a factor. "Another pair [of rocks] came from the south in straight lines, make sharp 90 degree turns to the west and then each made a big arc *towards* each other." This phenomenon, called "convergence," is difficult to explain.

Slippery When Wet

The most common theory is, of course, that the lakebed becomes slippery with mud or ice, and the boulders are pushed by the wind, which can reach up to 70 miles per hour as it is funneled through the narrow mountain passes. The rocks themselves are known to come from the dolomite mountains that frame the playa. And, in fact, most of the movement of the stones occurs at the southern shore area of the playa, where the wind funneling between two mountains reaches its greatest intensity.

Besides the ice/mud theory, there have been speculations ranging from extraterrestrials, to magnetics, earthquakes, and even demonic spirits. While a frosty desert surface may seem like an attractive solution, remember, Death Valley is the driest place in the United States. While this remains the favored theory among scientists, it still doesn't explain why nobody has ever seen it happen, how the stones can move in different directions, and why it happens nowhere else on Earth!

Direct

Observations

My own expedition to the racetrack raised more questions than answers. My brother and I arrived there early in the morning. We found two main locations where the moving stones were clustered — one near the entrance, and a bigger patch at the far end of the racetrack. Sure enough, there were long tracks where the rocks had moved. Most were pretty small, though seemingly too heavy for the wind to move! Furthermore, I found several cases of "convergence," and at least one rock that moved in the opposite direction of all the others. And I also couldn't help but wonder how these rocks got here in the first place. The lakebed was absolutely flat and empty for miles around.

I took several photographs and returned to the car to get out of the ferocious sun. I could only shake my head in wonder. It's definitely one of the strangest California locations I have ever visited.

And so the Racetrack Playa Sliding Stones of Death Valley remain a mystery. Maybe you can be the first person in history to catch one of these rocks moving by itself.

See for Yourself
Driving Instructions

The site is located in Death Valley National Park, 38 miles south of Ubehebe Crater. The dirt/gravel road starts here and leads to the site. Once you reach Tea Kettle Junction, you know you're getting close. There is a sign at the entrance to the playa, detailing the story of the sliding rocks. It is a half hour's hike to see the rocks themselves. Visitors are warned to be prepared for very extreme weather conditions! Bring lots of water!

5. Weird Trees

Trees have always held a strong fascination for human beings. True to its nature, California has produced some of the most unusual trees in the world, including the tallest and the oldest species.

Trees of Mystery

If you drive four miles north of Klamath on US 101, you will find yourself in the middle of the "Trees of Mystery Park." The Klamath National forest covers about 1,726,000 acres, most of which is untouched wilderness. Only a small area (120 acres) comprising the Trees of Mystery Park, however, has trees that are growing in highly unusual ways. Shaped by the harsh elements, or perhaps other unseen forces, the trees in this particularly area are more like sculptures than normal trees. The early Native Americans actually refused to enter the area, believing it to be cursed by evil spirits. Once you see the strange trees, you will understand.

Once Wonderland

While the trees attracted attention for years, it wasn't until 1931 that Carl Bruno of Lone Pine purchased the property. He had observed the many strange trees and was deeply fascinated. He soon opened the area to the public, calling it, "Wonderland Park."

Today, it is called the Trees of Mystery Park and has been in operation for more than fifty years. As it says in the brochure to park, "[It] is a unique and unusual forest. So many of the trees grow in unusual forms that very few are what is considered 'normal'."

Untouched by Human Hands

Still, the owner denies that the trees have been manipulated by human hands in any way. As he says, "Only the hand of Mother Nature has shaped these trees as most are in the 1000 to 2000 year old range."

Visitors to the park agree that the trees are definitely unusual. Writes one witness. "They're twisted and gnarled into elaborate formations: a tree shaped like an elephant. One that resembles a bolt of lightning. And another that grows upside down, its roots springing forth from some high-hanging branch. I spent an hour wandering amid these ancient monsters. A tree shaped like a candelabra caught my eye…people may be weird, but Mother Nature is the greatest mystery of all."

Cathedral Tree

A favorite attraction is "Cathedral Tree," a cluster of six redwoods growing out of a single root in a tight semi-circle. Nobody has ever been able to explain exactly why these trees are growing in such unusual and bizarre ways.

For the more adventurous, take a hike along the Trail of Tall Tales to observe unusual Redwood sculptures carved by chainsaws. The sculptures depict the story of Paul Bunyan and other logger legends. A visit to the park is said by the attendants to be a "super natural experience." (www.treesofmystery.net)

See for Yourself

Directions to a Super Natural Experience

The park is located 65 miles north of Eureka and eighteen miles south of Crescent City along Highway 101. Address: 15500 Highway 101 North, Klamath, CA 95548. Phone: 800-638-3389. website: www.treesofmystery.net."

The Drive-Thru Trees

California is definitely known for its trees. The forty-mile long stretch of highway along Highway 101 between Garberville and Pepperwood is actually called "The Avenue of Giants" or "the Redwood Highway." Located about 150 miles north of San Francisco, it is here that you will find the largest and tallest trees in the entire world. The trees are so massive that they are now a preserved species. Driving along this highway is an experience that cannot be adequately described. The majesty of these trees is literally breathtaking. They tower more than 300 feet high, sometimes literally disappearing into the clouds. As we shall see later on in the book, this area is also a favored realm for the legendary Bigfoot. Once you see the actual gigantic size of the trees, you can see how Bigfoot would feel right at home.

Business people looking to make a profit have found a way to make money with these trees. Most popular are the "drive-thru trees," which are found only in northern California.

Chandelier Tree, A Rare Breed

Probably the most famous is the Chandelier Tree, in Drive-Thru Tree Park on US 101 and Scenic Route 1 in the town of Leggett. The tree in question towers 315 feet into the air and has a diameter of 20 feet. What makes this tree so unusual, however, is the hand-hewn tunnel that is carved through the base of the tree. The tunnel is big enough to drive a Volkswagen Microbus through it. Today, conservationists have successfully lobbied to make it illegal to carve up any more trees to drive through. Therefore the few remaining few drive-thru trees are very valuable and increasingly rare. To get to the Chandelier Tree, you have to drive a mile down a narrow bumpy road to reach the tree-tunnel. Location: Leggett, US 101. Phone: 707-925-6464.

Another drive-through tree is called "Tour-Thru Tree." Located in Klamath, for a few bucks you can drive your car through the hand-hewn opening. Picnicking is also available. Phone: 707-482-5971.

A third example is the Shrine Drive-Thru Tree located in Myers Flats. The opening in this tree is naturally angled. To help preserve the site, the owners have strapped steel cables to the trunk. Shrine Drive-Thru also has a "Step-Thru" stump and a "Drive-On" tree. Who knew that there were many different ways for people to maneuver through a tree?!

The Immortal and Eternal

Several other weird trees along "the Avenue of Giants" have also established themselves as tourist attractions, including The Immortal Tree, The Eternal Tree House and the Living Chimney Tree. Another popular tourist spot is the "Cross-Section of Time." This is a cross-section slice of a redwood tree trunk with its growth rings marked, stretching back before the time of the birth of Jesus Christ!

North of "the Avenue of Giants" in Phillipsville is also the "One Log House," a unique structure built out of a single giant hollowed-out tree-trunk.

World's Tallest Room!

You might also want to check out "The World Famous Tree House". Built on a 4000 year-old-tree 250 high, 33 feet in diameter, and 101 feet in circumference, the tree house itself is built in a 50-foot-high cavity inside the tree. It claims to be the world's tallest single room. Location: Piercy, CA. For more information call 707-925-6406.

The Methuselah

Trees

High on a 10,000 foot section of White Mountain in the Inyo National Forest just north of Death Valley is something incredible: the scientifically verified oldest living creature on earth. The oldest creature is, in fact, an ancient weather-worn Bristlecone Pine tree (Latin name, Pinus longaeva.) Sur-

prisingly, this species is found only in California, Nevada, and Utah. It is probably the most extraordinary of all trees in California, and has been officially named the Methuselah Tree. Predating the birth of Jesus Christ and even the building of the Egyptian Pyramids, this amazing tree celebrated its 4768th birthday in the year 2005. There was one slightly older specimen, but it was destroyed in the attempt to determine its age!

The Methesulah Grove (also known as Patriarch Grove) trees are filled with mystery. Scientists have long known that trees were among the longest-lived of Earth's creatures, but it wasn't until the 1950s that botanists launched a scientific study to locate the world's actual oldest trees. As all dendrochronologists know, the age of a tree can be easily determined by counting the concentric rings in a horizontal slice of the tree's trunk.

Samples were taken from the oldest forests around the world. After decades of study, it was determined that the oldest trees were, in fact, Bristlecone Pines, and specifically a grove which grew just at the timberline in the White Mountains of the Sierra Nevada near California's Death Valley.

Secrets of Old Age

This was a surprise because scientists at first believed that the oldest trees would need an optimum environment to thrive and survive to an old age. In fact, exactly the opposite turned out to be the case. The environment of the Methesulah Grove is among the harshest on the planet. This, it turns out, is the surprising secret to their longevity. Writes Peter Tyson, "Here, in the rain shadow of the Sierra Nevadas, which block

weather approaching from the west, the average annual precipitation is less than twelve inches, and most of that falls as snow in winter. In summer, which can provide a few weeks of warmth for Bristlecone Pines to generate growth and reserves for overwintering, precipitable moisture ranks among the lowest recorded anywhere on Earth. Moreover, the soil the Bristlecones cling to is not dirt as most plants know it but dolomite, a limestone substrate with few nutrients. With so little time to get energy from the sun, and so little energy to be had from the soil, growth is grindingly slow. A Bristlecone Pine may add to its girth no more than an inch per century…The oldest Bristlecone Pines live on the most exposed sites." (Tyson, 1-4)

In other words, Bristlecones have their growth process retarded by an extremely harsh environment, apparently causing them to age more slowly. In fact, a single pine needle from a Bristlecone lives for up to forty years!

The harsh environment, however, is not the only secret. It turns out these trees are able to do something no other trees can do: hibernate. In times of severe drought, the entire growth system of the tree can come to a complete halt. Writes dendrochronologist Edmund Schulman (who spearheaded the decades-long search to find the oldest tree), "There is something a little fantastic in the persistent ability of a 4000 year-old tree to shut up shop almost everywhere throughout its stem in a very dry year, and faithfully to reawaken to add many new cells in a favorable year."

Bristlecones are also extremely dense and resinous, making them highly resistant to disease.

> **Predating the birth of Jesus Christ and even the building of the Egyptian Pyramids, this amazing tree celebrated its 4768th birthday in the year 2005. There was one slightly older specimen, but it was destroyed in the attempt to determine its age!**

Exact Location a Scientific Secret

In order to protect it, the *exact* location of the Methuselah Tree itself is a closely guarded secret known to only a few select scientists. Visitors are told only that it is one of the many trees located in the so-called "Methuselah Grove," which is located on White Mountain just north of Death Valley. Take Highway 395 and go east on Highway 168. Go thirteen miles to the White Mountain Road. Turn left and go seven miles up to Schulman Grove. Thirteen miles beyond Schulman grove is Patriarch Grove. Information: White Mountain Ranger District. 798 North Main Street. Bishop, CA 93514. Phone 760-873-2500.

As equally impressive as the Methuselah Tree is the tallest tree in the world. This majestic Sequoia tree grows in the coastal Redwood forest of Montgomery State Reserve, near Ukiah. The tree towers an incredible 367 feet high. There may be taller trees around, but as yet, this one tree remains the world's single tallest tree on record.

The Circus

Trees of Gilroy

Bonfant Gardens in Gilroy is the location of the little-known Circus Trees. You won't believe these trees until you see them. They look more like sculptures than trees. That's because the trees *are*, in fact, sculptures.

The trees do not grow naturally into these formations and have been forced to grow in various beautiful man-made shapes. One tree has a trunk that is growing in the shape of a heart. Another has a trunk that looks like a double helix. Another is actually six Sycamore trees that have been made to grow in the shape of a giant basket.

Arborsculptures: Rare and Fleeting

These trees were the pride and pleasure of the man who originated them, Alex Erlandson. Taking literally the old adage of "as the twig is bent, so the tree grows," Erlandson patiently grew scores of trees into intricate shapes. He grew his unique "arborsculptures" for more than forty years at his home in Scots Valley, near Santa Cruz.

When the trees later began to suffer from lack of care, Bonfant Gardens acquired the trees and transplanted them fifty miles away to Gilroy. Today only twenty-nine trees have survived.

The Petrified Forest

Although the Petrified Forest is well known, it is still one of the most bizarre places on earth. Nowhere else in the United States can you find a forest that has been turned to stone. The forest is located five miles outside of Calistoga, on Petrified Forest Road. It contains a museum and picnic facilities. Phone: 707-942-6667.

As can be seen, the trees of California have a lot to offer. I have personally visited several of the above sites and can assure the reader that it is worth the visit. Nothing can compare to hiking through a forest of gigantic trees, or wrapping your arms around a tree that is *thousands* of years old.

See for Yourself

Bonfant Gardens is located at 3050 Hecker Pass Highway (Hwy 152) in Gilroy. Take 101 to Masten Avenue Exit west until it turns into Fitzgerald. At end of street, turn left on Santa Teresa Boulevard and Right on Hecker Pass Highway (Highway 152.)

6. The Ruins of Mu

Do the Santa Monica Mountains contain the ruins of an ancient civilization?

Stone formations at the top of Las Flores Canyon in Malibu, allegedly near the site of the ancient civilization of Mu.

One of the most persistent and powerful legends of all times is the lost continent of Atlantis. The idea that advanced civilizations have already risen and fallen is an attractive one. It would definitely explain some of the curious anomalies that have been found in certain parts of the world. While Atlantis is the most famous of ancient civilizations, it certainly isn't the only one.

Ancient California

A lesser-known ancient civilization is known as Lemuria or Mu. What makes this legend interesting is that it takes place right here in California. According to several researchers, California is actually very ancient land and portions of it were formerly inhabited by a great civilization.

The Santa Monica mountain range in southern California is the one of the only transverse mountain ranges in the continental United States. While most mountain ranges run north-south, for some unknown reason this one runs east-west.

The entire mountain range was once under water, as evidenced by the numerous fossils found in the area. In fact, there is an area in the mountains – a stretch of road along Old Topanga Canyon Road — that is well-known to fossil-hunters around the world as it is one of the richest fossil finds in southern California.

The legend of Mu appears in many ancient texts, but the modern accounts are the most interesting. Which brings us to the story of Robert Stanley.

In 1973, Stanley became interested in UFOs when a series of sightings happened over his home in Malibu. At the same time, strange crop circles appeared. Stanley was only thirteen-years-old at the time, but the experience left him forever changed. The world suddenly became a much more mysterious place, and he devoted himself to learning (and trying to solve) as many of the mysteries as he could.

But one of the mysteries that intrigued him more than the others was the concept of ancient civilizations.

Writes Stanley, "Throughout my life, I have had recurring dreams of an ancient city of stone located in the mountains. I traveled 57 countries and visited many of the Earth's wonders, such as the Great Pyramid in Egypt, Stonehenge in England, and the Parthenon in Greece in search of finding this city, but I never saw anything like it. In the fall of 1985, I finally discovered what I believe are the ruins of this ancient city located in the Santa Monica Mountains of Malibu."

Ancient Mu

Stanley's first step was to thoroughly explore the area. Writes Stanley, "I was amazed by the incredible megalithic monuments carved out of stone, and the remnants of a series of walls which surround the city."

At first, Stanley kept his find to himself. He wanted to be sure that what he found was real. After satisfying himself that the formations were not natural, he started to tell others. "I became so intrigued with this area that I began to invite my friends to share in the experience."

To his delight, people who he brought to the site were so impressed that they told their friends and brought them to visit the area. Soon Stanley was getting so many requests for tours that he formed "Mystic Mountain Expeditions."

For several years in the 1990s, Stanley brought small groups of people to the area. As the advertisement reads, "Step into the ancient land of Mu. There is a fascinating hiking expedition which takes you through the ruins of an ancient stone city located in the scenic mountains of southern California. Your guide, Robert Stanley, will lead you on a vision quest, back into time, to a lush coastal valley called Mu. Much of Mu is now buried underwater, but some of the ruins are still visible in the higher elevations, such as the walls which once surrounded the temple grounds. Marvel at the megalithic sculptures which are carved into steep rock terraces, such as the sixty feet tall balancing Brahma's head, a two hundred foot tall Sphinx face, and the Asian Buddha. Experience the powerful energy vortexes, and learn about the amazing star people who once inhabited this sacred land. Why are UFOs still being seen and photographed in this area? Hear the incredible facts about the extraterrestrial connection to this region." (Stanley, 12-13)

See for Yourself

While Stanley no longer conducts tours, the location is found at the top of Las Flores Canyon in Malibu. You will know you're there when you see other parked cars and hikers. Follow the fire-trails along the ridge and you will come upon the stone formations.

I spoke with another gentleman who said that similar formations can be found further up the coast in the Santa Barbara mountains. And then of course, there is the story of Mount Shasta, which is so complex that it deserves its own chapter.

7. Mount Shasta

Of all the supernatural locations in California, Mount Shasta tops the list. In fact, there is so much weirdness there that it's difficult to know where to start! There are UFO sightings and abductions, Bigfoot encounters, religious miracles, underground cities with golden caverns, seven-foot tall Lemurians, ancient civilizations, unexplained noises, New Age psychics and channelers…and this is just the beginning!

Largest

Lone Peak

Which sounds like a good place to start. Mount Shasta is not only a magnet for the strange and unusual, the mountain itself has always been unique. First of all, unlike nearly all the other volcanic mountains in California, Mount Shasta stands alone, with no close neighbors. Incredibly, the mountain has the largest base and greatest mass of any "lone peak" in the world. It rises to an altitude of 14,162 feet, with a cubic volume of more than 80 cubic miles.

It is also among the youngest mountains in the United States, with an age of about 700,000 years. The mountain contains eight glaciers, and, despite having four cones, is incredibly symmetrical.

Strange

Denizens

The early local Native Americans had always considered the mountain holy, and claimed that a race of dwarves lived in caves along the slopes.

The first person to record firsthand supernatural experiences was Frederick Oliver Spencer. In 1884, he published his book, *A Dweller on Two Planets*, which he claimed was actually channeled from an entity named Phylos. The book tells the account of Walter Pierson who had an incredible experience on Mount Shasta during the California Gold Rush.

More than a dozen people claim to have been taken to an ancient Lemurian city hidden beneath Mount Shasta. In several of these cases, witnesses claim to have seen priceless gold artifacts.

Pierson had befriended a Chinese Laborer who turned out to be a mystic adept with access to the secret Shasta caverns beneath the mountain. Pierson was taken into a tunnel with walls that he said were polished and glowed. He was then taken into a carpeted cavern with a luxurious divan around the perimeter. Here he began his own initiation as a mystical adept.

In 1931, author Wishar Cerve published his landmark book, *Lemuria – The Lost Continent of the Pacific*, which presented his theory that Mount Shasta was the refuge of the survivors of the lost continent of Lemuria. Cerve maintained that Lemuria was an advanced civilization that suffered a fatal disaster about 12,000 years ago. According to Cerve, only a handful of Lemurians survived, and have been living in an underground city inside of Mount Shasta ever since.

Cerve's book contained several testimonies in support of his claims. According to Cerve, local residents reported encounters with strange individuals who would emerge from the local forests to trade gold nuggets and dust for supplies. Writes Cerve, "Those who have come to stores in nearby cities, especially at Weed, have spoken English in a perfect manner with perhaps a tinge of the British accents, and have been reluctant to answer questions about themselves. The goods they have purchased have always been paid for in gold nuggets of far greater value than the article purchased, and they have refused to accept any change, indicating that to them gold was of no value and they had no need for money of any kind."

According to Cerve, the strangers were actually Lemurians. They looked like normal people, only they were "tall, graceful and agile, with distinctive features such as large foreheads and long curly hair; the strangers wore unusual clothes, including headdresses with a special decoration that came down from the forehead to the bridge of the nose." (Cerve, 250-251)

Local residents began to investigate the area. Some reported coming upon areas of the mountain that glowed with "powerful illuminations." Others heard strange music or bells. Still others would find themselves tempo-rarily paralyzed, or would be accosted by a "heavily covered and concealed person who would lift him up and turn him away." A lucky few reported encounters with tall, friendly people dressed in long flowing robes who would hold deeply philosophical conversations about love, spirituality, and the fate of our planet.

The strange encounters brought more visitors. However, those who attempted to chase or photograph the tall strangers were invariably unsuccessful. The strangers would either run away or simply vanish. However, as more people came to visit, the number of firsthand accounts began to grow.

Hidden Mines, Strange Caverns

In 1904 J. C. Brown was prospecting for gold on Mount Shasta when he found a strange hidden cave. He dug into the opening and climbed into the cave, which turned into a tunnel winding deep inside the mountain. The tunnel stretched for miles and Brown realized that it must have been mined centuries earlier by a race of advanced beings. He kept going deep inside the mountain until he came upon caverns filled with copper and gold tablets, all inscribed neatly with strange hieroglyphics. He kept exploring and found more corridors lined with golden shields and other strange artifacts. He came upon one chamber that he said contained 27 skeletons, each about 10 feet in height, each clad in colorful robes.

Brown encountered no living beings, and spent several days exploring the various caverns. He then returned to the surface, taking nothing with him, and spent the next thirty years of his life investigating his experience, which he wrote about in his book, *The Lost Continent of Mu*. In 1934, Brown finally organized an expedition to return to the site. However, when the time came to go, Brown was nowhere to be found. He died two years later, never revealing the exact location of the tunnel into the mountain.

Around the 1930s reports of UFOs and Bigfoot began to turn up. The UFO and Bigfoot aspects of Mount Shasta are presented in later chapters. However, it should be kept in mind that the area is a major hot spot for both Bigfoot and UFO activity. This decade also marked a flood of reports from people who claimed to have been taken to a beautiful city beneath the mountain.

Strange Drinks

In Autumn of 1930, government-worker Guy Ballard visited Mount Shasta as part of his job, and instantly fell in love. In fact, he found himself spiritually transformed by the mountain, and spent all his time taking long hikes along the slopes. One day he was hiking near McCloud River when he suddenly realized that there was a man standing next to him. He was a Lemurian. The man promptly manifested a cup filled with a strange liquid, which he gave to Ballard. Then followed a long and deeply spiritual conversation about God, self, truth, love, desire, and other philosophical concepts. The man said he was Saint Germaine, believed by many to be an ascended master. Ballard later received numerous visits from Saint Germaine. Like other visitors, he was told that the earth is going to experience future catastrophes, but that peace will eventually reign. Ballard wrote his experiences in his book, *Unveiled Mysteries*. Writes Ballard, "To those who read this work, I wish to say that these experiences are as real and true as mankind's existence on this earth today, and that they all occurred during August, September, and October of 1930, upon Mount Shasta, California." (Frank, 69)

Strange Domes

Sometime around 1931, Professor Edgar Lucin Larkin, Director of Mount Lowe Observatory made a remarkable observation with one of his telescopes. Training his instrument upon Mount Shasta, he was shocked to see a golden glittering dome, such as found on top of Oriental buildings. Expecting it to be an optical illusion caused by a trick of light, he kept his telescope trained on the object. However, to his amazement, as the light changed, instead of disappearing, the golden dome remained. Furthermore, Professor Larkin observed two additional golden domes, and what appeared to be a marble structure. After the sun set, he checked the area again and was surprised to see "great lights around this dome." According to Cerve, the spectacle remained visible for more than a week.

Lemurian Guides

Also in 1931, an anonymous gentleman became lost while deer-hunting on the northeast side of Mount Shasta. He wandered around until he was completely exhausted. It was 3:00 a.m. when he suddenly realized that there was a seven-foot tall man standing next to him who said, "I am a Lemurian. What are you doing here?"

The hunter explained his position. At that point, the Lemurian took him through a hidden tunnel in the mountain. He was led to a palace, gardens, and a golden cave. The Lemurian told him that there were numerous tunnels beneath the mountain, one of which led to the rural areas of Del Norte, 90 miles to the west, near a monastery. Says the witness, "I saw plates and gold-lined shafts, and tables and chairs unbelievably monstrous in size." The witness was shown numerous other golden artifacts. He was also shown enormous fruits and vegetables grown by the Lemurians in large gardens.

The anonymous gentleman was then returned to the surface, where he told his experiences to his friend Abraham Mansfield. As it turned out, Mansfield himself claimed to have had similar encounters, during which he was also taken inside the mountain. Mansfield revealed his story in his book, *The Golden Goddess of the Lemurians*. Like other witnesses, Mansfield insisted that the stories were true, that there really was a giant city beneath the mountain. He said that the Lemurians are incredibly advanced technologically and spiritually, and that they have vast amounts of wealth and a complete understanding of science.

Lemurian Artifacts

Mansfield was actually able to produce numerous gold artifacts which he said were given to him by the Lemurians, including a bracelet, a pendants, several rings, a fork, a spoon, and other items. A photograph of the items is presented in Emilie Frank's excellent book, *Mount Shasta: California's Mystic Mountain*.

By Invitation Only

Also in 1931, Dr. M. Doreal claims that he received an invitation from the Lemurians to visit the city under Mount Shasta. He and two friends were mysteriously transported from Topanga Canyon in southern California [also a UFO hotspot] to a spot two-thirds up the slope of Mount Shasta. There they met a Lemurian face-to-face, and were taken inside a hidden structure built entirely out of rose-colored stone. Doreal says they were then taken underground to the top of the mountain, to a large flat rock that functioned like an elevator. They were then taken seven miles beneath the surface to an enormous cavern extending twenty miles long and ten thousand feet high. They were shown the Lemurian city, which was built of marble and stone, and exhibited incredible architectural designs. They were shown gardens and zoos containing never-before-seen plants and animals. They were also shown a temple of learning, and told that the Lemurians were working to gradually enlighten humankind. Dr. Doreal was shown that the Lemurians had mastered all the disciplines of science and was told the complicated history of the Lemurian race. He wrote about his experiences in a small booklet called *Mysteries of Mount Shasta*.

Investigative Journalism

In 1932, Los Angeles reporter Edward Lanser [Lancer] was assigned to do a story on the legendary Lemurians of Mount Shasta. Lanser had heard the many accounts and wanted to investigate firsthand. He climbed up into the foothills of the mountains where many of the reports had originated. To his amazement, he actually saw unexplained bright lights flashing in the wilderness. He returned for several evenings and was amazed to see more of the mysterious lights. He asked several local residents and was told that everybody knew about the lights and believed that an advanced race of beings actually live under the mountain. They told him that the Lemurians had supernatural powers: they were able to blend into the scenery and remain undetected. They told him that in the early 1930s, a forest fire on Mount Shasta was mysteriously extinguished by unknown forces. Also, they believed that nobody is able to penetrate into the mountain without being invited.

Ascended Masters, Ancient Philosophy

Lanser returned convinced, writing that his trip was "incredible" and that the "Lemurians have succeeded in secluding themselves in the midst of our teeming state."

From 1930 to 1940, Christian Scientist Nola Van Valer claims to have met "Phylos the Tibetan" and numerous other "ascended masters" on the slopes of Mount Shasta. Her adventure began while camping one day on the mountain. She and her husband were approached by a tall, graceful man dressed in a long, flowing robe. The man said that he had been observing them for a while, and had many things he wanted to tell them. Van Valer was intrigued and listened to what the strange man had to say.

The man proceeded to share vast amounts of deeply spiritual and philosophical information. Van Valer was awed by the information and recorded all of it in shorthand.

Van Valer claims that after this meeting, she continued to meet the Lemurians every year for ten years, recording volumes of spiritual wisdom. On each occasion, she was taken to a marble temple inside a cavern in the mountain. In 1963, she founded "The Radiant School of the Seekers and Servers," in order to share the knowledge she had been given by the Lemurians. The school lasted for many years, attracting students from across the world. Following Van Valer's death, the school disbanded. And yet, the stories continued.

Disappearing

Tents

In 1971, Lynn Ferrin was climbing Mount Shasta above Horse Camp when she saw an amazing sight: someone had set up a large medieval-looking pavilion-type tent, in an area that was totally inaccessible. The tent was actually high up on a butte, overlooking a tall sheer cliff. At first Ferrin assumed that some hippies had climbed up there and built the elaborate structure. However, she looked away, and when she looked back the tent was gone. As we have seen, she is not the only person to have encountered strange things on the slopes of Mount Shasta.

Intrusive Vapors,

Secret Missions

In January of 1976, a Mount Shasta resident and her friend were watching television in their home when they noticed a strange movement coming from the window. As they watched, a strange vapor-like substance came through the closed window and then materialized into several different entities. Writes the anonymous witness, "The first form [was] about eight feet tall…There were four more beings that stood behind the first who were about seven feet tall. Their faces were super-elongated and you couldn't see a mouth. They had on long robes." (Frank, 21-23)

According to the witness, the beings generated an enormous amount of energy. Her daughter emerged from her bedroom and also observed the beings. On impulse, they brought out a Ouija™ board and began to communicate with the beings who said they were from Lemuria, but now lived under Mount Shasta. They said that the daughter was actually one of them, and had been given a mission. The mission was kept private, known only to the daughter. However, in the days and weeks following, the family was able to make contact with the Lemurians on several different occasions. The daughter was reportedly too upset by the revelations to complete the mission entrusted to her by the Lemurians.

Strange Lights

for the Lost

In September 1981, welder Don Corder and a friend were hiking around the Whitney Glacier area on Mount Shasta when they became lost. When darkness fell, they realized that their situation had suddenly become dangerous. They knew they were near Horse Camp, but couldn't seem to find it. Suddenly, they saw some strange lights. Says Corder, "By golly, about 9:30 we saw a flash. It looked like somebody coming through the woods with a flashlight. We thought, boy, this is great. They're going to bring some hot coffee to us or something warm and help us get off this damn mountain."

The flashes of light continued, so the two men flashed their own flashlights back in response. To their delight, the lights flashed back, yet seemed to stay in the distance. Corder and his friend changed their direction and followed the lights. The lights then moved and appeared to be guiding them through the darkness. Several minutes later, the lights disappeared and the two men saw the bonfire of Horse Camp. The mysterious lights, they realized, had saved their lives. Says Corder, "As soon as we got far enough to see those bonfire lights at Horse Camp, we never saw them again. They were out. It kind of gave us an odd feeling…At the time

it wasn't weird or odd, but looking back…you've heard these stories about the mountain. I'm not much of a believer about the supernatural, but I'll tell you, we had a helping hand. And it's not our imagination." (Frank, 101-102)

Temporarily

Human

I have personally met people who have also had strange experiences on Mount Shasta. In the late 1980s, a young blond woman named Bonnie gave several lectures at a few local southern California UFO groups. In her lectures, Bonnie claimed that she was actually a Lemurian and that she lived in a large underground city with thousands of other Lemurians. She had only temporarily taken on a human form. I looked at her closely and agreed, she looked human. She said that the Lemurians are very advanced when it comes to science, and are easily able to provide power and illumination to the city without any pollution. She explained that her mission was to help enlighten humankind.

Strange Sleeps,

Mysterious Makeovers

Probably the strangest story I have heard from Mount Shasta concerns an anonymous young man who was hiking alone in the foothills of Mount Shasta in the late 1980s. He suddenly became unaccountably fatigued and fell asleep. When he woke up, he got the shock of his life: his long hair had been mysteriously braided with small crystals, various sticks, and leaves and flowers. It had all occurred while he was asleep and totally without his knowledge. He had no idea who would do this to him or why. He couldn't understand why he didn't wake up or how it could it have happened. Incidentally, the witness is tall, fair-skinned, with long flowing hair – somewhat like the descriptions of the alleged Lemurians. It is interesting that the alleged Lemurians are also known for wearing fancy headdresses. Could it be that they were responsible for his strange experience? The witness can only wonder.

Perplexing

Archaeological Ruins

If UFOs, Bigfoot, guiding lights, unexplained noises, underground cities, and golden caverns inhabited by a race of advanced Lemurians are not enough to boggle the mind, there is more. Mount Shasta and the surrounding areas also contain perplexing archaeological ruins. Author Richard Tierney writes that in the area around Black Butte there are numerous strange mounds about thirty feet high, made of piled-up rocks. According to Tierney, the mounds looked very much like unexcavated temple mounds that he had also seen in Mexico.

Tierney also wrote that strange stone circles can be found between Weed and Lake Shastina, north of the city of Edgewood. He counted at least two dozen stone circles, and estimated that there were many more. Each circle was formed from stones ranging in size from one foot to a few inches. Each circle was fifty to sixty feet in diameter, with a stone ring of about three feet thickness. Tierney raised several theories to account for the circles and mounds, but his favorite was that they were the remains of an ancient civilization.

Mount Shasta researcher Emilie Frank has also researched stone circles outside the adjacent town of Leaf, which cover an area of about 600 acres. Writes Frank, "The circles at Leaf surround slight mounds about 60 feet across and two to three feet high. They're located on a knoll and they're well covered by sagebrush. These circles consist of stones of all shapes and sizes and lie in a shallow ditch about one-foot deep by two-feet wide. The ditches are filled with rocks just to the surface of the surrounding areas and give the appearance of a stone pavement or mosaic."

Several scientists of various disciplines have examined the sites but have been unable to make a definitive conclusion. Writes Frank, "The mounds and circles of Edgewood, Leaf, and the Black Butte area still remain a mystery. Do these strange formations have anything at all to do with the controversial and mystic mountain which rises so majestically above them? No one seems to know." (Frank, 91-100)

Strange Attraction

Countless spiritual and religious groups continue to be attracted to Mount Shasta and hold regular rituals in the area. The Radiant School of Seekers and Servers, the Saint Germaine Foundation, the Association Sananda and Sanat Kumara, Elizabeth Clare Prophet's The Keepers of the Flame, and the Zen Mission Foundation are only a few. The mountain is considered sacred by many people of various disciplines. It has attracted virtually the entire range of New Age schools. The Harmonic Convergence in 1987 typified the mystique when the mountain was literally overrun by hundreds of spiritual seekers.

Perfect

Petroglyphs

If there still isn't enough mystery surrounding Mount Shasta, there are always the Castle Crag Petroglyphs, located in Little Castle Creek, Mt. Shasta. According to archaeologist Frank Bascom, "The fact stands out that the petroglyphs or symbols show greater skill and symmetry and a higher degree of culture than any found elsewhere in different places of the southwestern United States."

The petroglyphs do not match any local Native American culture, and instead appear to be either Mayan or Lemurian. One of the symbols is a swastika. Writes Bascom, "The swastika symbol is pre-Christian in origin and was found in the ruins of the continent of Lemuria...Church, in his 'Lost Continent of Mu' lists six of the symbols found at Castle Crags: the swastika, a form of the Maltese cross, the triangle, the all-seeing eye, the serpent and the three steps to the throne."

All Things

Supernatural Lead

to Mount Shasta

What more can be said about Mount Shasta? It covers the entire range of the supernatural. I have been researching UFOs and the paranormal for twenty years. Early into my investigations, I began to hear stories about the mountain. Whether a UFO sighting, a Bigfoot encounter or a Lemurian visitation, the accounts came in on a fairly regular basis. However, I never really made the connection between all these accounts until I began the research for this book. Now that I know about the large number of people who have had unusual experiences on Mount Shasta, I am awed by its undeniable power. It is hard to remain skeptical in the face of so much strangeness. Mount Shasta is considered one of the seven sacred mountains of the world. One needs only to visit it to find out why. As the leading researcher of Mount Shasta's supernatural side, Emilie Frank, writes, "Nothing anywhere can equal the beauty and the otherworldly occult charm of Mt. Shasta. Of that I am sure." (Frank, ii)

See for Yourself

Location: Mount Shasta is located in northern California. The city is spelled Mount Shasta. The mountain itself is usually designated Mt. Shasta. There are numerous campgrounds and hotels to accommodate visitors.

8. The Mystery Walls of Northern California

Don't Know Much ...

Nobody knows who built them or why. Nobody knows how old they are or exactly how many exist. In fact, nobody seems to know much about them at all! Whatever the reasons for their existence, numerous strange stone walls can be found in various locations all across northern California. The area around San Francisco, including Oakland and Santa Cruz, seems to hold the greatest number of these bizarre mystery walls.

The walls are built completely of large loose stones which have been carefully stacked. They stand about four feet high and two feet thick. Some run for only a few feet, while others extend for several hundred yards. Some are straight, others curve around hillsides. They are located both on public and private property. They are surprisingly numerous, extremely durable, and totally mysterious.

Theories Abound!

Countless people have studied them and countless theories have been raised to explain them. Some think they were built by Native Americans, others by early ranchers. Some have postulated that unknown settlers or perhaps stranded sailors or pirates were responsible. What is so bizarre about the walls is that they seem to be placed haphazardly. Some walls are short; some are long. They wind around the hillsides seemingly going nowhere. If there is a purpose to the walls, it isn't easy to find.

One of the many Mystery Walls located across northern California. Who built them, and why? The mystery remains unsolved. *Photo credit: Steve Bartholomew.*

Toltecs, Atlanteans, *Mongolians*?

Back in 1904, a journalist for the *San Francisco Chronicle* wrote, "Do the miles of mysterious stone barriers, which serve no modern purpose, bespeak of a lost civilization of Toltecs or Atlanteans?" That same year, professor Dr John Fryer of U. C. Berkeley wrote, "This is undoubtedly the work of Mongolians."

The Walls Described

Modern researcher Andy Asp writes, "Up to a meter high and a meter wide, the walls run in broken sections ranging from ten meters to over a half mile long. Some look to be careless piles of melon-sized rocks, while others are carefully constructed dry-laid masonry, occasionally using large sandstone boulders weighing a ton or more. The walls appear to be very old, perhaps even ancient. Many of the formations have sunk far into the earth, and others have accumulated thick calico coats of lichen. They are often completed obscured by dense thickets of poison oak and other brush....Scholars and amateur archaeologists have been puzzled by the walls' origins for over a century, due in large part to their apparent lack of purpose. The modest height would seem to rule out their functions as fortifications, and the rambling start-and-stop patterns render them useless as corrals or containment fences. Examples can be found as far north as Berkeley and as far south as Milpitas, near the Silicon Valley. One researcher estimates that if the walls were strung together, they would probably stretch for 20 miles or more." (Asp, 1-20)

Recent Investigations

One of the few people who have taken the time and effort to study the structures is local resident Steve Bartholomew. He has been researching and writing about stone structures in northern California for several years. Several of his articles have been published in *Ancient American Magazine*.

In 1998, he had the opportunity to study one of the walls that had apparently never been studied before. It had been discovered accidentally by Bartholomew's friend, Patrick, who was hiking in Lake County on private property when he came upon the abandoned wall.

After the discovery, Bartholomew couldn't resist the lure of examining a brand new "unseen wall," so he organized an expedition and went to the site. Writes Bartholomew, "At last we came upon Patrick's stone wall. Rocks and boulders which had gone into the wall's construction all originated from the ravine below…Someone had gone to a great deal of effort, long ago, to haul them up a hundred feet or so of steep hillside. The amount of sheer manpower involved staggers the imagination. It would have been impossible to accomplish such labor with horses or mules, due to the steepness of the incline. Work like this must have required great dedication on someone's part. And for what purpose? Looking around, we found ourselves in a relatively flat clearing, falling off to ravines on all sides. What could have been the reason for this construction?

"From here, there were no signs of civilization visible, save the wall itself. We might have been thousands of miles into the wilderness…One of the standard explanations for California's enigmatic walls is that they were built during the 19th Century to keep cattle from wandering off. But the vicinity in which the Lake county site lies is no cattle land. The surrounding territory is extremely rugged. Anyone trying to herd cows here would be constantly dragging animals out of ravines."

Bartholomew and his group examined the construction of the walls, but it only deepened the mystery. Writes Bartholomew, "The closer I examined the wall, the more amazing it seemed. Although primitive, it had every aspect of extreme age. In many places, large boulders were stacked on top of smaller rocks, the opposite of what one would expect. But this method appears to have been an identifying aspect of the State's anomalous ramparts. In some places, Patrick's wall has crumbled to only a foot or two in height; in others it remains five to six feet high. In some spots, it has been reduced to a mere pile of rocks. Despite our best efforts, we were unable to determine the structure's total length; vegetation of the hill on which it stands is almost impenetrable. We could see about a quarter of a mile before it disappeared into dense oak forest and underbrush."

After examining the wall, Bartholomew was suitably impressed by it. As he writes, "Altogether, I have seen literally dozens of similar old rock walls in Northern California. But the Lake County specimen is by far the strangest, for three reasons: Its location is extremely inaccessible; extraordinary difficulties must have gone into its construction; and a complete absence of any reason for its existence."

While the above wall is on private property, numerous other sites are located on public lands. Writes Bartholomew, "There are other mysterious stone artifacts throughout northern California. At Tilden Park in Berkeley are found stone circles and walls miles in length. They are all anomalies – they serve no apparent purpose, no one knows who built them or when. Sometimes a wall will disappear in the side of a hill, only to reemerge several hundred feet away. There are numerous theories about them. No one knows how old they are. Yet no professional archaeologist has ever taken enough interest to excavate." (Bartholomew, 1-5)

> Someone had gone to a great deal of effort, long ago, to haul them up a hundred feet or so of steep hillside. The amount of sheer manpower involved staggers the imagination.

More Theories

Theories to explain the many mysterious stone walls continue to circulate. The first known inhabitants, the Ohlone Native Americans do not seem to be responsible as they did not build any permanent structures. Ohlone scholar and author Malcolm Margolin writes, "It sure beats the heck out of me what those walls are doing up there."

Dr Robert Fisher writes, "These walls are just enigmas. They predate the Indians. They predate the Spaniards. It doesn't fit in with any of the later history."

According to researcher Andy Asp, the local legend is that the walls were built by Celtic Druids. Another theory is that they were built by early Amish farmers. Writes Andy Asp, "A shortage of formal scholarship on the East Bay walls has added to their mysterious appeal…While portions of the wall appear just moments from the campus of U.C. Berkeley, there has been little research done in the modern era using contemporary techniques. Russell Swanson, an amateur wall researcher, has tried in the past to arrange for tree core samples, Carbon-14 dating tests, and lichen dating tests, but was largely met with ambivalence by the scientific community." (Asp, 1-20)

See For Yourself

As can be seen, the mysterious Oakland walls are widespread. Some accessible ones are located in Tilden Park. Others are located east of San Francisco Bay in the East Bay Regional Park District. Another famous site is located near Mission San Jose. Just take the public hiking trail leading from the mission.

9. The Standing Stones of Point Reyes

Unknown to many people, there are numerous unexplained stone structures throughout California. The majority of these are located in the northern California area. We have already examined the Mysterious Oakland walls. Even lesser known are the mysterious Standing Stones of Point Reyes.

The site is located near Tomales Point at the tip of the Point Reyes Peninsula, among the grassy fields lining the rocky 600-foot sheer cliffs. The environment here is harsh, with a constant ocean breeze. No trees are able to take root on the wind-swept granite soil.

Elusive Stones

It is here that the Standing Stones of Point Reyes can be found. What makes these walls so strange is that there are rumors that they disappear and reappear in various locations!

The Standing Stones of Point Reyes, one of several locations in California containing strange stone formations. *Photo credit: Steve Bartholomew.*

One theory is that the standing stones were placed by local ranchers. Another is that they are the remnants of unknown Native American settlements. Finally, there has been speculation that Spanish Explorers constructed them. The truth is, nobody knows who built these structures or what their purpose is. All that is known is that they are not natural formations.

One person who made a fascinating study of the area is local resident Steve Bartholomew. Armed with his camera and vague directions, he ventured to the alleged site of the standing stones. Writes Bartholomew, "Point Reyes is strange…But where was this mysterious stone wall I had been told of? … there was supposed to be a stone wall here, or the remnant of one. Why wasn't I seeing it? It was then I had what I can only describe as an 'anomalous experience.' Recently I'd heard someone discussing these strange rock walls. He'd mentioned in passing that the walls themselves have the ability to make themselves invisible, unless you're ready to see them. I certainly didn't believe that. Nevertheless I decided on a small experiment.

"Standing on the trail with my eyes closed, I said a little prayer or request. I wasn't even sure who I was asking – Nature spirits, or the guardian rocks? I merely asked permission to see the wall for myself.

"What happened next still gives me gooseflesh when I remember. I opened my eyes and heard – a sound. I could not begin to describe it, except that it was like a voice in the wind. I didn't understand what it said but it was a human voice, as if I heard a voice from miles away on a freakish gust. At the same moment I had a sensation of giddiness, like a brief dizzy spell. Something strange was happening. I took two or three steps off the trail, as if trying to regain my balance. I looked down at my feet. And saw the wall."

Bartholomew whipped out his camera and took a photograph of the mystery structure. As he says, "It wasn't really a wall so much as a line of stones on the ground…a perfectly straight line of rocks imbedded in the ground, stretching from one cliff to the other. Now I felt a reverent sense of awe. Who had laid these stones, how long ago and for what unknown purpose?"

Bartholomew became even more impressed when he realized that several other stone structures were situated in meaningful patterns, showing the compass directions much like Stonehenge. Says Bartholomew, "The more I looked, the more amazed I became. I seemed to find traces of an ancient civilization everywhere. There were numerous places where stones from the field had been gathered together and piled into mounds, exactly like those ancient graves in the British Isles. Why had no archaeologist ever excavated this place?" (Bartholomew, 1-6)

Bartholomew has since made several other expeditions and has taken other people to the area. While the theories are numerous, the facts are few. All that is really known is that the structures were built long ago by some unknown people.

See for Yourself … *If* You Can!

Directions: Drive to the Point Reyes National Seashore towards the north end of the peninsula, called Tomales Point or Pierce Point. Park at Upper Pierce Ranch Historic Site and take the north hiking trail. The standing stones are lined up along the western cliff.

10. Ogams in California

One of the few rare Ogams found in California. Who were the mysterious stone writers of this ancient script? Photo credit: Steve Bartholomew.

Close-up of a California Ogam. These strange carvings are among the earliest form of writing known to humankind. Photo credit: Steve Bartholomew.

Original Mystery

One of the greatest mysteries on earth is the origin of humankind. Experts are still unable to decide whether modern humans first walked the planet 40,000 years ago, or perhaps much earlier.

This is also true for California, and we have the artifacts to prove it! Among the first alphabets developed by humans is one known as Ogam. Closely related to Hittite cuneiform, Ogam was written on notched sticks and carved in stone. Conventional wisdom states that Ogam was invented by the Irish during Roman times. However, as researcher Steve Bartholomew writes, "This belief flies in the face of overwhelming evidence of its use on the European Continent and elsewhere millennia before the Romans."

Not surprisingly, researchers have uncovered several Ogams right here in California. And like other mysterious stone structures found throughout the state, their origin remains a mystery.

Willits Rock

Bartholomew has studied one little-known Ogam known as "Willits Rock." It is located outside the front door of the Willits Museum in Mendocino County. It was donated to the museum in 1972 by the Hansens, a local ranch family only a few miles east of town.

Willits Rock is conventionally believed to have been carved by the Pomo Native Americans who occupied the area for at least 10,000 years. Writes Bartholomew, "The Willits stone has prominent Ogam style script, but only on one side. The other side is occupied by a large number of cupules, small round depressions which are a typical trademark of West Coast Native Americans. No one knows the meaning of these shallow depressions, except for the fact that they probably had some ritual purpose."

Reading Ogam

Bartholomew is able to read Ogam script and was actually able to decipher part of the meaning of Willits Rock. "Another interesting detail, and one that makes me suspect an astronomical meaning, is one of the round cupules located near the edge of the Ogam area. This one has three vertical lines extending from its lower edge, giving it the shape of a comet – or the sun with descending rays. Just to the right is the letter 'L,' inscribed vertically. The three lines below the cupule form the letter 'L-B' turning it into a rebus. A rebus, of course, is a picture formed with letters which spell the name of the picture. In this case we have the ancient sun god Bel, or Baal, spelled right to left, in the Semitic style. The circular cupule therefore represents the sun. And just to the right is the prominent letter 'L'.

"There is only one word in modern Irish or Old Gaelic which can be spelled with the single letter 'L.' (The older form of Ogam usually included no vowels.) This word is 'la,' written with an accent in English letters. 'La' turns out to be an Indo-European cognate related to a Sanskrit word, 'latha'; the most common meaning in several different languages is 'to shine.' In modern Irish the meaning is 'day.'…Thus our unknown rock writer did his best to make sure we understand his meaning. He draws a picture of the sun, with the name of Bel. So that we don't miss it, he repeats the name 'Bel' above, and the word 'shine' to the right. Thus the three glyphs have the meaning 'sunshine!'"

Bartholomew has examined other sections of the Willits Ogam which remain untranslated. As he writes, "There are other glyphs here I do not understand. There is, for example, a vertical line with a curve starting from its top and descending to the right. I suspect this may have some astronomical meaning, or it may be a map."

Bartholomew admits that, although he has extracted some information from the carvings, most of the background behind the Ogam remains a mystery. As he writes, "[It] appears to be composed of…hard andesite, or so I thought at first. At some point in its history it has broken through the middle – probably decades ago, judging by the degree of erosion…I'm not sure of the mineral composition of the Willits rock, but some parts of the surface look like marble or possibly obsidian. It's an extremely hard type of rock. Given its advanced state of weathering, it must be quite old."

A Private Ogam

Bartholomew had the opportunity to study another Ogam a mere fifty miles from Willits Rock and located on private property. This private Ogam is even more impressive and displays numerous markings that appear to indicate times of solstice and other significant astronomical dates.

When one considers that Ogams have been largely overlooked and misunderstood, one can only guess at how many other similar sacred mysterious stones may be lying around, unseen, undiscovered, and unknown.

Ogam Origins

Mystery

The central mystery concerning Ogam script is, where did it come from? Writes Bartholomew, "How did Ogam arrive in California in some remote past age? I have no idea. It is a mystery. I can only hope that with further study by qualified scholars, it may not remain a complete mystery forever." (Bartholomew, 1-11)

Thankfully, the Willits Rock Ogam remains preserved. While its origin remains a mystery, writes Bartholomew, "Its existence and location are no secret. Anyone can go and look. Personally I have spent many a long, hot day in the countryside peering at rocks, looking for possible ancient writing. The only reason I did not discover this one earlier is that no one told me it was there."

"There are other glyphs here I do not understand. There is, for example, a vertical line with a curve starting from its top and descending to the right. I suspect this may have some astronomical meaning, or it may be a map."

The central mystery concerning Ogam script is, where did it come from? Writes Bartholomew, "How did Ogam arrive in California in some remote past age? I have no idea. It is a mystery. I can only hope that with further study by qualified scholars, it may not remain a complete mystery forever." (Bartholomew, 1-11)

See For Yourself

Willits Rock Ogam

To view the Willits Rock Ogam, go to the Willits Museum in Mendocino County. It is located outside the front door. A plaque next to the rock reads: Pomo Petroglyphs.

Recent Discoveries, Other Ogams to Visit

Even today, other California Ogams are being discovered. In the late 1990s, another large Ogam was discovered in the Angeles Forest just north of the town of Pasadena. While a photograph of the mysterious stone appeared in the *Pasadena-Star News*, the exact location is being kept secret pending further study.

However, another Ogam that is available for public viewing can be found in the small town of Cherokee, California. This large coffin-shaped stone can be found in the local Cherokee museum. According to one researcher, the Ogam script translates into the following message: "I am striped and in pain from Bel's poison arrows. I give an uproar at the smiting of my mindful body."

Yet another Ogam can be found about thirty miles north of the town of Laytonville. Researcher Steve Bartholomew investigated the stone firsthand and verified that it contains true Ogam script. The actual stone is about the size of a large car. The rock stands alone in a field along a dirt, logging road about eleven miles off Highway 101. The rock itself is covered with graffiti, both modern and ancient. Some comes from today's residents. Some comes from earlier local Indian tribes. But some of it appears to be much older.

According to Bartholomew, the Ogam script is located on one portion of the rock, and is extremely weathered. Nevertheless, the script is obviously Ogam. Writes Bartholomew, "Judging by the degree of weathering, compared to other inscriptions on the same rock, this Ogam inscription may well be more than a thousand years old ... Personally, I have no explanation nor am I about to present one. The fact is, Ogam inscriptions exist in California. Before a theory evolves, we must deal with the facts."

As can be seen, Ogams remain one of many mysteries that are just waiting to be solved. Who were these mysterious stone writers? Hopefully further research will uncover additional Ogams and the mystery will one day be solved.

11. The Oriflamme Mountain Ghost Lights

Earthlights or ghost lights. These rare and mysterious lights usually appear over large mountains. The Oriflamme Mountain and Mount San Gorgonio are California's most famous locations to observe this dramatic phenomenon.

Ghost lights present a persistent mystery; they appear in rare and highly specific locations across the world. Also called spook lights, phantom lights, *Will o' the Wisps*, and earth lights, certain geographically defined areas (usually large mountains) seem to produce an as-yet-unexplained type of illumination. The lights are usually small. There may be one or more of them at one time. They may move or hover in place. They are usually white in color. They may flicker briefly or be sustained for hours. They appear regularly, but sporadically, with no apparent predictable pattern.

Many Theories, Little Illumination

These strange lights have been viewed for hundreds of years. Nobody knows their exact cause, and countless theories have been raised to explain their existence. Early observers usually attributed the lights to ghosts or nature spirits. Others have speculated that UFOs are responsible. Skeptics claim they are caused by weather inversions, swamp gas, fireflies, or perhaps a bizarre feature in the landscape that allows headlights from passing cars to shine in a way that creates an illusory effect of dancing lights. Other theories include ball lightning or more ghoulishly, burning methane venting from old burial sites, long before coffins had cement liners to prevent escaping gasses. Such "cemetery lights" were believed by some to be premonitions of upcoming deaths. Probably the most popular theory, however, is that the lights are generated by some type of geological or seismic force. There are many well-verified accounts of "earthquake lights" or a light source coming from the ground during an earthquake. This phenomenon has been verified by an ingenious experiment. When small fragments of granite are placed under extreme pressure, they emit tiny, short-lived balls of light. While this experiment has been repeated by numerous geologists, it is not without its problems.

bizarre phenomenon. Probably the most famous are the Brown Mountain lights in Tennessee and the Marfa Lights in Texas.

One of the least famous is the Oriflamme Mountain in the southern California desert town of Anza-Borrego. Located on the western edge, the Oriflamme Mountain is composed of granite and schist bedrock. It has several streams flowing from it. Oriflamme Canyon is lined with oaks, sycamores, willow, and cottonwoods. It is a popular site for hiking, camping, and biking and remains a largely untouched wilderness area.

The Golden Flame

The Oriflamme Mountain is also known for its mysterious ghost lights. The name "Oriflamme" actually translates as "Golden Flame." Apparently, the accounts of these lights reach so far back in history that the mountain was actually named for them. The lights occur all over the mountain and range out over the adjacent Borrego Valley desert.

While the oral traditions were well-established for centuries, the first recorded account came in 1858, when a stagecoach driver passing by the mountain observed "phantom lights" dancing on the mountain. From that point on, reports began to pour in from other witnesses, including settlers, prospectors, and soldiers.

Money Lights?

At first, the lights were thought to be from the spirits of the Native Americans who once inhabited the area. Several ancient Indian burial grounds are located in Oriflamme Canyon and the surrounding areas. True to their profession, however, prospectors generally theorized that the *money lights*, as they called them, indicated the presence of treasure or gold, and in fact gold has been found in the area.

One of the strangest and most famous of the sightings occurred in 1892, to a group of three prospectors camping near Grapevine Canyon. One of the men, Charles Knowles, described what happened. He and his companions suddenly observed three "lights" which looked like "fireworks" or balls of fire. The strange lights seemed to rise directly from the ground. They traveled in an arching pattern, reaching an elevation of about 100 feet. As they started to fall back down to the earth, the lights exploded.

About thirty minutes later, the lights returned. On this occasion, the lights behaved very differently. They rose from the ground and arched up to 100 feet, but instead of exploding, they returned to the ground where they stopped, reversed in direction, and traveled back to their starting location. Clearly these are not normal lights!

Bootleggers, Smugglers?

The sightings continued. Miners periodically saw the lights over the adjacent Vallecito Mountains and across the Borrego desert. At times, the lights reportedly lit up the night sky like a fireworks show. During the Prohibition era, it was speculated that the lights were caused by bootleggers. And at one point, the Oriflamme lights again came under suspicion for indicating the presence of illegal immigration or smuggling activities.

Still, the lights continued to appear. Reports have continued on and off, reaching to the present day. In the 1930s, a sighting of one of the mysterious ghost lights bobbing up and down along San Felipe Creek was reported to the *American Society for Psychical Research*, which printed the account in their journal.

Scientific Investigations

More recently, in October 2002, the *International Earthlight Alliance* (IEA) conducted a field investigation into the lights. The IEA is composed of scientists with various disciplines devoted to studying the phenomenon of earth lights.

Other theories include ball lightning or more ghoulishly, burning methane venting from old burial sites, long before coffins had cement liners to prevent escaping gasses. Such "cemetery lights" were believed by some to be premonitions of upcoming deaths.

Despite the popularity of the seismic theory, earth lights are *not* more common in areas with large earthquake activity. In fact, some areas with no earthquake activity produce remarkable displays. Furthermore, the earth lights are sometimes viewed for a period of hours.

Ghost Light Locations

There are only a handful of places in the United States that are known to produce this

On October 18, 2002, Marsha Adams of the IEA headed a team of researchers for an on-site investigation. While the team did not observe the lights, they were able to interview firsthand eyewitnesses from the nearby town of Butterfield who confirmed that the lights still appear.

Still, no explanation to account for earth lights has ever been found. One recent scientific theory is as bizarre as any other theory. It states that when strong winds blow sand up against large quartz outcroppings, they create a strong charge of static electricity. When the static-electric charge is strong enough, it discharges and causes the lights to flash.

See for Yourself

The area is now preserved as Anza-Borrego Desert State Park. To reach Oriflamme Canyon, take Highway S-2 one mile south of the Box Canyon historical site. There is a small sign that reads "Oriflamme Canyon." It is a three-mile dirt road that may require four-wheel drive. Stay left as the road forks and it will lead you to the base of the canyon. Here you will find some of the ancient Indian "morteros" or gravesites. The canyon leads up to the southwest.

The mountain itself can be observed from Highway S2, four miles west of Butterfield ranch. Two dirt roads lead up to the mountain. The Butterfield Ranch Resort is located at: 14925 Gt. S. Overland, Julian, CA 92036. Phone: 760-765-2179.

Other Sites for Mysterious Lights

Other locations in California do have possible potential for producing earth lights. The IEC was alerted to the location of a private ranch in the town of Campo where mysterious recurring lights were appearing.

Mysterious lights have often been seen around Mount Shasta up in northern California (see chapter on Mount Shasta). And in central California, Mount San Gorgonio has been the location of a few possible earth light sightings.

In the summer of 1983, eight climbers had just reached the top of San Gorgonio Peak when they observed a large unexplained light hovering overhead. Says one of the witnesses, Mark Grant, "It was about three or four hundred feet above us. I mean, it was very close and the whole area around us lit up…. It was brighter than it was comfortable to look at. As a matter of fact I remember it was very uncomfortable to look into the light because it was so bright and so intense…there was no noise whatsoever with this. And the light just kind of hovered overhead and circled around, and all of a sudden it vanished – it was completely gone. It just narrowed down into a pinpoint and poof, it was gone." (Dennett 1997, 27-30)

None of the climbers could explain what they had seen. They thought of helicopters, but the object made no noise and moved away too quickly. The light may have been a UFO or it may have been caused by earth lights. Certainly mountain peaks are known to be sacred places in many cultures, and many earth lights are reported along mountain peaks. That San Gorgonio produces earth lights like Oriflamme Mountain is strengthened by the below account.

In the summer of 1993, Jason Adams and three friends were backpacking in the San Gorgonio Wilderness Area. They spent the second night on the northeast slope of Mount San Gorgonio at an elevation of about 10,000 feet. They were completely isolated from all civilization. It was then that they sighted what appeared to be earth lights. Writes Adams, "As we were climbing into our sleeping bags I noticed a bright bluish-white light to the southeast of us, uphill. The light appeared to be about 200 yards away and approximately three inches in diameter. The light source appeared to 'bounce' across the top of the ridge, reverse course, and then 'bounce' back to the other end of the ridge. Overall it was visible for about ten seconds, then it abruptly disappeared. Upon conferring with my friends I learned that one of them had seen the light just as I had. Another had been lying in his sleeping bag, looking up, and had seen a similar light at the peak of the tree under which we were sleeping."

The next day the men went to investigate the area. Writes Adams, "We walked up to the ridge where we had seen the light. On the other side was a sheer cliff, dropping several hundred feet. The ridge itself was sparsely forested and, aside from the view, there was nothing noteworthy about it. We found no possible light sources." (Adams, 1)

The experience of Adams and his friends is highly reminiscent of the British myths of Will O' the Wisps, nasty creatures who used lights to lure unwary travelers off the beaten path and to their doom: in this case, off a sheer cliff hundreds of feet high. Fortunately for Adams and his friends, they waited until morning to investigate.

As we have seen, earth lights can be found all across California, though the majority of them seem to be centered around large mountains. They are usually viewed only at night, though daylight sightings cannot be ruled out. While the Marfa Lights and the Brown Mountain lights have been captured on film, nobody has yet been able to photograph any California earth lights.

There are numerous theories, but as of today they remain – like so many other things in California — unexplained.

12. Giants in the Desert

Located in the small southern California desert town of Blythe, a small farming community with a population of about 8000 inhabitants, just outside the town, are dozens of *intaglios*, the giants of the desert. In fact, they are huge human and animal representations etched into the desert floor.

Their existence itself is not so unusual. The big mysteries are: who made them, why, and what do they mean? There are only a half dozen of them, scattered across a small area of the desert outside Blythe. They are only visible from the air, so whoever made them had no way of seeing them in their entirety. There are a few human figures and a few animal figures. One of the animals is obviously a snake. The other is a four-legged creature, but nobody is quite sure what type of animal is represented. Some say it's a coyote. Others say that it looks like a horse, which would mean that horses were in America at least 500 years ago, the estimated age of the intaglios. The figures themselves are enormous. One of the human figures is a 171 feet long. Another is 94 feet in length. A strange arc that cuts across one of the figures is believed to be the symbol of a ritual dance.

The figures were discovered in the 1930s. Professional archaeologists investigated the site in 1952, but were unable to provide any conclusive explanations. The theories to explain the intaglios range from possible Native American sacred sites to attempts to contact or communicate with extraterrestrials. The main mystery is who made them? It is just one of the many California mysteries that remain unsolved.

The theories to explain the intaglios range from possible Native American sacred sites to attempts to contact or communicate with extraterrestrials.

See for Yourself

The intaglios are located seventeen miles north of Blythe on Highway 95.

Part Two
Cryptozoological Creatures

1. California Lake Monsters

As civilization continues to encroach upon the shrinking wilderness, more and more reports are coming in of strange, unexplained animals. Known as *cryptozoological* creatures, these are species that remain unknown to mainstream science. One of the most popular of cryptozoological creatures is Bigfoot, also known as Sasquatch or the Yeti. Some of the earliest recorded accounts come from California, which continues to be one of the world's leading Bigfoot producers. In fact, Bigfoot reports have come in from virtually every corner of the state.

However, Bigfoot is not the only unexplained creature in California. As it turns out, there are several lakes that evidently contain their own unexplained aquatic creatures, including Lake Elsinore, Lake Tahoe, Lake Hodges, and others. Each of these locations has a long tradition of encounters with what appear to be a lake monster much like that of the famous Loch Ness in Scotland. Then there are the gigantic sea serpent-like creatures that make regular appearances along California's long coastline, and the giant mountain salamanders seen by only a few lucky witnesses. And, of course, we can't forget the nefarious *chupacabra*.

Is it actually possible that so many unexplained creatures are lurking through California's vast wilderness? The evidence says, yes! If you want to see a cryptozoological creature for yourself, it might be much easier than you think.

California has at least four lakes that produce reports of unknown "lake monsters."

Thwarting

Conventional Wisdom

For those skeptics who don't believe in cryptozoological creatures, it should be pointed out that many new species are discovered each year. A small portion of these include large animals. Mainstream science has a tendency to become a closed system. New evidence that goes against conventional wisdom can be easily suppressed, distorted, denied or disbelieved. For example, nineteenth century zoologists were reluctant to admit the existence of such creatures as gorillas and the platypus, even when confronted with credible evidence. For cryptozoologists, this skepticism can represent a major obstacle to serious research.

California has more unexplained lake monsters than any other state in the United States. The creatures have been sighted regularly by multiple independent witnesses for more than a century and even photographed. And yet, the mystery remains. Nobody has been able to produce conclusive evidence of their existence. But, as we shall see, proof is often in the eye of the beholder. Literally *hundreds* of people have seen these creatures for themselves. For them, there is little room for denial. They know the truth. The California lake monsters are real.

Elsie, The Lake Monster of Lake Elsinore

While Nessie of Loch Ness, Scotland, is the world's most famous lake monster, there are actually hundreds of lakes that produce similar accounts. The truth is, these lake monsters are being reported in various lakes around the entire planet. The incredible similarity of these different accounts soon makes it clear to the serious researcher that lake monsters are, in fact, real. There are simply too many people who have reported seeing the same thing in completely different locations.

There are various theories to explain lake monsters. Skeptics claim that witnesses are only seeing large fish, perhaps giant sturgeon, which can grow up to twenty feet long. Another theory is that the creatures are actually aquatic dinosaurs that have somehow managed to survive the various mass extinctions that killed off most of the other dinosaurs, and have still remained undetected by modern science.

One lake that has gained a reputation for having its own mysterious creature living in its depths is southern California's Lake Elsinore. The town of Lake Elsinore is built around the lake, which is the area's main industry, mostly tourism and recreation. Thousands of people flock to the lake on a daily basis to enjoy its fresh waters.

Is it actually possible that an unknown creature could remain so elusive around so many people? The answer of course is, no, it can't, and it hasn't. The fact is that numerous people *have* seen the monster – so many that the monster actually has its own name, Elsie.

Early Elsie Accounts

The first reports of the lake monster of Lake Elsinore came from the *Paí ah' che'* Native Americans, who told visiting Spaniards that their lake, which they called "Etengvo Wumoma," was inhabited by a gigantic monster which would surface from time to time, belching steam and fire.

This has led to some speculation that the accounts are caused by mysterious hot springs which might bubble to the surface. With sulfuric gases escaping, this might make a believable lake monster.

Modern Elsie Sightings

These theories, however, are easily pushed aside by the several modern accounts of sightings, which actually stretch back more than 100 years to 1884.

As one local writer, David Allen Russell, reports, "There are still many reliable witnesses who claim that they have seen the monster following their boats under the water late at night, terrifying them so much that they headed pell-mell for the banks and beaches as fast as their water vessels could carry them, and never came back." (Russell, 1-2)

Most of the accounts describe a serpent-like creature, which shows the humps on its back as it propels itself through the water. Only a few claim to have seen its head and face, which is described like a snake, with a dog-like snout.

Lake Elsinore has actually dried up at least twice in its recorded history, making skeptics conclude that monster sightings would therefore be impossible. However, because we know nothing about the species of creature, it is entirely possible that it simply hibernated in the mud, or perhaps even laid eggs and reproduced.

In any case, the stories circulated so widely, that Elsie soon became California's most famous lake monster. During the winter of 1970, residents and state recreation officers had several sightings of the creature, whose humps appeared to move up and down like a gigantic snake.

In the late 1980s, a local company, Poppy Graphics, offered to create a life-size statue of Elsie, and make the creature the city's official mascot. The idea gained wide approval, and eventually more than 200 volunteers donated time, money or supplies to build the fiberglass statue. Today, the statue stands more than twenty-five feet high and a hundred feet long. It is painted in bright colors and shows a friendly, inviting lake monster. It is being held captive on Lakeland Beach, where it can be viewed by visitors.

Tessie, The Lake
Monster of Lake Tahoe

Lake Tahoe. There are numerous reports every year involving sightings of an unknown lake monster roaming the depths of this freshwater lake. *Photo credit: Roger Anderson.*

Lake Tahoe is a beautiful alpine freshwater lake located in central California along the Nevada-California border. The lake is an enormous tourist attraction, bringing in thousands of water-sport enthusiasts in the summer, and just as many skiers and snowboarders in the winter.

Unknown to many people, however, is that Lake Tahoe has its very own lake monster. Unlike most lakes, Lake Tahoe is incredibly deep, with an estimated depth of 1645 feet. And with a length of twenty-two miles, an unknown creature has plenty of space to hide.

Early Reports and Tessie's Lair

Reports began soon after early American settlers arrived at the lake and have continued until the present day. Like Lake Elsinore, the first sightings were actually recorded by the Native Americans, in this case, the Washoe and Paiute Tribes. In the mid-1800s, the two tribes often fought over the right to hunt and fish in the lake area. Both tribes also had legends of a monster that lived in the waters. They held sacred meetings in a large cavern called "Cave Rock" which is located above another large underwater cavern, and supposedly the lair of the lake monster.

More Recent Reports

In the 1930s, a series of sightings revived the legends, and people began to take the reports more seriously. Over the years, the sightings of Tessie became so numerous that eventually a museum was created to document the history of the lake monster. The museum was full of Tessie souvenirs and newspaper clippings of various sightings. Unfortunately, the museum has recently been shut down.

Tahoe Tessie is braver than most lake monsters and its many regular appearances lend credence to its reality. In the summer of 1979, a visiting couple was convinced that they observed a "sea serpent" in the lake off of Tahoe Vista. The couple reported their account to local newspapers.

Sightings continued sporadically. In 1984, there was a series of highly publicized sightings by various witnesses from different locations on the lake. In 1985, a tourist saw the creature and shot several frames of footage showing a large "something" swimming through the lake. Embarrassed officials downplayed the recent sightings and even attempted to suppress the film.

Another recent dramatic sighting occurred to Gene St. Denis and his friend, while walking along the beach along Cave Rock. Says St. Denis, "We saw a blotchy gray creature about ten to fifteen feet long. It turned a corner and produced a V-shaped wake in front of it."

The unknown creature surfaced briefly, and then plunged back into the depths of the lake, leaving St. Denis and his friend totally amazed.

This was not St. Denis's only sighting. He is a local resident, and actually makes a living from the lake. He is the owner of Blue Ribbon Fishing and Tahoe Trophy Trout. Because of this, he spends much of his of time on the lake. This puts him in the perfect position to have repeated encounters. His next experience would be considerably more dramatic.

St. Denis was swimming along the shoreline with another friend when, suddenly, the water seemed to explode underneath them. As the water began to calm, they observed a sixteen-foot long snake-like creature slithering quickly away.

Looking down in the water beneath them, St. Denis and his friend observed more evidence of the creature's passing. Says St. Denis, "We waited for the silt to settle and found large fin prints where the creature had been."

St. Denis has found other bits of intriguing evidence. On two occasions, while he was reeling fish into this boat, *something* attacked the fish, leaving what looked like enormous teeth marks. Says St. Denis, "About halfway to the boat, these fish – they were big fish – got raked…the holes left by the teeth were big enough to put a pencil into." (Louise, 1-3)

Theories Countered

Skeptics claim that the sightings of Tessie could be caused by an unusual or rare fish. One popular explanation is the sturgeon, which can reach a weight of 1500 pounds, a length up to twenty feet, and can live for more than 100 years. Another possible candidate is the muskie, a large aggressive fish that can reach a length of more than eight feet.

However, these theories both have major problems. One is that sturgeon have no teeth. Another is that neither muskie nor sturgeon are actually found in Lake Tahoe. And finally, the descriptions of most witnesses involve a *much* longer serpent-like creature (most reports say about sixty feet) that bears little resemblance to a normal fish. It is usually described as being snake-like, with dark skin and reptilian features.

In 1984, Charles Goldman, Professor of Limnology (the study of Lakes) at Davis University came to study the accounts and give a lecture on the topic. He remained unconvinced. Says Goldman, "We think that a lot of the Tessie reports are actually colliding boat wakes which produce a series of waves." Goldman says that this creates an illusion of a series of humps rising out of the water, looking like a giant serpent. He also claimed that a mother goose being followed in single file by her gosling babies would create the same type of illusion.

Tessie Persists

Most of the witnesses, however, believe that Tahoe Tessie is exactly what she appears to be: an unidentified species. According to researcher Cherie Louise, Tessie sightings occur at a rate of about a dozen per year, or once a month. A Tessie phone hotline was established at Kings Beach, the former site of the Tessie museum. Unfortunately, the hotline has been discontinued.

And yet, like all lake monsters, Tessie remains elusive, showing herself only just enough to keep the legend alive, and not enough for conclusive proof.

Tessie and Jacques Cousteau

There have been unconfirmed rumors that Jacques Cousteau conducted a search for Tessie and after successfully finding her, decided not to reveal his discovery because "the world wasn't ready." If true, perhaps he feared that Tessie would be hunted to her death.

While not as famous as Nessie, Tessie is quickly becoming one of the world's best-verified lake monsters. In fact, Loren Coleman cites Lake Tahoe as one of the top ten best locations in the world to look for a lake monster.

Tessie Returns

On April 26, 2005, Tahoe resident Ron Talmadge and his friend Beth Douglas were walking along the west shore of Tahoe Park Beach when they had a dramatic sighting. Only a few dozen yards offshore, Talmadge and Douglas were amazed to see an enormous snake-like creature undulating on the water's surface. Talmadge was already familiar with the stories of Tessie, and he recognized the monster instantly. Says Talmadge, "There were these solid black humps…there was no wake as it came towards us."

He quickly exclaimed, "Damn, that's Tessie!" His friend, Beth Douglas was amazed and awed. "It was so cool…the way he said it was so calm. I thought it was an everyday occurrence." Needless to say, both Douglas and Talmadge are now believers. As Talmadge says, "This sucker's real!" (Sheffield, 4)

As can be seen, Tessie is still alive and kicking. Incidentally, Lake Tahoe contains an estimated fish population well in excess of 6500 prey fish (not including Tessie), supplying plenty of food for a large sea-monster.

> **Tahoe Tessie is braver than most lake monsters and its many regular appearances lend credence to its reality.**

See for Yourself

For those who would like to see Tessie for themselves, Lake Tahoe is a tourist's haven, with all kinds of fun things to do, including snorkeling, boating, bike-riding, hiking, water-skiing, snow-skiing, snow boarding, and more. And for the more adventurous, there's always a good time in having a Tessie "stake-out." A good place to start might be cave beach. Many of the sightings have occurred in this area, which contains large underwater caverns. Again, there is speculation that Tessie makes her home somewhere in this area. Another possible hideout is a deep hole at the bottom of the lake in Carnelian Bay. Yet another favored spot is King's Beach, also the former location of the Tessie museum. The entire lake is surrounded by roads and pathways that offer many secluded spots for Tessie observations. Good luck!

Hodgee, the Lake Monster of Lake Hodges

One of the most impressive and yet virtually unknown lake monsters is that of Lake Hodges, located in southern California, about thirty-one miles north of San Diego. While other lake monsters have received a good deal of publicity, "Hodgee" is almost unheard of. This is surprising because the evidence of his existence is very impressive.

Lake Hodges has a surface area of 1,234 acres and twenty-seven miles of shorelines. It is a long, thin, winding lake. Its depth has not yet been determined. Its waters are replenished by the Del Dios river, which has run through the valley for 40,000 years.

Lake Hodges Secret Resident

Lake Hodges used to be a much smaller lake, which was regarded by the local Kumeyaay Native Americans as sacred. On the south side of the lake they created a sacred site to honor the area. It is called *Piedras Pintadas* or Painted Rocks, and is today still considered sacred to the Kumeyaay.

Then in 1916, Colonel Ed Fletcher convinced the Santa Fe Railroad to create a dam at the western end. The Kumeyaay protested, and for the first time, revealed the presence of a large unknown creature that guarded the lake.

The Union Railroad went ahead with the project anyway, dismissing the warnings as "ramblings attempting to stop the project." After two years the dam was completed and the Del Dios canyon became permanently flooded, tripling the size of the lake.

Disturbances, Vandalism, Escalating Sightings

The first modern reports of Hodgee have been traced back to 1921, when fishermen from San Diego and local fishermen reported seeing "a large disturbance" in the waters of the lake. These reports continued for two years.

Then in 1923, events began to escalate. Two mines next to the lake had been in operation for two years with no problems. Then, four days apart, both of the mines were vandalized. Heavy rock extraction equipment had been toppled over and partially crushed. When the two competing mine owners began to blame each other, the police were brought in to investigate. The only conclusion that could be drawn, however, was that the culprit must have used the lake to access the mines as there were no footprints. Some people raised the possibility that the monster of Lake Hodges was responsible.

In 1925, the city of San Diego purchased the lake for $490,000 dollars. The property was turned into a recreational and fishing area. It was at this time that the reports of Hodgee increased dramatically. More and more people began to report seeing a large snake-like creature.

Official Investigations

By 1929, the reports had become so numerous that the mayor of Escondido began to feel pressure from local citizens to take action. The mayor agreed and formally requested the San Diego Mayor, Harry C. Clark, to fund an official investigation into the claims. Incredibly, Mayor Clark agreed and turned the project over to the San Diego University of California and the Scripps Institute of Oceanography.

In 1930, the official investigation announced that they had found no hard proof or conclusive evidence of the existence of a monster in Lake Hodges. However, one research assistant reported his own sighting. He was out on the lake when he saw a head that was "lizardlike...protruding from the water." Because of this, the Scripps Institute concluded that more research was needed.

Meanwhile, the sightings continued. In 1931, a small boat docked along a pier was mysteriously destroyed. Police were called in to investigate. No footprints were found, but according to the police report, there was evidence of a "great turmoil under the water along the base of the pier, from a boat or underwater vessel...or perhaps a large creature."

This prompted the Scripps Institute to take drastic action. Thomas W. Vaughan, the director of the Institute, headed the project that involved the construction of an enormous metal cage, the size of a small house to capture the creature.

In 1932, the cage was submerged in the lake and a small sea lion was secured inside as bait. At the same time, several cameras in glass containers were placed underwater, tied to buoys around the cage.

The trap was complete and expectations for success were high. When the cage was raised a short time later, investigators were amazed to see that the bait had been taken, but the trap remained un-sprung. Then they checked the cameras.

To their amazement, one of the cameras produced a very intriguing photograph which appeared to show the shape of a large underwater creature. The photo was later digitally enhanced and clearly shows a large dinosaur-looking shape. The creature appears to have a long snake-like neck and head, a large thick body, and wide, flat fins. While Hodgee wasn't physically captured, it appeared that his image was. This inspired several subsequent attempts to capture the creature. Incredibly, these numerous attempts resulted only in smashed cameras and buoys. Apparently, Hodgee realized that his safety was in danger.

While Hodgee defended himself, the project itself ran into further problems. The public had learned that defenseless sea lions were being used as bait, which began an animal rights protest. By 1933, the project was cancelled.

Meanwhile, sightings continued. In 1941, scientists from the Scripps Institute received funding from the United State's Navy's Office of Naval Research to conduct a new type of investigation.

Their first step was to place a large portion of the lake off limits to all people. They then carefully placed a huge length of "trip-wire" at a depth of twelve feet, attached to a large rack of cameras on the surface. The system was placed in operation for three months with no signs of any activity. However, on the third month, the trip wire was activated and the most famous of all Hodgee photos was taken. It clearly shows a very large hump protruding from the water, along with another section of the body.

The photo finally provided the solid evidence researchers needed to prove the existence of Hodgee.

However, at that time, World War II was growing in influence, and all research was stopped while attention was diverted towards the war effort.

Rotenon Death?

Meanwhile, the sightings continued. Then in 1956 came one of the strangest and saddest chapters in the history of Lake Hodges. The lake was being overrun by one type of fish, the carp. Officials decided that the only solution was to kill all the existing fish in the lake and restock it with new fish. Thousands of pounds of the highly toxic chemical, Rotenon, were poured into the lake, causing the vast majority of fish to asphyxiate. The lake was then restocked.

There was reportedly some controversy about whether the real reason was to kill and capture the lake monster. The lake was closed for two years while studies took place.

Hodgee Resurfaced

The lake was then re-opened to the public. It appeared, at first, that Hodgee had been killed. However, it wasn't long before the locals began to report sightings of the same creature that they had seen many times before. Hodgee was back. In 1966, two families were picnicking along the shoreline. Suddenly, about fifty yards offshore, a large creature surfaced. It was witnessed by seven people, one of whom snapped several photos, one of which shows a dark hump protruding from the water.

In 1985, Lake Hodges dam-keeper, Morgan A Tidwell, held a press conference during which he publicly announced that Hodgee was a real creature of an unknown species which inhabited the lake.

Research Continued

Sightings of Hodgee have continued to the present day and are currently being studied by the Lake Hodges Scientific Research Center. The center takes the Hodgee sightings very seriously. As they say, "The LHSRC is a not-for-profit research organization that is dedicated to learning more about the unexplained phenomena related to Lake Hodges. In particular, we are focused on the so-called 'Lake Hodges Monster' known locally as 'Hodgee'." (www.hodgee.com)

In 1999, the center set up sophisticated cameras along the shoreline of the lake, hoping to catch another photograph, which remains a high priority. They also have plans to study a deep earthquake fault that runs through the center of the lake, analyze fish counts, and collect local testimonies.

There are surprisingly few skeptical explanations to account for Hodgee. Because the fish population has been strictly monitored and controlled, it is impossible to explain away Hodgee as a giant sturgeon. The lake contains numerous small fish, including largemouth bass, crappie, bluegill, channel catfish, bullhead, and carp, but nothing big enough to account for Hodgee.

However, Lake Hodges is a big lake and some of these fish have reached record size. In 1985, the second largest bass ever caught in the United States was reeled out of Lake Hodges by fisherman Gene Dupras. The enormous bass weighed in at twenty pounds, five ounces. Although large, it comes nowhere near to accounting for the Hodgee sightings.

Today, Lake Hodges remains among the largely untouched wilderness sites. It is a popular local recreational area, with picnicking, boating, wind-surfing, horseback riding, mountain biking, hiking, and other activities. The Lake Hodges Interpretive Center is being planned for the southeastern portion of the lake. The center will contain a research institute and a museum about the lake.

A Monster

In Lake Elizabeth

Seventeen miles west of Palmdale on Elizabeth Lake Road lies a small, remote body of water called Lake Elizabeth. Among the first to report unusual activity in the lake was rancher Don Pedro Carrillo, who reportedly abandoned his ranch in 1830 after a mysterious fire burned down his property. He felt that the lake was cursed by the Devil. In 1855, American settlers moved into the area, but reportedly abandoned it, saying it was haunted.

Early Observations

The first recorded sighting occurred around that time, when rancher Don Chico Lopez and two others observed a "huge monster with bat-like wings" emerge from the lake. Lopez had been losing his livestock regularly, and now it seemed he knew why. He sold his ranch at a loss. The property was purchased by rancher Miguel Leonis, who also claimed to see the creature. In 1886,

yet another rancher, Don Felipe Rivera, also reported seeing the gigantic reptilian.

Dead or Gone?

And there the sightings seem to end. Perhaps the creature decided to remain hidden, or maybe it died. Or perhaps it simply moved locations, as there are rumors of similar sightings in a nearby small lake known as Sag Pond, which also goes by several other names, including Una Lake, Lake La Rush Lamar, and the Bottomless Lake. This particular body of water is located in Palmdale along the Sierra Highway.

Other Lakes, Other Creatures

In any case, California has numerous other lakes with legends of unknown creatures. Scattered reports of unknown creatures have come from the Blue Lakes east of Ukiah and from Clear Lake in northern California.

Yet another lake that has been long rumored to hold a lake monster is Lake Laguna. Located in Fullerton in southern California, this seven-acre lake has produced a number of unsubstantiated reports of a large, unknown, prehistoric-looking creature lurking in its depths. The reports stretch back at least forty years. Believers called the creature "Old Bob." Witnesses claimed he had a huge head that would peek above the surface for a moment before diving back beneath the surface.

Still, the rumors remained just that, rumors.

Landed Lake Monster

Then, on September 9, 2004, these rumors were proven to be true when workers hired to pull fish from the lake captured something very unusual in their fishing nets. The lake was undergoing a two million dollar renovation that involved dredging the entire lake.

When the workers pulled up their nets, the last thing they expected to find was "Old Bob" himself. Yet, there he was, tangled in the nets, the lake monster of Lake Laguna – a giant alligator snapping turtle.

See for Yourself

The lake is located thirty-one miles north of San Diego, and can be accessed from Interstate Highway 15. Exit on Via Rancho Diego, go west to Lake Drive, then south on Lake Drive to the lake entrance on your left. There is no overnight camping allowed at the lake, however ten miles east of the lake is Lake Dixon, which does allow camping. For reservations call 760-741-3328.

While your there, be sure to check out the sacred site, the Piedras Pintadas (Painted Rocks), located on the south side of the lake.

Alligator snapping turtles are the largest of all freshwater turtles in North America. They grow up to 250 pounds and live longer than 100 years. They are native only to the South and East Coast, and are actually illegal in California.

Old Bob weighed about 100 pounds and was estimated to be about fifty years old. He had the characteristic huge head, wormlike tongue, hooked beak, and a three-foot-diameter ridge-like shell. How Old Bob got into the lake is a mystery. Officials speculated that perhaps he was a pet that grew too big for his pond and was deposited by his owner into the lake.

Sharon Paquette is the vice president of the Orange County chapter of the California Turtle and Tortoise Club. According to her, the alligator snapping turtles have changed little since the age of dinosaurs. Says Paquette, "No wonder folks get excited. It's an awesome sight to see what looks like a prehistoric creature."

But, according to Paquette, "Old Bob" is also dangerous. As she says, "These are powerful animals. A human could lose a foot or fingers."

Because Old Bob was illegal in California, he was carted away and taken to a refuge on the East Coast where he remains today.

However, there is a lesson to be learned from Old Bob. The fact that a creature of his size remained undetected for so long in a lake of that size lends credence to the many other accounts of unknown lake monsters in the much larger California lakes.

> **Because Old Bob was illegal in California, he was carted away and taken to a refuge on the East Coast where he remains today.**

2. Sea Serpents of the California Coast

Overlooking the Santa Catalina channel, the location of many sightings of an unknown sea serpent.

California leads the nation with reports of unknown sea serpents reaching back nearly 100 years.

Cryptozoologists theorize that the various reports of sea serpents may have their origins in a prehistoric creature perhaps similar to the plesiosaurus.

California has a thousand-mile-long beautiful coastline with some of the most crowded beaches in the world. If sea serpents are real, one would expect that there would be numerous reports up and down the coast. As it turns out, this is exactly the case. In fact (and true to its nature), California is one of the world's leading hotspots for sea serpents. These reports reach back more than 125 years and continue to the present day.

"See" Serpents, Sightings Studied

The first person to examine these reports systematically was the father of modern cryptozoology, Bernard Heuvelmans. While studying cases from across the world, he focused on the California coast and discovered that the area was an active sea serpent hotspot. As he writes, "[T]he territory of one type of sea serpent, the maned it would seem, probably stretches all along the west coast of North America – at least in the temperate zone." (Heuvelmans, 478)

Sea serpents were first noticed and recorded throughout the 1910s and 1920s, when a flurry of sightings occurred as far north as San Francisco and as far south as San Clemente. However, earlier reports have been since located by ardent researchers.

As uncovered by Bernard Heuvelmans, the first known sea-serpent account off the coast of California occurred on December 21, 1879. Captain G. Verschuur of the ship *Granada* was sailing along the southern California coast off Cape San Lucas when he and his crew observed a thin-necked, serpent-like creature rise three feet out of the water in full view of all aboard. Heuvelmans speculated that it was either a giant eel or a baby sea serpent. The ship's second officer recalled having seen another larger sea serpent eight years earlier off the coast of Australia.

This, however, was just the beginning. The first reports to generate widespread attention occurred off the coast of Southern California, along the Santa Catalina channel. Starting in 1914, numerous local fishermen reported their sightings of an enormous sea serpent-like creature. For the next five years reports poured in, becoming so numerous that it became impossible to pass them off as mere rumors.

Then, in 1919, world-famous fisherman Ralph Bandini confirmed all the rumors when he came forward with his own account of having seen gigantic sea serpents. Bandini was an expert big-game fisherman, and later authored three classic books on the sport. He was a secretary of the Tuna Club, a member of the California fish and game commission, a lawyer, and a champion of coastal conservation — your basic pillar-of-the-community type — in other words, the perfect witness.

The San Clemente Monster

Bandini's first sighting of what came to be known as "the San Clemente Monster" occurred in 1919 off the coast of Santa Catalina Island, when he and his crew saw a creature off in the distance rising higher and higher out of the water. Before they could get a closer observation, the creature plunged beneath the surface.

However, one year later in September 1920, Bandini and his fishing partner, Smith Warren, had an unforgettable close-up encounter with the San Clemente Monster. It was eight o'clock in the morning and the two men were off the coast of San Clemente Island when the monster made its dramatic appearance. Writes Bandini, "All of a sudden, I saw something dark and big heave up. I seized my glasses. What I saw brought me straight up! A great columnar neck and head, I guess that is what it was, lifting a good ten feet. It must have been five or six feet thick. Something that appeared to be a kind of mane or coarse hair, almost like a fine seaweed, hung dankly. But the eyes – those were what held me. Huge, seemingly bulging, round – at least a foot in diameter! We swung around it...Then, even as I watched through the glasses, the Thing sank. There was no swirl, no fuss...just a leisurely majestic sinking – and it disappeared, about a quarter mile away."

Bandini estimated that the creature was considerably larger than a blue whale, the largest known living animal on earth. He was amazed by the way it didn't rise with the waves as a whale would have done, but instead remained as motionless as a rock. He knew this meant that, like an iceberg, most of the creature was underwater, and it must be incredibly huge. Bandini later sighted the creature on two separate occasions, both times in the Santa Catalina channel.

During that same time period, several other prominent witnesses also claimed to have seen the unknown creature. George Farnsworth, the president of the Tuna Club observed the creature and gave an identical description as that of Bandini. Writes Farnsworth, "Its eyes were 12 inches in diameter, not set on the side like an ordinary fish, but more central. It had a big mane of hair about two feet long. We were within a hundred feet of it before it went down. This was no sea elephant. It was some kind of mammal, for it could not have been standing so long unless it was." (Heuvelmans, 479)

Other witnesses include former Tuna Club president, Jimmy Jump; millionaire George C. Thomas III; inventor of the Coxe reel, Joe Coxe; and fishing author, J. Charles Davis II. In each case, the monster appeared in the same general area, along the Santa Catalina channel.

Examining the Dead

That strange creatures do exist off the California coast was proven in 1925, when the carcass of an enormous unknown sea-creature washed up on the beaches of Santa Cruz. The creature was badly decomposed. It measured 36 feet in length, had a long slender neck, small eyes, a large head, and a beaked snout. Serpent enthusiasts announced what appeared to be proof at last of the existence of the giant creatures. Eventually, the skull was examined by scientists from the Museum of the California Academy of Sciences and determined to be of an extremely rare species of beaked-whale, one that has only been seen a few times in recorded history. The appearance of a long neck had been an illusion caused by the decomposition of the skin separating from the rib cage.

Although the Santa Cruz monster turned out to be a known species, it proved that the coastal areas do, in fact, harbor a wide variety of rare marine animals. Supporting this assertion is that the extremely rare oarfish has washed up on the California coast on three occasions. In 1901, an oarfish washed up on Newport Beach. Later, another oarfish was captured off the coast of Malibu. Also, the island of Coronado, immediately north of the Mexican border was also the location of an oarfish capture. Oarfish can reach lengths of up to 23 feet, and look very much like a small variety of sea serpent.

The Old Man
of Monterey Trench

While there are many interesting coastal areas along California, one of the strangest is Monterey Bay. What makes this particular area so unusual is the deep submarine canyon located in the bay. In 1992, Monterey Bay was declared a federal marine sanctuary. It covers 5312 square miles, extending 200 miles along the coast, and is the largest marine refuge in the United States. The canyon, known as Monterey Trench, is extremely deep with some sections deeper than 9000 feet. Its exact depth is not known, but it is at least twice the depth of the Grand Canyon. It is the deepest underwater trench in North America.

The area is protected because of the vast variety of marine life found there. Writes one researcher, "The canyon has more biological diversity per square centimeter, or mile, than the richest habitat on earth, including the rain forest."

The bay contains more than 340 species of fish, 30 species of marine mammals, and 116 species of birds (at the time a world record!). Therefore, it should not be too hard to believe that this bay has produced literally dozens of sightings of giant sea serpents and other strange sea monsters. In fact, the sightings were so common that the sea serpent was given its own name: "Bobo" or "The Old Man of Monterey Bay."

The sightings actually reach down to Cape San Martin, which produced a plethora of sightings throughout the 1930s and 1940s.

Researcher Randall Reinstedt is the world's expert on the Monterey Bay Sea monsters. Writes Reinstedt, "Stories of encounters with frightening monsters and snake-like serpents have circulated throughout the Monterey Bay area for countless years." (Reinstedt, 9)

In fact, the sightings reach back nearly 100 years. Rumors of sightings began in the 1920s, when local fishermen came to shore with claims of sightings. Most of these involved single witnesses who were not believed. But as more fishermen made their livings on the rich fishing in the bay, it was only a matter of time before more sightings occurred.

A Human-looking Head

On an eventful morning, at around 11:00, in September 1930, a fishing boat was off Point Joe at the south edge of Monterey Bay. As the boat traversed the waters, the crew noticed a large creature in the water eyeing them from a distance of about eighty feet. They were trying to determine what the creature was when it rose out of the water to a height of six feet. The men were shocked to see an almost human-looking head perched on a four-foot thick neck. The enormous creature dived beneath the surface and swam underneath the boat. The crew was then able to see that the "sea monster" had large fins and a huge tail. It quickly disappeared into the depths.

> One crewmember said the creature had "a very old man's or monkey's face, with eyes twice the diameter of breakfast buns, and a mouth like a crescent moon.

Also in the early 1930s, a Monterey resident, then fourteen years old, was walking along the shore when he saw a creature rising out of the water only about 200 yards from shore. Suddenly, the creature stuck its head out of the water to a height of twelve feet! The witness was amazed to see a head like a giraffe. The creature suddenly dived back in and disappeared.

At first, these accounts and others were considered rumors or failed to gain widespread attention. But the sightings continued and soon more people began to take notice. Another early sighting occurred in 1938. The crew of the ship *Dante Allighieri* was crossing over the deep part of Monterey Trench when they saw a strange object floating in the water. As they approached, they realized it was a creature about thirty feet long, with a fish-like tail, and a surprisingly human-like face. The boat had apparently surprised the creature, which was dozing on the surface. As the boat drew alongside of the creature, it woke up, looked at the ship, and dived into the depths … but not before the crew got a good look at the monster. One crewmember said the creature had "a very old man's or monkey's face, with eyes twice the diameter of breakfast buns, and a mouth like a crescent moon. Barnacles were all over the head, and also along the black body. Folds of white skin hung beneath the neck. The body was as big around as a pick-up truck. It must have weighed maybe eight or nine tons." (Reinstedt, 22)

Local newspapers picked up the story and the sea serpent of Monterey became forever established. Another dramatic and highly credible sighting occurred in 1940, to the captain and crew of a sardine-boat. As they sailed across the bay, they noticed a large object floating directly above the Monterey Trench. They approached up to ninety feet and saw that the object was actually a large creature rising four feet out of the water. The captain circled the creature, which turned in the water to keep the boat in view. The creature had a human-looking head and a gray-brown body about three feet wide. The stand-off lasted about ten minutes. The captain was considering trying to capture the creature when it suddenly plunged beneath the water and disappeared.

These sightings marked the beginning of a long and continuing series of sightings of the strange sea monster. Writes Reinstedt, "In the late 1940s there was a rash of such sightings in the Pacific Grove, Monterey, and Fort Ord areas. Almost to a person, witnesses who made sightings from shore described the creature as extremely long, approximately four feet in diameter, and multi-humped. Reports of the coloring indicated the body was either tan or gray. The serpent-like head was said to have been flat in appearance, with eyes like those of an African crocodile."

According to Reinstedt, the descriptions of the monster (or monsters) vary, but the reports of the human-like face were "remarkably consistent."

On November 7, 1946, a report came in of a sea-monster off Cape San Martin. One of the witnesses described the creature as having a face like a gorilla.

Another encounter occurred one morning at around dawn in July of 1948. A crew of nine men were sailing at the mid-point of Monterey Bay, directly over the Monterey Trench, when they saw the now-famous "Bobo." Bob-

bing in the water about 175 yards away, they observed an enormous creature rise about six feet out of the water. The face looked human-like with a "flat nose and large, blinking eyes." The monster and the sailors watched each other for a few moments, until one of the crew grabbed a rifle and opened fire on the creature, which immediately disappeared beneath the surface.

By this time, sightings were so common that they were regularly reported in the local newspapers. When the stories attracted the attention of the United Press, reporters learned that the sea-monster had been reported for decades and was whole-heartedly believed to exist by the local population.

One local resident wrote to the *Saturday Evening Post*, "…Sea monsters have been sighted frequently in Monterey Bay, California, during the past twenty years. So common has the occurrence become that fishermen no longer mention it with tongue in cheek, and many are the tales of encounters with the 'Old Man of Monterey Bay' as it is called locally…length of the creature is estimated from 45 to 70 feet." (Heuvelmans, 478)

While the central California coast seems to attract the most sea serpents, sightings actually reach as far south as San Clemente. In his book, *Mysterious Sea Monsters of California's Central Coast*, Reinstedt presents more than a dozen additional sightings ranging up and down the coast, the vast majority occurring in the 1930s and 1940s.

Back to

San Clemente

The 1950s brought more reports of the San Clemente maned sea serpent. In December of

1950, postal worker Miss Opal Lambert was working in her office in the Summerland Resort, which overlooks the coastal area of the northern Santa Catalina channel. Says Lambert, "I was stamping Christmas cards when I looked up and saw it swimming in circles about 200 yards off shore."

Lambert called the police. By the time they arrived, the creature had left. Lambert reports that the creature swam back and forth for a period of ten minutes. She estimated that its head and neck rose about four feet above the surface of the water.

Three years later, on June 8, 1953, the creature made another appearance. Professional fisherman Sam Randazzo and his crew of eight men observed the creature when it surfaced near their boat. Says Randazzo, "We saw the Thing, estimated that it had a neck ten feet long and between five and six feet thick. Its eyes were cone shaped, protruding, and about a foot in diameter." Randazzo immediately called the Coastguard and reported their sighting.

The sightings continued. In October 1954, Barney Armstrong of the *Sea-Fern* was off the coast of Newport Beach when he saw a creature that he estimated must weigh at least twenty tons. Writes Armstrong, "I spotted the thing sticking up out of the water about four feet." The witnesses reported a large round head and a mouth at least two feet across.

Around the same time, aircraft worker Phil Parker and his friend, architect Grant King, were fishing off the coast of nearby La Jolla when they saw an enormous sea creature surface about fifty feet away. They watched it for twenty-five minutes, clearly observing that the

> "It wasn't a whale and it wasn't a sea lion…and it sure didn't look like a snake."

creature had a face and shoulders like a gorilla. Says Parker, "It wasn't a whale and it wasn't a sea lion…and it sure didn't look like a snake."

Meanwhile, the sightings continued. Throughout the 1970s and 1980s, reports poured in of a sea serpent-like creature swimming in the San Francisco Bay area. During October and November of 1983, a "dark eel-like creature" was observed by numerous witnesses swimming up and down the coast. Some of the witnesses observed the creature through binoculars.

Then, on October 31, 1983, a construction crew was working on the Golden Gate Bridge above Stinson Beach when they looked down into the water and saw a 100-foot-long creature swimming along the shoreline. One of the workers, Mark Ratto, reports that the creature was about five feet thick and propelled itself quickly through the water. The creature was actually being followed by a large flock of birds and a school of two-dozen sea lions. Ratto says that the creature lifted it head and neck up out of the water, and he could see several humps also coming out of the water.

The construction workers reported their sighting to local newspapers. After their story was published, numerous other witnesses came forward with reports of similar local sightings.

Another sighting occurred on the morning of February 5, 1985, off Stone Tower Point in San Francisco Bay. Two brothers, Robert and William Clark, noticed two seals swimming frantically across the bay. Looking behind the seals, they were amazed to see a gigantic "snake-like" creature, which propelled itself by forming its body into humps and moving them up and down. They also noticed small fins along its side. The creature quickly moved away.

Disbelieving their own eyes, the Clark brothers posted themselves as look-outs, hoping to observe the strange creature again. Their patience was rewarded a few weeks later when the serpent returned. Since then, they have observed the unknown creature several times, and have recorded numerous reports from other witnesses in the area.

Well Traveled Waters

As we have seen, sea serpents are real and have been regularly seen up and down the California coast for nearly a century. If you want to see your own sea serpent encounter, this is definitely the place to be. Leading cryptozoologist, Loren Coleman, places the California coastline as the top sixth out of eight locations in the world for serpent-hunters to view an actual sea serpent. As he writes, "From the channel near San Clemente to the waters of Monterey Bay, from the harbors near San Francisco to the cliffs overlooking Stinson Beach, the ocean just west of California may be a playground and migration route for Sea Serpents, as it is for a variety of cetaceans. The Santa Catalina waterway has frequently experienced waves of Sea Serpent encounters and sightings, and doubtless will have more in the future. The Tuna Club of Catalina Island has organized fishing parties that have experienced sightings. The reports of Bobo, the Old Man of Monterey, an apparent Classic Sea Serpent, and other sightings have fostered a minor tourist industry of booklets on Sea Serpents and led, at one time, to displays of Sea Serpent history at kiosks along walks around Santa Cruz." (Coleman & Hugye, 290-291)

3. Giant Mountain Salamanders

Meet the
Hellbender

Among the strangest and most mysterious creatures to be reported in the unexplored California wilderness are giant salamanders, ranging in size from five to nine feet long. Giant salamanders are known to exist in Asia, where they reach a maximum length of just over five feet. The largest salamander in the United States, however, is the two-foot long *Hellbender*, native only to the Appalachian Mountains and the Ozarks. At least, this is the currently accepted theory.

Trinity Alps Waterways Frequented

Throughout the 1920s, however, reports came in from hunters and explorers of gigantic salamanders swimming in the lakes and rivers of the Trinity Alps of northern California. The first credible account is that of hunter, Frank L Griffith.

In 1920, Griffith was hunting deer at the head of the New River near Trinity Lake. As he walked by one of the lakes, he was astonished to see five giant salamanders lying at the bottom of the river. Some of the salamanders, he noticed, were at least nine feet long. Griffith quickly got out his fishing gear and attempted to catch one. To his delight, one of the giant salamanders took the bait. Unfortunately, Griffith quickly realized he had made a terrible mistake. The salamander was much too large, heavy, and strong for him to pull out of the water, and it quickly got away. Unable to capture them, Griffith eventually left.

Confessions of a
Herpetologist

Through-out the years, more scattered reports came in. One intriguing case comes from herpetologist George S. Myers. A herpetologist is an expert on reptiles and amphibians. In 1939, Myers received a call from a commercial fisherman who fished the Sacramento River south of the Trinity Alps. The fisherman wanted Myers to examine a strange creature that he had caught in his catfish nets in the Sacramento River.

Myers went to the scene and was amazed at what he saw: a two-foot giant salamander. As a herpetologist, he recognized the species immediately as *Megalobatrachus*, which again is allegedly found only in Asia. While this salamander wasn't even a third the size of the mystery salamanders of the Trinities, Myers was still impressed. As he writes, "The creature exhibited coloration quite at variance with that of several live Japanese examples I've seen but also with the published accounts of the color of Chinese specimens. The dorsum was a uniform dark brown, with an irregular sparse sprinkling all over the back of rather well-defined dull yellow-spots, these being of irregular outline and about one centimeter in diameter. There were no small spots, darker than the ground color, which is the common color of all the examples of Megalobatrachus I have seen..." (Coleman & Hugye, 236-237)

Myers was able to examine the salamander for a half-hour, fully satisfying himself that the specimen appeared to be — with minor variations – an Asiatic Giant Salamander. The fisherman would not let Myers keep the creature. Myers later published his account, ensuring that the information would be recorded for posterity.

Rodgers
Strikes Out

In 1948, biologist Thomas L. Rodgers heard about Griffith's earlier sighting. Intrigued about the possibility that such creatures might actually exist, he made no less than

Trinity
Expeditions

four expeditions to the area. Unfortunately, he was unable to find any trace of the salamanders.

Then in 1958 and 1959, two brothers, one a Jesuit priest (Father Hubbard) and the other an army captain, (John Hubbard) organized a series of trips to the Trinity Alps to search for the creatures. Apparently, they had some success. In 1960, Father Hubbard announced that their expeditions had, in fact, established the existence of the giant salamanders in the Trinity region. While no further information surfaced, the sightings continued.

In January of 1960, animal handler Vern Harden and a friend were fishing in Hubbard Lake (named after the above Hubbard family) located in the Trinity Alps, when they came upon a dozen giant salamanders. Harden quickly tried to catch one of the creatures. He used his fishing line and to his amazement, managed to hook one, which he measured at no less than eight feet and four inches! Unfortunately, a snowstorm arrived, forcing Harden to give up the struggle, and the salamander got away. Their account, however, added fuel to the fire.

By now interest was high. Immediately after the Harden encounter, famed Bigfoot researcher, Tom Slick, joined the craze. He and his group mounted an expedition and searched for the mystery amphibians, but were unable to locate any hint of their existence.

Inspired by the growing number of accounts, three university professors and zoologists, Robert Stebbins, Nathan Cohen, and Thomas Rodgers (who had already conducted four expeditions), decided to organize another extensive search. On September 1, 1960, the three scientists thoroughly searched the area and found more than a dozen salamanders. Unfortunately, the largest one was just under twelve inches long.

Thomas Rodgers concluded that, in his opinion, the unknown creatures didn't exist, and he hoped that "this evidence will kill rumors about any Giant Salamanders in the Trinity Mountains of California." (Coleman & Hugye, 234)

Close

Encounters

Despite Rodgers' negative conclusions, reports continued to surface. Sometime in the early 1980s, a woman named Valenya encountered the giant salamanders not far from her home in the Siskiyou Mountains near Bluff Creek. Valenya was camping when she was woken up at around 2:00 a.m. to the sound of a large creature moving towards her campsite. When the sound broke into her campsite, she flicked on her flashlight and gasped in amazement. Writes Valenya, *"That's a damn dinosaur!* Was my first thought…The form was that of a salamander, but it looked like it measured some three feet long from nose to tail tip. A mottled pinto pattern alternating between black and orange gave its smooth skin a festive Halloween touch…it was much flatter-bodied and more heavily built than a salamander, and its head looked really odd. Unlike little salamanders' pretty heads, with their big pop-out eyes and rounded faces, this fellow had a head as flat as a rattlesnake's, and about as ugly. Its eyes were tiny and deeply set."

Valenya's first instinct was to capture the creature so she would have proof. But she instantly realized it was too large. She stepped aside and watched it walk away. She later discussed the incident with several of her neighbors and learned that there had been other witnesses to the same type of creature. Writes Valenya, "One lady found the same critter (or an identical one) on her doorstep when she opened the front door one morning. She assumed it was a rubber toy, a trick her kids were playing on her, and she smiled. Then it moved and she screamed. Another man was confounded upon discovering one living under the floor he was tearing off an old building on his land." (Valenya, 62-67)

Recent

Expeditions

Expeditions to locate the creatures have continued to the present day. In 1997, Bigfoot researcher, Kyle Mizokami, organized yet another expedition, and searched several of the remote lakes in the Trinity Alps. Unfortunately, he was unable to find any evidence of the salamanders.

According to prominent cryptozoologist, Loren Coleman, the mystery salamanders of the Trinity Alps – assuming they exist – are probably related to the species *Megalobatrachus*, normally found only in Asia. As he says, "These inhabit swift-moving mountain streams in Japan and China – an environment very similar to the mountain streams of the Trinity Alps where the Mystery Salamander has been reported." (Coleman & Hugye, 233)

While the mystery salamanders may be rare, the above reports seem to confirm their existence. The smoking gun proof, however, is waiting for the first intrepid explorer with enough courage and luck to find the elusive, mysterious giant mountain salamanders of northern California.

> While the mystery salamanders may be rare, the above reports seem to confirm their existence. The smoking gun proof, however, is waiting for the first intrepid explorer with enough courage and luck to find the elusive, mysterious giant mountain salamanders of northern California.

4. Bigfoot in California

California has one of the largest Bigfoot populations in the world, with hundreds of reports coming from every corner of the state.

By Any Other Name...

Many mysterious creatures roam our planet. Probably the most famous of these is the giant Bigfoot. Known throughout the world by various names (Sasquatch, Wildman, Skunk Ape, Yeti, Abominable Snowman...), sightings have occurred since early human history and continue to the present day.

While nobody has produced a verified Bigfoot body, there is a surprisingly large amount of evidence to support its existence. The evidence comes in many forms including thousands of multiple, independent eyewitness testimonies, footprints and body prints, hair samples, dung samples, animal effects, audio recordings, moving films, and photographs.

While Bigfoot is seen across the world, researchers have concluded that the Pacific Northwestern United States is the location of the highest population concentration. Writes Loren Coleman, "It has been estimated that the population of Bigfoot in the Pacific Northwest is between two thousand and four thousand individuals, with the greatest concentration around Bluff Creek, California..."

Appearing Live Throughout California!

There have been literally thousands of sightings in California, way too many to include in a book of this size. The sightings come from every corner of the state. In fact, Bigfoot has been seen virtually *everywhere* in California. Up and down the coast, in the lush forests of northern California, the desert regions near San Diego, the Angeles Forest north of Los Angeles – all are major Bigfoot hotspots. The truth is, you can't travel more than a few hundred miles in the Golden State without running into a place where Bigfoot has been seen.

Some of the earliest records of Bigfoot's actual existence come from California. Native Americans have long reported the creature, and have given it many names. Starting in the 1850s, gold prospectors and miners reported sightings in such areas as Antioch, Round Valley, and San Joaquin. One such early encounter was reported by a gold prospector in the Mount Shasta area who claimed that a Bigfoot smashed his sluiceway against a tree.

Murderous Rampage at Deadman's Hole!

Around this time, a series of murders outside the southern California city of San Marcus were blamed on Bigfoot. The actual location was a remote valley called Deadman's Hole. In 1858, an unidentified man was found beaten to death in the area. In 1870, a Frenchman said that he was attacked in his cabin by a tall, hairy creature. Then in 1888, two more badly crushed bodies were discovered. Also in that year, two hunters came upon a cave filled with human bones. As they examined the bones, they were attacked by a tall, hairy, man-like ape-creature with a human-looking face. The hunters shot at the creature and then ran away in a panic.

Two additional deaths occurred as late as 1922. Later, more hunters again claimed to confront the hostile Bigfoot, which ran away when they opened fire on it. Since then, no further deaths have been reported. And this type of murderous Bigfoot case remains unique.

Meanwhile, the early sightings began to grow in number. In Autumn of 1869, a hunter was hunting along nearby Orestimba Creek when he saw a Bigfoot approach his campfire, grab some burning sticks, and start swinging them around. The next year, numerous residents of Mount Diablo reported a wildman in the area that left thirteen-inch tracks.

The One That Got Away

One dramatic encounter occurred in 1882 in the Owens Valley. After several people had reported seeing a large hairy bipedal creature in the area, several men decided to go hunting for it. Incredibly, they found the creature lying down asleep in a field, and attempted to capture it. John Clarke reports that he tried to lasso the creature but it woke up and ran away screaming. His associate, Paul Myrtengreen, fainted unconscious when the creature turned and charged him. Hunter John Ferral followed the creature and a few days later came upon it while it was feeding. He fired five bullets into the creature, but the shots seemed to have no effect. The creature charged him, causing his horse to panic and gallop uncontrollably. The horse broke both its front legs as it tried to escape. Ferral himself was badly bruised and the Bigfoot got away.

Native Americans Speak Out

Scattered encounters occurred throughout the northern California area, but few people seemed to believe or pay attention to the accounts. The local Native Americans, however, were well aware of Bigfoot and began to reveal some of their encounters too. In the summer of 1897, a Native American who lived in Tulelake reported that he was approached by a Bigfoot while fishing. He offered the Bigfoot one of the fish, which it accepted.

The Native Americans report other friendly Bigfoot encounters. In the early 1900s, a native of Mount Shasta reports that he was hiking in the wilderness when he was bitten by a poisonous snake. Incredibly, he was then approached by a Bigfoot, which lifted him up and carried him back to his camp.

Red-eyed and Hostile

In 1938, a gentleman from Los Angeles went camping outside of Anza Borrego in southern California when he was approached by several hostile white-haired Bigfoot with red eyes. He was able to keep the creatures at a distance by building up his campfire and holding up burning sticks.

Mostly Harmless

While Bigfoot encounters can be scary, the creatures rarely harm humans. Some cases, however, definitely push the limits of fear. During World War II, two friends, O. R. Edwards and Bill Cole, were hunting in the Siskiyou Mountains when they had an unforgettable encounter with Bigfoot. Today there are several accounts of people being kidnapped by Bigfoot. This case is one of the earliest on record.

Hunter Bagged by Bigfoot

The two hunters walked around some bushes. Both men suddenly saw the head of an ape-like creature dart out of the woods, look at them, and dart back in. In a matter of seconds, they heard the Bigfoot running towards them in the forest and Cole was attacked. Says Edwards, "I heard the *pad-pad-pad* of running feet and the *whump* and grunt as their bodies came together. Dashing back to the end of the bush I saw a large manlike creature covered with brown hair. It was about seven feet tall and it was carrying in its arms what seemed like a man. I could only see legs and shoes."

Edwards looked to his side and saw that Cole was gone. The Bigfoot, he suddenly realized, had just kidnapped his friend.

Cole himself reports that he had no warning and that he suddenly found himself being carried through the forest by the creature, which held him tightly for a short time, then dropped him and sent him rolling down the hill. Cole jumped up and grabbed his rifle. As he says, "I stood there some time and looked and listened. I had a feeling I was being watched and hunted."

The two men kept their encounter secret for many years. Says Edwards, "I would not believe what I had seen."

Says Cole, "Funny, neither of us has the guts to say what happened to us." (Coleman 2003, 193-194)

Bigfoot Crossings

As time went on, the accounts increased. In 1947, Mr. and Mrs. Russ Tribble observed two Bigfoot outside the city of Round Mountain. The Bigfoot crossed the road in front of them. One of them stopped and looked in the car window. After the creatures left, they explored the area and discovered large footprints.

Road Rage

In 1952, an anonymous gentleman was driving along a dirt road through the forest outside of Orlean, near Bear Valley, California, when he saw a Bigfoot along the road. Although it was rainy and dark, he got out of his car to observe when the Bigfoot turned towards him in a threatening way. The creature then walked back into the forest. However, the encounter wasn't over yet. The man got back in his car and started to drive when the Bigfoot leapt out of the forest and attacked his car. The witness accelerated, but the Bigfoot held on for 200 yards before finally letting go.

Fleeting Encounter

One of the most common types of Bigfoot encounter occurs when witnesses are driving late at night. In 1956, Mrs. J. Pomray was driving along Interstate 5 near Mount Shasta when she saw a Bigfoot run across the road and disappear into the forest.

Sidewalk Supervisors

The first encounter to gain widespread media attention and bring Bigfoot permanently into public awareness occurred in August of 1958 in the town of Bluff Creek in northern California. A large construction crew was building the Bluff Creek road when strange things began to occur on the job site. On August 3, foreman Wilbur Wallace was puzzled to find a 700-pound tire that had been thrown away from the work-site.

A few weeks later, on August 22, worker Jerry Crew was leaving the work-site when he discovered dozens of giant man-like footprints around his tractor. He told Wallace, and the news of the footprints spread like wildfire. The account was soon leaked to the press by the wife of one of the workers.

Then, on October 1 and 2, Jerry Crew discovered more tracks, of which he made plaster casts. The story instantly became a media sensation, and the attention of the world focused on the then unknown town of Bluff Creek.

On October 12, two workers, Ray Kerr and Bob Braezle, were driving at night near Bluff Creek when they saw the eight-foot tall figure of Bigfoot run across the road in full view of their headlights. The witnesses report that the Bigfoot traversed the entire road in two strides.

Bluff Creek, Bigfoot's Capital

Then on November 1, 1958, more footprints were discovered. Later, there would be allegations that Wallace had either hoaxed the footprints or taken financial advantage of the situation, though this was never conclusively proven. In either case, Bluff Creek became firmly established as the Bigfoot capital of the world. And as a result, hundreds of people found the courage to share their own accounts. Bigfoot had finally earned respectability. Bigfoot hunters converged on Bluff Creek and began the never-ending search for the elusive primate.

In 1958, a woman and her daughter were outside in the Hoopa Valley near Bluff Creek when they saw two Bigfoot, one large and one small, as they hiked along the hillside.

Numerous Encounters

At the same time, in nearby Weaverville, two doctors drove along Highway 299 late at night when they had the most common type of Bigfoot encounter – they observed the creature through the car headlights as it bounded across the road in front of them.

In June of 1959, an anonymous gentleman became sleepy after driving for several hours. He pulled over late at night outside of Weed, California, to rest. While resting, he was alerted to the noise of somebody walking through the forest in front of his car. He turned on his headlights and observed Bigfoot, which quickly disappeared into the forest.

Also in 1959, a private pilot and his wife were flying over Bluff Creek when they spotted a trail of huge footprints on the ground. They followed the tracks from above and further ahead, were amazed to see the Bigfoot that was making them.

Making Tracks

While all these sightings were occurring, dozens of other witnesses reported numerous Bigfoot tracks all over the area. In some cases, the tracks numbered over 1000! The Bluff Creek sightings would continue for decades. Today this area continues to produce the largest number of encounters in California.

Bigfoot on the Hill

Meanwhile the sightings continued. In 1960, two men in Quartz Hill, located at the west end of the Antelope Valley in southern California, observed what appeared to be a giant bipedal figure silhouetted against the sky on a nearby hill.

Mount Shasta Born

Mount Shasta is one of the many lairs of Bigfoot. In 1962, a unique encounter occurred when a local woman, Bonnie Feldman, claimed to have observed a pregnant female Bigfoot give birth to a baby Bigfoot on the mountainside. She watched the event from the porch of her trailer on the eastern slopes of the mountain.

Too Close Encounter

In June of 1962, Robert Hatfield was in his home in Fort Bragg when his dogs began barking outside. Looking out, he saw the head and shoulders of a Bigfoot as it walked behind a six-foot-tall fence. He ran inside to get his friend, Bud Jensen. They returned outside, but by then the Bigfoot was gone. Jensen returned back inside, but Hatfield kept looking. He then walked around the house and smack into the Bigfoot. The creature knocked him to the ground, and Hatfield scrambled back into the house. Meanwhile, Jensen looked out the window and observed the Bigfoot approaching the front door, which Hatfield had left open. He ran up to close it, but the Bigfoot also ran forward and held it open. The two men got ready to shoot the creature if it entered, but at that point it suddenly left. They found a handprint on the door that measured 11 1/2 inches long. They also found several 16-inch footprints outside.

Among the Lava Beds

On August 10, 1962, Joseph Wattenberger was hiking east of McCloud, near the Lava Beds National Monument when he observed a Bigfoot off in the distance.

Bigfoot Benevolence

While some accounts of Bigfoot have a menacing aspect, some accounts are decidedly benevolent. For example, in 1963, a man was deer hunting on the slopes of Mount Shasta when he slipped and fell, badly injuring himself. The witness reports that a nine-foot tall, smelly, white-haired Bigfoot appeared, scooped him up in its massive arms, and carried him about three miles back to the safety of his campsite.

Another account of a friendly Bigfoot occurred on Mount Shasta when two men said a Bigfoot approached their campsite, came right up to them, and handed them a quartz crystal, then bounded off into the forest.

Multiple Witnesses

Many Bigfoot encounters involve multiple witnesses of high credibility. On January 27, 1963, the police department in Sonora received a call from an anonymous gentleman who said that he saw Bigfoot while driving along the Sonora highway. A sheriff and deputy went to investigate and heard the sound of Bigfoot screaming in the woods.

One month later, on February 28, private pilots Lennart Strand and Alden Hoover were flying through the same area when they saw a ten-foot-tall brown Bigfoot wandering through a remote area of the wilderness. They took photos of the creature but the pictures were too blurry to be conclusive.

In March 1963, Mr. and Mrs. Campbell were honeymooning at the Jack and Jill Ski Lodge in Strawberry, California. Unknown to them, the owners of the ski lodge had recently had several run-ins with Bigfoot. As the Campbells hiked along the many remote trails in the area, they were amazed to see a hairy figure about nine feet tall in the nearby fields. They later learned that they were not the only witnesses to this particular Bigfoot.

Fleet of Foot

Despite its enormous size, Bigfoot is incredibly agile. On August 3, 1963, a father and his son from Hoopa, California, observed a Bigfoot that easily leapt over a five-foot high fence and ran off into the forest.

Car Alarm

On the evening of September 13, 1964, Benjamin Wilder was driving near Blue Lake in northern California when he became sleepy and pulled over in his car to rest. Suddenly he woke up to find Bigfoot shaking his car. Shortly thereafter, the Bigfoot ran off and Wilder immediately left the area.

The Hairy Animal Man

One month later, in the southern California city of Fillmore, several youngsters were playing in an abandoned dairy when they observed a "hairy animal man."

Camping with Bigfoot

Bigfoot often seems to be attracted to people's campsites. A typical encounter occurred in the summer of 1965. Jim and Jan Gorrell were barbecuing at the Bowen's Ranch campgrounds on San Gorgonio Mountain when they were approached by a ten-foot-tall Bigfoot, who calmly observed them from a distance. The Gorrells were too nervous to remain there and quickly packed everything up and left.

While there are only a few reports of people being harmed by Bigfoot, there is something about the creature that makes people often react with unrestrained terror. It was 2:00 am, in January of 1966, and friends Bob Kelley and Archie Bradshaw were in their cabin in Wildwood. Without warning a Bigfoot suddenly approached and stared at them through the window. Kelly quickly grabbed his shotgun and fired. Although he was sure he hit the creature, it ran away. They went outside and measured its tracks at 18 inches.

In July and August of 1966, several Bigfoot reports came from the southern California city of Fontana. One family reports that a tall, red-haired Bigfoot ransacked their car while they were picnicking. Two teenage boys were hiking outside Fontana when a Bigfoot actually attacked them. The Bigfoot grabbed one of the boys, who suffered scratches and torn clothing as a result.

Another rare Bigfoot attack occurred in the same area on August 27. Jerri Hendehall and a friend saw a Bigfoot from their car. To their shock, the Bigfoot quickly approached, reached through the car window, and grabbed the arm of the witness, causing painful scratches. Both witnesses report that the Bigfoot was covered with slimy mud and emitted a putrid odor.

Corroborating the above encounters, around the same time, two young men were hiking in nearby Quartz Hill when they observed a Bigfoot standing still on a distant hilltop. By this time, it was becoming clear to researchers that southern California was also a major Bigfoot hotspot.

Still, the vast forests with their towering Sequoia and Redwood trees remain the preferred Bigfoot habitat. In 1966, Richard Sides was hiking near Bluff Creek when he saw a Bigfoot squatting down by Bluff Creek, drinking water with cupped hands.

Keep Your Eyes to Yourself!

Also in 1966, Larry Browning was camping in the Trinity Alps outside of Weaverville when he saw a Bigfoot walk by his campsite. He was so amazed that he returned to the campsite several times in the hopes of another sighting. His patience was finally rewarded. However, he learned the hard way that Bigfoot isn't always particularly friendly. Two years later on April 6, 1968, he observed a Bigfoot wading across the Salmon River. He returned the next day and saw a female Bigfoot. On this occasion, the Bigfoot also saw him and began to chase him. Browning reports that the Bigfoot followed him for a half-hour and, at one point, charged him menacingly before finally going away.

The Memory Lingers On

In early 1967, Russel Summerville was on Highway 299, just west of Willow Creek when he observed a nine-foot tall Bigfoot walking along the highway. The creature stayed parallel to the highway for about fifty feet before dashing back into the undergrowth. Summerville reports that a terrible odor lingered for several minutes.

Caught on Film

Many professional and amateur Bigfoot hunters have mounted various expeditions in search of Bigfoot. Most of these searches concentrated around the Bluff Creek area. One of these hunters included a man by the name of Roger Patterson. He heard about new Bigfoot prints in the area of Bluff Creek, and in October 1967, he went to Bluff Creek to make a film documentary about the increasingly popular creature. So began one of the most influential and controversial events in Bigfoot history.

On October 18, 1967, Roger Patterson and his associate, Robert Gimlin, were riding through the area of the footprints, occasionally taking film footage of the surroundings to use as background material.

Early in the afternoon, they came around a corner on the trail and saw a tall hairy figure a few hundred yards away. Patterson quickly retrieved his movie camera and filmed 952 frames of moving film of the creature as it walked away into the forest. The film became a media sensation, and still is today. Controversy surrounds the film, and there have been numerous claims of hoaxes. The primary witnesses have never recanted their stories, though today experts are divided as to the film's authenticity. Nevertheless, it is only one of many cases. And Bluff Creek and the surrounding areas continued to produce a constant parade of solid reports.

Into the Woods

In June 1968, Steve Martin and Bruce Cornwall were hiking in the Bluff Creek area when they saw and smelled a Bigfoot in a clearing in the forest.

On July 11, 1968, a family was camping along the Trinity River when they saw a Bigfoot walk closely by their campsite and back into the forest.

In the Heat of the Night

Also in July, Harold Lancaster was hiking through the southern California desert outside of Borrego Springs. It was late at night when he saw a "giant apeman" walking towards him. It then bounded away and disappeared.

Buzzing Bigfoot

Although rare, there are several accounts on record where people have seen Bigfoot from the air. In January 1969, private pilots Robert James Jr. and Larry Larwick were flying a small plane over north Yosemite Park when they saw a long line of what looked like Bigfoot tracks. Intrigued, they followed the tracks. To their amazement, the tracks were fresh and led them directly to the Bigfoot himself. They buzzed the creature with their plane, getting as close as fifty feet to the creature. They took blurry photographs of the creature, and estimated that it was about twelve feet tall with twenty-inch-long footprints.

Up Close and Personal

Many witnesses have made close-up observations of Bigfoot and can provide detailed descriptions of their appearance. A perfect example occurred on April 16, 1969. Mr. and Mrs. Robert Behme were driving late at night outside of Paradise, California, when they encountered Bigfoot crossing the road in front of them. Says Behme, "As we started a long curve, our headlights lit what seemed to be a man in fur, crossing the road…our impression that it was more than six feet high, completely covered with short black hairs which seemed to be marked either of white spots or of mud. Its face was white…the head was small and finished at a peak at the top. It was heavily built with particularly heavy legs." (www.bigfootencounters.com)

Around that same time and in the nearby city of Oroville, Ed Saville and Eldon Butler were rabbit hunting. To their shock, their rabbit calls attracted an eight-foot tall green-eyed Bigfoot, which came to investigate the noise.

In June of 1969, Ben Foster, Bob Kelley and his family, and several others were at the Wildwood Inn in Wildwood when they were drawn outside by the sound of barking dogs. The group of witnesses then observed a six-foot-tall dark brown Bigfoot fighting with the dogs, which had surrounded it. The creature then ran off into the surrounding forest.

One month later, on July 4, 1969, Eldon Brackett was hiking north of Wildwood when he observed a seven foot tall Bigfoot. After it left, he examined the tracks, which measured 16-1/2 inches with a four foot stride. On July 17, brothers Charles and Kevin Jackson were burning rabbit entrails in their backyard in rural Oroville when they saw an 8-foot female Bigfoot walk by the nearby outhouse.

Also in July 1969, Don Ballard and a friend were horseback riding through the Trinity Alps when they had a rare daylight sighting of the creature. Ballard reports that the creature appeared to have no neck and left several 16-inch tracks. Around the same time, Homer Stickley observed a Bigfoot walk through his backyard in the outskirts of Oroville. In the months that followed, he found several tracks measuring about eleven inches.

Bigfoot Wave of '69

July of 1969 was a major Bigfoot wave. In the city of Twain, three teenagers were driving home from a movie when they observed a Bigfoot crouching in the middle of the road in front of them. They swerved to avoid it and came to a screeching stop. When they turned around, the creature was gone.

A rare interactive encounter occurred to an anonymous female prospector working outside of Orleans. She reports that during the summer of 1969, she observed a male and female Bigfoot on several occasions. After seeing them several times, she left out apples and grapes for the creatures, which they took.

In the fall of 1969, Oroville again showed itself as a Bigfoot hotspot. Ron Sanders was hiking along French Creek in Oroville when he saw two Bigfoot across the reservoir. The Bigfoot were turning over large rocks and appeared to be eating something. Around that same time, Charles Maudlin was hiking along the nearby Feather River when he saw a Bigfoot running along an abandoned dirt road. On October 31, Wes Strong was in his home in Oroville when he saw a Bigfoot squatting in his yard. Strong says that the Bigfoot stared back at him, obviously aware that it was being observed.

About a week later, Mike Scott and a friend were in Calaveras, in Big Trees National Park when they saw a Bigfoot about thirty yards away. Scott fired three rounds of ammunition at the creature, which quickly escaped, apparently unharmed.

The sightings continued regularly throughout the 1970s. In April 1970, Buzz McLaughlin and several others of Hyampom, California, observed a nine-foot-tall Bigfoot outside the Manzanita Ranch School. They described the creature as looking like "a giant gorilla."

On May 14, 1970, Archie Buckley was hiking at Stuart Gap, south of Wildwood, when he observed a seven-foot-tall Bigfoot. After it left, he measured its tracks at 15 inches. Buckley was so awestruck by his experience that he began researching other accounts and conducting his own Bigfoot stakeouts. One month after his first encounter, on June 18, Buckley returned, hoping to have another encounter. He was incredibly successful. He was actually able to attract a Bigfoot to his camp by laying out freshly caught fish as an offering. This is one of very few cases in which people were actually able to initiate an encounter.

Be Very, Very Quiet …

Also in 1970, two hunters in Cooper Canyon near Quartz Hill, southern California, were out hunting in the forest when they encountered what they at first thought was a very large unidentified animal. However, when the "creature" stood up, they looked through their gun scopes and observed what appeared to be a large human-looking figure. Unable to determine if it was a person or an animal, they didn't shoot. A short time later, the figure ran off into the forest.

On September 1, 1971, an anonymous Lieutenant Sheriff was driving southeast of Mammoth Mountain when he observed an eight-foot-tall hairy Bigfoot standing along the roadside with arms outstretched.

Around that same time, but farther south in Palmdale, an anonymous young man says that he encountered Bigfoot and fired four shots at it with a 30-30 rifle. As in virtually all cases where people shoot at the creature, the Bigfoot was apparently unharmed and fled the area.

High Sierras Bigfoot

In late 1971 and early 1972, several reports of Bigfoot came in from the high Sierras. Campers Warren Johnson, Larry Johnson, Bill McDowell, and others reported several incidents where Bigfoot would prowl around their campsite, howling in the distance. They were able to capture some of the vocalizations on audiotape.

Bigfoot, UFOs, and the Boys from Balls Ferry

There is no doubt that Bigfoot is real and that California is a hotspot. Take the following encounter, which occurred in January 1972 to four teenage boys from Balls Ferry. This particular account is one of the extremely rare Bigfoot-UFO encounters. The boys were driving when they saw an unidentified large glowing object swoop down over their car. They continued driving, and later parked along Battle Creek. It was there that they heard a blood-curdling scream. They trained their flashlights on the sound and saw a seven-foot-tall creature covered with dark brown hair. Suddenly afraid, they left the area and immediately returned with an adult. Again, all of them heard the creature howling loudly, scaring them off the scene. Says the adult, Dean Rich, "It sounded like a real deep growl. It was a real weird type of sensation. It was something I've never experienced before." (Coleman 2003, 175)

In the Southern California Wilds with Bigfoot

Covering more than 650,000 acres, the Angeles National Forest just north of Los Angeles is a vast remote wilderness and a haven for all kinds of large wildlife including bear, deer, cougar, and even Bigfoot! While the northern California Bigfoot sightings are well known, many people are not aware that southern California has produced literally hundreds of reports.

And when you take into account that most people never report their encounters, the number of accounts probably runs into the thousands. Just one visit to the vast mountains covered with thick pine forest is enough to convince anyone that many mysteries lay beyond the little explored pathways that wind along the borders of the untouched wilderness.

For whatever reason, the southern California sightings increased, and by the mid-1970s, the area was producing a flood of reports.

In February 1972, four teenagers were hiking in the Lake Isabella area of southern California when they saw a Bigfoot prowling around their campground in the late moonlight.

On October 8, 1972, Randy Norton and Steve Gillespie were in the city of Redding when they observed a Bigfoot traverse Clear Creek at the Placer Street Bridge. The next day they saw what appeared to be the same Bigfoot in the same area, running away.

The year of 1973 brought a flood of reports from the Lancaster/Palmdale area. On March 14, 1973, three U. S. Marines observed a "large, bipedal hairy creature" on the outskirts of Lancaster. According to the witnesses, they were driving along when the creature leapt directly in front of their car. That same month, a local woman went outside to see why her dogs were whimpering. Suddenly, she was shocked to see a tall, hairy, ape-like figure stand up from the tall grass and run off.

On April 22, 1973, three men from the San Fernando Valley, William Roemermann, Brian Goldojarb, and Richard Engels, went camping at Sycamore Flats Campground in Big Rock Canyon, near Lancaster. They were out exploring together when they observed a hairy man-like creature towering at least eleven feet tall. According to the witnesses, the creature paced their pick-up truck along the road for about twenty seconds.

One month later, Ron Bailey observed an eight-foot tall Bigfoot standing next to a telephone pole along the road in Palmdale. After it left, he approached the site and found large footprints.

One month after that, in June 1973, siblings Bret and Stefanie Baylor were playing outside their Lancaster home when they saw Bigfoot observing them from behind a boulder.

And one month later, in July, an anonymous naturalist was researching in the Castle Craggie Mountain area when he observed an eight-foot-tall Bigfoot with a human-looking face for a period of about forty-five minutes.

Rock Throwing and Other Antisocial Behavior

In August of 1973, Margaret and Joyce Baylor of Lancaster observed a 12-foot tall Bigfoot along the roadside. After it left, they found its footprints. Around the same time, Mike Pense was driving his motorcycle through the desert area north of Lancaster when a Bigfoot appeared and threw rocks at his motorcycle.

Meanwhile, back up in northern California, things were also heating up, specifically in the Shasta-Trinity National Forest. Writes Loren Coleman, "In August…during a fishing trip and other visits, several Bay Area-based Bigfooters, including Sharon Gorden, Richard Foster, Ben E Foster Jr., and Archie Buckley, had multiple Bigfoot sightings there including seeing a Bigfoot throw a rock, one prowling around a campfire, another flipping a car aerial, some communicating by gesture, and another being attracted nearby. Tracks, a dead fawn, and feces had been found. It was an active area…" (Coleman 2003, 217)

Meanwhile, the Bigfoot wave of southern California continued strong. One evening in September 1973, two people were in their driveway in Quartz Hill. They turned on the headlights and were amazed to see a Bigfoot with tangled hair standing at the end of the driveway. After it left, they also observed large footprints.

Strides, Leaps, and Bounds

In October 1973, large 21-inch footprints were discovered at the nearby South Fork Campground. Measurements taken of the distance between the footprints registered a twelve-foot stride!

On December 27, two siblings were hiking near their home in Palmdale when they saw a Bigfoot which they estimated was about 12 feet tall. As they watched, it bounded away at very high speeds, and disappeared into the desert.

Buttes Stakeout

Also in 1973, a team of researchers set up a Bigfoot stakeout in the Mojave desert near The Buttes. Kent Lacy and the other researchers achieved their goal of an encounter when they all observed a large hairy Bigfoot standing off in the distance. At the same time, they smelled a powerful "rank odor."

Sitting Tall

In 1974, a Quartz Hill family was startled by the appearance of Bigfoot in their backyard. Meanwhile, the nearby Big Rock Canyon Campground continued to generate a number of reports throughout the 1970s. Most of the people who encountered the creature were campers, hikers or hunters. In August of 1974, Bruce Morgan was at Big Rock when he saw a shaggy white-haired Bigfoot sitting down on the ground. In a sitting position, its height was about six feet!

Near Misses and Big Prints

Around that same time, Terry Albright was driving through Big Rock along the mountain roads when he nearly hit a seven-foot-tall black-haired Bigfoot.

In September of 1974, Neil Fern and Rich Engles were hiking at night in Antelope Valley when they saw a seven-foot-tall black Bigfoot standing on a hilltop. After it left, they explored the area and found 15-inch, three-toed footprints.

A few months later, a group of children were walking near the Canyon High School in Newhall-Saugus when they saw a nine-foot-tall dark-colored Bigfoot raise its arms and jump off into the wilderness.

The wave continued strong into 1975. On August 14, Irene Rambo observed a 10-foot tall Bigfoot peer over her backyard fence in Corona. Three days later, James Mihalko, Ernest Palmeira, and two others were near their home in Corona when they saw the same 10-foot tall Bigfoot wandering through a citrus grove.

Further north, in Sequoia National Park, John Clark was camping when he saw a nine-foot tall Bigfoot that appeared to have blond hair, or had covered itself in light-colored vegetation.

On September 3, 1975, Mark Karr was driving outside Oroville in the early morning when a seven-foot tall Bigfoot appeared along the roadside. Karr was so amazed, he lost control of his car and smashed into a tree. When he looked up, the Bigfoot was gone.

Bigfoot Hunts and Other Sightings

In 1975, an anonymous man was driving outside of Saugus when he saw a Bigfoot, holding a small animal in its hands as it stood in the light of a flashing road sign.

Back up in northern California, near Pine Grove, two teenagers, Rick Van Deli and Joe Coughlin, saw Bigfoot twice over a period of a few weeks.

On March 23, 1976, Ed Johnson and police patrolman Dan Murphy observed a Bigfoot leap over an eight-foot wall in rural Mill Valley. The next day they investigated the area and found the corpse of a freshly killed deer.

In the summer of 1976, two brothers were fishing late at night at Morris Dam when they observed a very tall "human-like" creature walking along a deer path. A few months later, a hunter reported his sighting of the creature along the West Fork River. In this case, he also heard the Bigfoot scream in a weird mixture of howling and roaring.

... More Effin' Afraid ...

In 1977, a man was camping in the woods outside of Mendocino when he was woken up by a large bipedal creature running through the woods outside his tent. Says the anonymous camper, "...I was more effin' afraid than I could ever remember, praying that what I was listening to wouldn't start moving towards my tent. The noise sounded like a two-legged monster crashing through the woods hastily." (www.bigfoot encounters.com)

The camper didn't see anything; however, he reports that in the area where he was camping, many disemboweled animals had recently been found.

More Bigfoot Crossings

As with UFOs, many Bigfoot sightings occur to people who are driving late at night. Again, the most common type of encounter is a road crossing, as in the following case. Late one evening in 1978, a truck driver was driving near the Lake Hughes area when he observed a very tall, hairy man-like creature run across the road in front of his headlights.

Throughout the 1980s and '90s, southern California researcher Ann Druffel investigated numerous Bigfoot cases throughout the Tujunga Canyon area.

Bright Lights and Moaning Bigfoot

A very interesting case of a Bigfoot sighting with a UFO connection occurred in the backyard of radiologist Robert Murphy. This case was personally investigated by the author. The Murphy home is located in the outskirts of Canyon Country, immediately north of the sprawling megalopolis of Los Angeles. One summer evening in 1978, Murphy was startled to see an object flashing extremely bright red and white lights landing in his backyard. He first thought it was a helicopter because there are no roads or structures behind his house. Then Murphy realized the object was totally silent. He jumped up to go outside and the lights quickly disappeared.

Murphy was very puzzled, but it was the next night that he got a real scare. Says Murphy, "This is the one that gets me. I have three dogs, and they were terrified out of their minds. They were huddled together on my patio. All three of them were huddled together and they were obviously terrified out of their minds. And they were looking at the same spot where that thing with all the lights was the night before, right in the corner of my yard.

"They were barking at something up there. And they were barking furiously, like they've never done before in their lives. And they were huddled all together.

"And then I heard this thing, this...creature. And this thing moaned – and moaned in an unearthly fashion that's very hard to describe, only other than it had a very low, long-toned eerie moan that sounded like it was resonating in a very large creature, like a big barrel-chested kind of creature. You just hear the resonance of this thing. And it moaned really long, like ten seconds."

At this point, Murphy mentioned something that is familiar to Bigfoot researchers, but unfamiliar to most people – that Bigfoot is *telepathic*. "It seemed like I was reading its mind, and it was irritated with the dogs. That's what I thought. And it moaned again a second time, same thing as before, about the same duration. And then the third time, it moaned again, but this time it was really, really loud. And it moaned for a real long time, and I was so scared that I was afraid to go look." (Dennett 1997, 197-206)

Murphy retreated into this house. The next morning, he went to investigate and found what appeared to be partial footprints.

Finishing Out the '70s

Meanwhile, the sightings continued strong and steady. On May 30, 1979, Bill Ifftiger was driving along US Highway 395 outside Yosemite when he saw an eight-foot tall Bigfoot dash across the road in front of his car.

In June of 1979, Shirley DeWolfe and her family observed an eight-foot-tall Bigfoot walking down 140th Street East near their home in Lancaster.

While the 1970s was a very active decade for Bigfoot in California, the next three decades brought a steady stream of new reports.

Bigfoot in the 1980s

The area around Mount Saint Helens has long been a Bigfoot hotspot. In the days following the eruption of the mountain in May of 1980, Bety Ann Almo and her friend observed a Bigfoot there on three separate occasions. Each time, they saw the creature wandering through a walnut tree grove located along the Feather River.

A few months later, on June 9, 1980, two men, Dave Wilhelm and Ben Larson, from Scotts Valley, California, noticed a horrible garbage-like smell near their campsite. Going to investigate, they drove around the area slowly. At one point, they heard loud footsteps and heavy breathing. Suddenly, a 12-foot tall Bigfoot appeared in their headlights. The next day they returned and observed large footprints.

On September 3, 1980, Clyde Williams was driving through Lake Hughes late at night when a Bigfoot leapt in front of his car and bounded quickly up a steep mountainside.

The Angeles National Forest just north of Los Angeles has produced a steady stream of Bigfoot encounters.

In 1984, Bigfoot was seen crossing this road located at the northwest end of the San Fernando Valley in southern California. Campers in the area have also reported encounters.

This tree was damaged when a Bigfoot climbed into it and snapped several large branches. The witnesses have reported numerous Bigfoot encounters around their home in Acton. I had my own Bigfoot encounter along the Angeles Crest Highway only a few miles away.

On January 6, 1981, an anonymous witness was hiking through the Angeles Forest looking for Bigfoot tracks when he had an incredible encounter. As he searched, he suddenly heard a loud metallic noise. At the same time all animal sounds stopped. Looking around, he observed a large metallic saucer landed nearby. Looking to his left, he saw two tall Bigfoot-type creatures in the distance. Both of the creatures were making long loping strides directly towards him. The witness snapped one photograph and then ran away in a panic. Unfortunately, the photograph was inconclusive.

In 1982, Marcie Honstead was in her home in Eureka when she looked out her window and saw the head and shoulders of a Bigfoot. It quickly moved away, leaving Honstead forever convinced that Bigfoot is real.

Urban Bigfoot

There are many accounts on record in which Bigfoot has approached densely populated urban areas. On the northwest end of the highly populated San Fernando Valley in southern California lies the Santa Susanna Mountains. One evening in January 1984, two men were driving along a curvy mountain road of Santa Susanna Pass when they encountered an eight-foot-tall hairy creature standing in the road. They swerved to avoid striking the creature and crashed their all-terrain vehicle. The creature quickly ran away.

One month later, three hunters in the same area said that they witnessed another (or the same) eight-foot-tall hairy man-like creature walk by their campsite.

In 1987, a group of retired firefighters were enjoying a volleyball game in the Obrien Campground near Mount Shasta Lake when a Bigfoot walked through the nearby field, apparently oblivious to all the human activity going on around it.

A Cross Between a Skunk and Something Dead

This next dramatic case exhibits many details that are typical of Bigfoot behavior, and contains most of the elements of an extensive Bigfoot encounter. In June of 1988, Sean Fries was camping alone in an isolated wilderness area along the Feather River in northern California when he had a terrifying encounter with Bigfoot. He was alone in his tent with his dogs sleeping outside. He woke up to find his dogs running into his tent, shaking in fear. Outside, all the animal sounds of crickets had stopped. Fries grabbed his rifle and, overcoming his fear, went out of his tent to put more wood on the fire. He had the sensation of being watched. Then, says Fries, "I heard some very heavy footsteps right behind me in the trees. There was also a very strange odor, almost like a cross between a skunk and something dead." Fries spun around, but whatever it was stayed out of view in the thick forest. However, the encounter was not over yet. Says Fries, "This thing circled my camp all night long."

When morning finally arrived, Fries had had enough. He decided to leave immediately. Little did he know, he was about to be chased by the creature. Says Fries, "At first light, I packed up and started out and this thing followed me almost the entire day. I could smell it and even saw it through the woods about 75 yards away from me, taking an almost parallel trail to me as if to make sure I left its territory." (www.bigfoot encounters.com)

A few months later, in August of 1988, Todd Wilheim was driving through the eastern Sierras when he saw two Bigfoot cross the road in front of his vehicle.

1990s Bigfoot

In 1995, filmmaker Craig Miller was filming a movie in the scenic Jedediah Smith Redwoods State Park outside of Crescent City in northern California when he and Colin Goddard (the husband of one of the models) observed and filmed a Bigfoot. Goddard was driving the crew in a large RV when he observed an eight-foot tall, hairy, human-like form walking across the road in front of their vehicle.

He shouted to Miller to look. Miller grabbed his video camera and managed to capture five seconds of video of the creature as it crossed the road and disappeared into the wilderness.

Bigfoot Greets Tourists

While most witnesses only catch a fleeting glimpse of Bigfoot at night, some cases involve close-up daylight sightings. This following case may be unique in Bigfoot literature. In August 1995, an anonymous couple from Pennsylvania traveled to northern California for a vacation. They rented a car and drove to various locations. Little did they know, they were about to have a highly dramatic Bigfoot encounter. Very early one morning, they were driving outside of Crescent City along the coast when they spotted a beautiful beach. They stopped the car and prepared to get out and take a walk when, with no warning whatsoever, Bigfoot showed up.

Says the main witness, "I turned to see this big thing standing right in front of my car. At first I thought it was a bear until our eyes met. I couldn't move or speak. We just locked eyes for what seemed to be forever. It stood about six and a half to seven feet, dark brown matted hair, and was holding what looked to be seaweed, which it used both hands to carry. It didn't seem startled. In fact, I felt it was looking at me with anger in its eyes. It let go a snort and a glob of snot hit the windshield right in front of my face. It then took three or four steps and completely crossed the highway while it was still looking at me." (www.bigfootencounters.com)

At this point, another driver drove up and they all watched the creature quickly bound off into the forest. The main witness has insisted upon complete anonymity.

Woodland Witnesses

While late-night drivers account for many Bigfoot reports, probably the majority comes from campers and hikers and other people who explore their local wilderness areas. At around 10:00 am, on August 4, 1996, several campers in the Inyo National Forest observed a Bigfoot from a distance of about 300 yards. The creature was eight or nine feet tall and moved quickly along a nearby ridge.

In September 1997, several reports came in from Lake Crowley. The first sighting was made by several campers who observed the creature while cooking their camp breakfast. A few weeks later, several fishermen were fishing around dusk when they observed a Bigfoot looking back at them from the banks of the lake.

In July of 1998, several mountain-bikers were biking along the base of Mammoth Mountain at around dawn when they observed a Bigfoot walking near the ski tram at the base of the mountain.

On October 17, 1998, several campers in the Plumas National Forest were woken up by the sound of a large bipedal creature walking around their campsite. The next evening, they heard a strange howling noise about two miles away. All were convinced that it was Bigfoot.

Bigfoot For
the New Millennium

Another even more recent case occurred in the town of Acton, which borders the Angeles Forest. I was also able to personally investigate this very important case. The main witness, Wendy Holcomb (pseudonym), reports that she had several encounters with a Bigfoot-like creature that roamed around her home for a period of a few months in the summer of 2001. Several members of the home also observed the creature, including her young son.

The case has generated a surprising amount of physical evidence. One morning after an encounter, the witnesses found chewed up animal bones on the doorstep. They concluded that the bones had been left as a gift by the Bigfoot. On another occasion, they have found skinned-animals. On numerous occasions, they have gone outside after an encounter and observed large footprints. They have also smelled powerful rank odors that they associate with the creature's presence. On one occasion they heard a loud noise on the roof. The next morning they went to investigate and found an enormous boulder perched on the top of the roof. It took two full-grown men to move the boulder off the house. On yet another occasion, Wendy's son observed the Bigfoot climb into a tree next to their home. There was a loud cracking sound as it broke several of the branches. The next morning, her son explained that he saw the "monkey man" last night, outside in the tree. Wendy went outside and observed that several thick branches in the tree were snapped off. There were also large footprints.

I conducted an extensive interview with the main witness, Wendy. She reports a telepathic link with the creature, as she could often sense it before it came. The encounters she said, had continued on and off for three years. She felt that the creature was friendly and felt that it was excited because it had found somebody who could communicate with it.

In late 2003, Wendy called me to say that she was still having encounters and did I want to see the Bigfoot for myself? My answer, of course, was an enthusiastic yes. Little did I realize that we would be successful. I should have expected it because Wendy had actually taken my sister-in-law (the artist for this book) out

Bigfoot hunting a few months earlier, and they both reported hearing a bipedal creature bounding through the darkened forest towards them. Unfortunately, they left in fear.

At the time, I was still a little bit of a Bigfoot skeptic and had trouble believing that I had run across another actual firsthand case. However, as Wendy's encounters continued, and the evidence mounted, it became clear that the case was real. In October 2003, Wendy, her friend Mike (pseudonym), and I hiked to a wilderness area a few miles from Wendy's home off the Angeles Crest Highway.

We had just pulled off the road and were getting out our cameras and recording equipment when we all three heard something: a very loud and continuous growling noise off in the distance, coming somewhere from the deep forested valley directly to our east. We all three stood immediately still and looked at each other with wide eyes. We whispered, "Did you hear that? What was that? Be quiet!"

We all listened and about one second later we heard it again, a long continuous loud growling sound in the distance, lasting about five full seconds. It was so loud I looked up to see if there could be a jet flying overhead. But it definitely seemed to come from a certain area, *down* in the valley to the east. It almost sounded like a chainsaw off in the distance, but it was somehow different. We looked at each other and fumbled for our equipment. But by then it was over and didn't return.

While I can't say for sure that we encountered Bigfoot, I still can't explain what we heard. It didn't sound like a mountain lion, coyote, bear or other animal. And we definitely heard *something*.

> **We all three stood immediately still and looked at each other with wide eyes. We whispered, "Did you hear that? What was that? Be quiet!"**

See for Yourself

In any case, the California Bigfoot cases number in the thousands. As can be seen, Bigfoot is alive and well all across the Golden State. So where do you go if you want to see Bigfoot? Amazingly, no matter where you are in the state, you don't have to travel far.

The Angeles National Forest/Antelope Valley/ Lancaster area, located just north of Los Angeles, is a major hotspot. With more than eighty campgrounds located across the sprawling forests and mountains in the Angeles Forest National Park, there are plenty of places for the intrepid Bigfoot hunter to explore.

Bigfoot expert Loren Coleman lists the Antelope Valley area as number eighteen of the twenty best places in the world to contact Bigfoot. As he writes, "Antelope Valley sees a lot of unusual Bigfoot activity but does not get much publicity, even though it is so close to Los Angeles." (Coleman 2003, 249)

If you want to contact Bigfoot, go to a remote location in the forest and meditate on making mental contact. You might be surprised what happens. In the three Bigfoot cases I personally investigated, each of them had a strong telepathic aspect. And as we have seen,

there are several cases on record where people went on Bigfoot stakeouts and were totally successful.

For those who are too afraid to venture out into the unknown forests, you can also drive through the area on the scenic Route 2, the sixty-four mile long Angeles Crest Highway. For more information on camping in the Angeles Crest Forest campgrounds, call the Angeles National Forest Supervisor Station at 818-574-5200.

For anybody even remotely interested in Bigfoot, the town of Willow Creek in northern California is a must-see. The small town is located in the center of a huge redwood forest of untouched wilderness. It is easy to see why Willow Creek is such a Bigfoot hotspot. It's the perfect place for a Bigfoot to live undetected. It is actually located adjacent to Bluff Creek, which as we have seen, is *The* Major Bigfoot Hotspot.

Each Labor Day weekend, the town holds its annual Bigfoot celebration. The entire town is saturated with Bigfoot influence. You can order a "Bigfoot Breakfast" at the local diner. At midday, there is Bigfoot parade down Main Street, complete with floats and costumed people commemorating the unknown creature. The evening closes with a Bigfoot Barbecue.

On May 6, 2000, Willow Creek opened the Willow Creek/China Flat museum, two wings of which are devoted entirely to Bigfoot. In front of the museum looms a nearly thirty-foot tall sculpture of the beast. The museum itself houses various exhibits displaying the evidence, including photographs, plaster-cast footprints, accounts of sightings and other interesting bits of evidence. There's also a local gift shop with all kinds of Bigfoot memorabilia, from key-chains and dolls to finger puppets and maps of various sighting locations.

Loren Coleman lists Bluff Creek as the *number one* best spot in the entire world to see a Bigfoot. As he says, "Bluff Creek is the Mecca of the Bigfoot field." (Coleman 2003, 247)

For those who want to visit Willow Creek or Bluff Creek and immerse themselves in Bigfoot culture, and maybe have their own sighting, the towns are located north of San Francisco, off Highway 299. Take Interstate 101 and turn east on Highway 299.

While Willow Creek is "Bigfoot Central," all of northern California could be considered a Bigfoot hotspot. Another place to learn more about Bigfoot is Garberville, also in northern California, which has a large Bigfoot statue standing outside The Legends of Bigfoot museum, dedicated solely to the mysterious creature.

Number five on Coleman's top twenty list is the Mount Shasta-Trinity Alps area. Says Coleman, "The Trinity Alps are also steeped in Native and modern Bigfoot lore. The Sisson Museum, southwest of Mount Shasta City, has Bigfoot exhibits and souvenirs." (Coleman 2003, 247)

Below is a list of some of the larger cities and counties were Bigfoot has been seen on multiple occasions, stretching from at least the early 1900s to the present day. Again, this is only a partial list. But as can be seen, no matter where you are in California, you don't have to go far to see a Bigfoot.

Acton, Alameda, Alpine, Amador, Antelope Valley, Anza Borrego, Big Rock, Bluff Creek, Butte, Calaveras, Canyon Country, Colusa, Contra Costa, Crescent City, Del Norte, El Dorado, Eureka, Fresno, Glenn, Happy Camp, Hayward, Hoopa, Humboldt, Imperial, Inyo, Kern, Lake Hughes, Lake Tahoe, Lancaster, Lassen, Los Angeles, Madera, Magalia, Mammoth, Marin, Mariposa, Mendocino, Merced, Modoc, Mono, Monterey, Mount Shasta, Orange, Oroville, Palmdale, Paradise, Placer, Plumas, Redding, Riverside, Sacramento, San Bernardino, San Diego, San Francisco, San Joaquin, San Luis Obispo, San Mateo, San Rafael, Santa Barbara, Santa Clara, Santa Cruz, Shasta, Sierra, Siskiyou, Solano, Sonoma, Stanislaus, Sutter, Tehama, Trinity, Tujunga, Tulare, Tuolumne, Vacaville, Ventura, Willow Creek, Yosemite.

5. The Chupacabra in California

The "Goat Sucker," New and Unique

In the mid-1990s, disturbing reports surfaced in Puerto Rico of animal mutilations in conjunction with sightings of a very strange creature dubbed the "chupacabra" or goat-sucker.

The chupacabra is unique among cryptozoological creatures in that it appears to be a brand new phenomenon. Its appearance seems straight out of a horror movie. It has glowing red eyes, fangs, a hairy body, spikes along it back, goat-like legs, and clawed appendages. Despite its chimera-like appearance, the evidence in support of the creature's existence is surprisingly extensive. At first, there were only anecdotal eyewitness testimonies. But as these added up, so did the physical evidence of animal mutilations. Author and researcher Scott Corrales has written a book, *Chupacabras and Other Mysteries*, detailing many impressive cases.

The chupacabra, as it turns out, is *vampiric* – it has a gnawing hunger for blood. It has left hundreds of carcasses in its wake – each of them with strange puncture wounds and arteries drained of blood.

Whatever the chupacabra is, many people are taking the reports very seriously. This is especially true when one considers that the chupacabra has now moved out of Puerto Rico, across the world, and into the United States, specifically, California.

The Chupacabra or "Goat Sucker:" Originally reported in Puerto Rico, it wasn't long before Californians also began to see this unexplained nefarious creature.

Theories Abound!

As is usually the case when strange things happen, theories to explain the reports range from the ridiculous to the bizarre. Some claim the reports are due to mass hysteria. Others have pointed out that California's large Latino population, with strong beliefs in local legends, may be a factor. Another popular theory is that the chupacabra is actually a genetically-manufactured creature which escaped from some secret government laboratory. And then of course there is the ever-popular extraterrestrial theory.

Because the reports are now so widespread, it is clear that there is more than one chupacabra. Another popular theory is that the chupacabra is an interdimensional creature that has somehow intruded into the physical world where it is creating havoc.

Many Sightings

In 1996, the local town of Poway, just a few miles north of San Diego and the Mexican border became the center of media attention when the chupacabra made numerous appearances. As reported in the June 30, 1996, issue of the *Advocate Herald*, "Recent sightings and a reported attack have put the entire community on alert."

The article went on to say that city officials have no knowledge concerning the creature, and speculated that the chupacabra was an escaped genetic mutant, (similar to Killer Bees.) Meanwhile, the entire town was living in virtual lockdown conditions. As the paper advised, "Anyone encountering one of these animals should immediately contact local authorities. Do not approach it and move indoors as quickly and quietly as possible."

The creature was described as standing about three feet high, with large claws and fangs, looking like a gargoyle.

Inland Empire Struck

The next area to be struck was about 100 miles up north, in Orange County and throughout the Inland Empire, the widely-spread group of desert cities located east of Los Angeles.

An anonymous witness from Phelan (outside Hesperia) provides a compelling testimony. This area is a remote desert area with an active wildlife population. The first strange thing the witness noticed was a sudden and rapid decline in the local wildlife population. First all the coyotes disappeared; then so did the rabbits.

One evening around this time, the witness was drawn outside to investigate why her dogs were barking and her pig was squealing. At that point, she came face-to-face with the chupacabra. As soon as it saw her, it disappeared off into the brush.

However, since that time, the witness and her husband have had several encounters. Writes the main witness, "…It usually appears after dark, and recently not as often. This creature stands on two legs and is a dark smoky gray. It seems to be covered by a sort of peach type fuzz in the same gray color. The eyes are enormous, almond shaped…the head is an oval shape that is much wider on the top. The arms have three digits that have very long claws on the ends…the arms themselves are very thin and give the appearance of limited power, and yet we watched in fascination as it tore open the chain link of the pigpen almost effortlessly. From some angles it resembled a mini person about three to four feet tall approximately 75 to 80 pounds. When it walks it has a slumped over gait. The one time my husband went after it at the pigpen, he noticed these spikey things on its back like porcupine quills that seemed to move independently." (Murphy, 1-4)

The witness states that they have seen the chupacabra a dozen times in 1996. They also remarked upon local UFO activity and a large number of military helicopters searching the area.

Chupacabra Stops Traffic

Another chupacabra encounter occurred on February 18, 1996, in Sherman Oaks, California. Two men were driving at 9:30 in the evening when they saw a bizarre-looking creature running parallel to the road, pacing their vehicle. At one point, the creature dashed in front of the car and the witnesses skidded to a stop on the roadside. At the same time, the drivers of two other vehicles also saw the creature and stopped suddenly. At this point, the main witness, Marcel X., noticed two other creatures running towards a bright light hovering in a nearby field. According to the witness, the creatures had scales and a row of spikes running down their backs, goat-like heads, red teardrop-shaped eyes, and two legs. They moved very quickly away. The witnesses filed a police report on the incident.

…Weird Rasping Screech

A more recent report comes from Santa Clarita, just north of Los Angeles. In 2001, two friends were walking along the streets in a rural part of town. They were actually talking about the Chupacabra because they had recently heard about sightings. Incredibly, merely discussing the creature seemed to call it forth, and they had their own very scary encounter. Says the main witness, "We both turned around when we heard a weird rasping screech. We had a flashlight, and flashed it at the street. [We] saw a weird creature that looked as if it was about to spring. It had red eyes, and when it turned and fled, we noticed its powerful hind legs. We heard the noise several more times, and some rustling in the tree. We turned and ran. We could hear one or two animals also uttering the attack cry. We didn't stop running 'til we reached my house. This made us sure never to go out in the dark again."

Chupacabra Hazing

Yet another recent sighting occurred to a young freshman college student from the University of San Diego. The student, who prefers to remain anonymous, reports that his ordeal began when he decided to join a fraternity. As part of his pledge, he was told to go and sleep out alone in the mountains outside of San Diego, where there had been a number of recent Chupacabra sightings.

The student was taken out by his pledge masters, told about the recent sightings – obviously to scare him — and then left alone. The student was not impressed by the stories and knew that his frat brothers were just trying to instill him with fear. Says the student, "Because it was so boring out there alone in the woods, I decided to go to bed. About an hour after I had gone into my tent I heard a rustling. I figured it was one of those [frat] guys trying to scare me, or an animal. Any-way, I tried to go back to bed. But then I heard it right outside my tent. I flashed my light against the tent and I could see this thing standing up with spikes along its head and back, right outside my tent."

Despite the strange shadow on his tent, the witness was convinced that his fraternity brothers were somehow responsible. As he says, "I screamed to what I thought was one of the guys, 'Ha, ha, funny…I'm trying to go to sleep.' But no one answered. I walked up to the tent and punched the side of it. They still didn't say anything. So I unzipped the tent and I stared right at it. Its red eyes looked right at me and then it fled into the woods."

The witness is absolutely convinced that he saw an actual chupacabra. As he says, "There is no way possible that the animal could have been one of my frat brothers. I asked them the next day and they seemed just as scared as I was. None of them have ever 'fessed up to it. I don't think they ever will 'cause I know that the thing was a chupacabra. It was in those woods, and it was big and scary." (www.elchupacabra.com)

California: Cryptozoo-logical Paradise

As can be seen, California is literally filled with all kinds of mysterious creatures. They inhabit our lakes. They swim along our mountain streams. They lurk along the coastlines. They hide in the dense forests. They wander through the isolated deserts. They come in all shapes and sizes, and appear regularly across California. Whether you want to see a Bigfoot, a lake monster, a sea serpent, a giant salamander or a chupacabra, California is apparently the place to be.

> California is literally filled with all kinds of mysterious creatures. They inhabit our lakes. They swim along our mountain streams. They lurk along the coastlines. They hide in the dense forests. They wander through the isolated deserts.

For those who are too scared to hunt for ghosts, UFOs or cryptozoological creatures, there are always more Divine pursuits available. While there are many haunted sites to explore, there are just as many sacred sites.

Ever since Jesus Christ made His appearance more than 2000 years ago, He has apparently continued to return again and again across the world. Also making regular appearances is the Mother Mary.

Religious visions are certainly nothing new. What makes some of these cases compelling, however, is that they have supporting witnesses and, in rare cases, physical evidence.

1. Crosses of Light

One Way

Cross

In Altadena, California, an apparent religious miracle is taking the community by storm. Starting in 1986, a brilliant cross of light appeared on the bathroom window of Reverend P. G. Pierce. The cross is only visible from the inside looking out.

Because of this, Reverend Pierce has allowed literally thousands of people into his home to view the cross of light. Pierce believes that the cross is a sign of the presence of Jesus Christ.

Several newspaper reporters have made the trip to Pierce's home. Writes the Los Angeles *Herald Examiner*, "Whether or not a miracle exists, it is clear that many people in Los Angeles want desperately to see and touch a fingerprint of the Creator."

In Altadena, California, an apparent religious miracle is taking the community by storm. Starting in 1986, a brilliant cross of light appeared on the bathroom window of Reverend P. G. Pierce. The cross is only visible from the inside looking out.

Numerous homes throughout California have become the locations for alleged religious miracles. Often this involves the appearance of mysterious "crosses of light" on bathroom windows.

As it turns out, crosses of light appearing in windows are regularly reported as a sign of divine intervention.

In 1988, the town of El Monte attracted worldwide attention when at least ten homes reported the appearance of mysterious crosses of light. Researcher

El Monte

Lights

Frances Robinson produced a video documentary on the El Monte crosses. During her research, she heard of similar phenomenon appearing in Baldwin Park, Montebello, La Puente, and East Los Angeles.

These crosses of light appear to be a relatively common phenomenon with new cases surfacing several times a year. On August 17, 1990, the *Los Angeles Times*

L.A.

Crosses

described the appearances of crosses of light on bathroom windows in Montecito Heights and Los Angeles.

Radiant Crosses

In 1990, the home of Leo and Loretta Alphonso in Los Angeles attracted hundreds of on-lookers to observe several "radiant crosses" appearing in a certain window.

No Phony Baloney ... But Weird

In 1992, the home of Maria Ruiz of Baldwin Park became the next target. As reported in the *Pasadena-Star News*, Ruiz first noticed the cross during a power-outage. As she stood in her darkened bathroom, she saw a bright yellow cross through the frosted glass of the bathroom window. Ruiz used to believe that religious miracles were "a bunch of phony baloney."

Now that her home has attracted a steady stream of worshippers, Ruiz is not so judgmental. As she says, "I can't say it's a sign from God or it's not a sign from God...It is weird."

"Inviting people here to pray and see crosses makes them feel good. They feel the Holy Spirit. They can feel all these warm feelings."

Bathroom Crosses

Only the Beginning

Why so many of these crosses appear in bathrooms is a mystery. Another case is that of Joann Noriega of Montclair. On December 8, 1992, she noticed for the first time a "big, beautiful cross" on her bathroom window. She had lived in the house for seventeen years and never noticed any such markings. She was convinced it was a sign from God. As she says, "It was the Virgin Mary. I had no doubt. I didn't even try to guess at it."

Heavenly Bells

However, that was just the beginning. Noriega began having visions of the Virgin Mary. At the same time, more glowing crosses appeared on various windows, weird rainbows appeared around the house, a candle in her bedroom began seeping oil, and the mysterious sound of heavenly bells rang through the hallways. Next came the scent of roses.

Holy Spirit

Following this flurry of activity, Noriega began holding services in her home. These became very popular and have now continued for years. Each week, she holds a Friday night prayer meeting in her living room. Today, years later, several thousand people have made the pilgrimage to her house. Says Noriega, "Inviting people here to pray and see crosses makes them feel good. They feel the Holy Spirit. They can feel all these warm feelings."

Healed and Transformed

Some people have come away from Noriega's living room healed and transformed. Hussem Farach told reporters that before he came, he was addicted to drugs, but afterwards, was free of his addiction. Says Farach, "I believe I've been in the worst places in my living hell. But now I know, whatever happens, God is there for me. He's already proved it."

Cries, Wind,

and a Cross

In 1994, the *Orange County Register* reported on the experiences of Margarito and Maria Ortega of Orange County. The experiences began when Maria woke up at 3:00 a.m. to the sound of a baby crying. She searched the house and entered the bathroom. Upon turning on the light, a loud rush of wind swept past her. She looked up and saw a white, glowing cross on the bathroom window. She fell to her knees in prayer.

The experience transformed the lives of the Ortega family, consisting of twelve members. The whole family has become more spiritual. One of the children stopped drinking alcohol. Says another family member, David, "I think it's a message to everybody. Something's going to happen, but we don't know what."

Word of the cross spread throughout the neighborhood, and before long there were crowds of people parading through the Ortega's home. The Ortegas are a little "tired" of the crowds, but at the same time, they believe it is wrong to deny people the right to see the cross.

Signs of

the Times?

Meanwhile, the phenomenon continued to manifest elsewhere. In 1996, Carlos and Ines Alvarez of Bakersfield opened their home to the public to view another glowing cross on a bathroom window. The cross appeared on March 7, 1996. Word soon spread and crowds gathered to gaze at the cross, which seems to have a powerful effect on the audience. While some people fall to their knees in devout prayer, others are moved to the point of tears, and some, say the Alvarezes, even faint.

Their bathroom became so popular that the family produced a video about it. Says Ines Alvarez, "A lot of people think it's a message to send us because we're in the last days."

The next cross of light to gain widespread attention appeared in 1998, in one of the light fixtures of Greenwood Community Church in Elk, California. The church was built in 1892 and is now more than 100 years old. In 1993, the then failing Methodist church was sold to the local community for $170,000, and is now open to all denominations. It was in this unique setting that the cross first appeared. A photograph of the glowing cross clearly shows a well-defined cross, glowing bright orange. Like other crosses, it has convinced many people that it is a true divine image, or an actual sign from God.

> "A lot of people think it's a message to send us because we're in the last days."

2. Living Statues

Common among religious miracles are statues that seem to come to life by either weeping, moving or consuming liquids. Some statues weep salty tears. Others bleed human blood. Some drink milk. Others appear to blink or sway back and forth. The phenomenon has occurred for centuries and appears to be worldwide. Nevertheless, it is very rare.

Thirty Statues

Seep Olive Oil

In 1995, Reverend Moueen Hana (a priest from the Eastern Orthodox Church in San Jose) revealed to the *San Jose Mercury News* that many of his religious icons were miraculously seeping olive oil! Hana says that he has counted no less than thirty of his statues that have exhibited this strange phenomenon over a period of several years. In 1995, eight of the statues were dripping oil.

Healing Oils

Hana reports that the dripping oil appeared to have been ignited by the visit from an incredible woman named Myrna Nazoor. In 1982, Nazoor, at that time living in Syria, had a vision of the Virgin Mary. After the vision, one of her statues of the Virgin Mary began to leak oil. Shortly thereafter, Nazoor herself began to perform healings, during which the palms of her hands would fill with oil.

In 1988, a total of 57 gallons of olive oil seeped from one of Nazoor's statues. A sample sent to a lab in Germany proved that the oil was 100 percent pure. Nazoor's miracle has been verified by three separate orthodox churches.

More Healings

It was then that his own icons began to exude oil. More recently, Hana has found that the miracle is affecting him personally. Twice his hands have dripped olive oil while he was immersed in prayer. And already, says Hana, two miraculous healings have been reported.

Weeping

Statues

Weeping statues are rare, but they are definitely not unique. A recent example is currently taking place [at the time of this writing] in an anonymous home in northern California. The couple is very religious and own several small religious statues. Suddenly, and without warning, several of these statues began to weep tears.

As reported in the *Spirit Daily.com* online newspaper, "The exudation began in 1997 with the Immaculate Heart of Mary and recently has included allegedly miraculous tears from an image of Divine Mercy – which the owners take to bear special significance…we can only say that the owners seem sincere, devout and straightforward."

Tears of Blood

One of these statues is of Padre Pio, a nineteenth century stigmatic. In 2003, the small statue began to bleed "tears of blood." The couple eventually contacted researchers and had the blood tested. On November 3, 2003, tests confirmed that the liquid coming from the statue was, in fact, human blood.

As the *Spirit Daily* reported, "We have followed this family's situation for years. Many statues allegedly weep in her home. Up until now, the exudations have been tears or oil. What does the blood mean?"

Thirsty

Statues

Not all miracles involve statues that weep. Some involve statues that appear to consume liquid. In 2002, statues of Ganesh all across India reportedly would drink milk offerings if held up to the mouth.

Hearing of this strange miracle, devotees in the United States gave milk offerings in numerous Hindu temples, hoping for another sign. The miracle devotees were hoping for actually occurred in the Sunnyvale, California, Hindu Temple. As reported by the Hindu Priests who witnessed the miracle, milk offerings left at the statues of Ganesh and the Lord Shiva were both apparently consumed by the statues! According to the priests, the phenomenon lasted for three days. The event was actually filmed and shown on several local television programs. The statue would drink a full bowlful of milk over a period of several minutes. The statues still remain in the temple, which is located on 420-450 Persian Drive in Sunnyvale, California. Phone: 408-734-4554.

Oily Photos

In 1988, Nazoor visited Reverend Hana's church in San Jose. She gave Reverend Hana a photograph of the miraculous oil-producing icon. Hana made 8000 copies to distribute to the masses. To his amazement, the miracle translated directly to the photos. Says Reverend Hana, "Many of these [photographs] have exuded oil."

3. Virgin Mary Trees

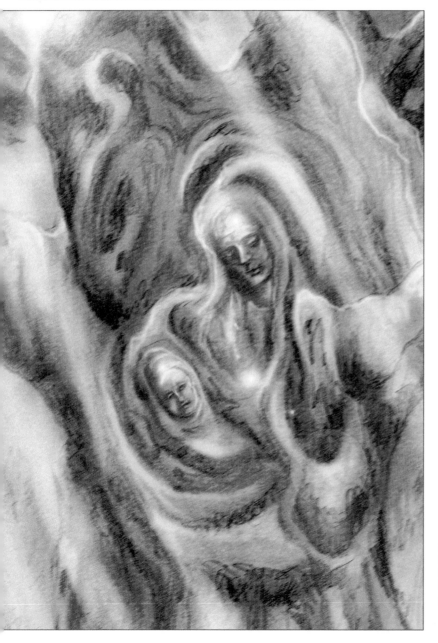

Among the strangest religious miracles are the so-called "Virgin Mary Trees." In these rare cases, images of the Mother Mary can be seen on the trunks of trees, or on the faces of sawed off branches.

> **Says Father Bunda, "For those who believe, no explanation is necessary. For those who don't believe, no explanation is possible."**

Meaningful Shapes

It is not unusual to see meaningful shapes in otherwise natural formations. The human mind has a tendency to find patterns and see everything from an anthropocentric viewpoint. This phenomenon, called *pareidolia*, has often been used by skeptics to account for these visions. Seeing meaningful shapes in clouds is a typical example. Whether or not this explains Virgin Mary trees, you will have to decide for yourself.

A Virgin Mary tree is a tree that carries the image of Mother Mary. Sometimes the image appears among the leaves or along the trunk. More often it appears after a branch is removed and the tree's sap seeps out of the severed limb to form an image.

Our Lady of Watsonville

On June 17, 1993, Anita Contreras traveled to Pinto Lake County Park in Watsonville. She was praying for her children under a small grove of trees when she noticed something peculiar on the trunk of one of the trees. It appeared to be an image of some kind. Looking closer, she was surprised to see that it was the Virgin Mary. Contreras told her friends, who also became convinced. They told their friends, and in a matter of months, more than 4000 people were praying in front of the tree daily.

A shrine to "Our Lady of Watsonville" was set up near the soccer fields and playgrounds of Pinto Lake. Six years later, the site was still popular. Father Roman Bunda celebrated Mass at the site on the sixth anniversary of the event. Says Father Bunda, "For those who believe, no explanation is necessary. For those who don't believe, no explanation is possible."

It is difficult to say how common Virgin Mary trees are as most of them receive little publicity other than through local newspapers. They do, however, seem to appear fairly regularly.

Colma –

City of Repose

More recently, in late 1997, the city of Colma gained local media attention for having several Virgin Mary trees. What makes this site particularly bizarre is that Colma is known as the "City of Repose." It is the official cemetery of San Francisco and contains more than 20,000 graves!

One of the Virgin Mary Trees is located at the back end of the Olivet Cemetery grounds. The image is on the trunk and shows "Madonna and Child." Several other trees reportedly contain images, but the main attraction is the tree at the southwest corner of the cemetery. On the side of the tree, twenty feet up, a sawed-off branch is exuding sap in the image of the Virgin Mary.

The trees are easy to locate because of the numerous flowers, candles, ribbons, messages, and religious items that have been placed at their bases. At its peak, the site attracted large crowds of up to sixty people at a time.

> What makes this site particularly bizarre is that Colma is known as the "City of Repose." It is the official cemetery of San Francisco and contains more than 20,000 graves!

See for Yourself

The site is located in the city of Colma, just south of San Francisco. Olivet Cemetery is located at the intersection of Hillside and Hoffman, two blocks northeast of Highway 82.

4. Religious Apparitions

La Loma
and Our Lady

It was Christmas day, 1984, in the little town of La Loma, just southeast of Bakersfield, when it happened. Was it a miracle? Some residents of the mostly Latino neighborhood believe it may be. On that day, numerous people throughout the town observed the beautiful glowing apparition of Our Lady of Guadalupe. The apparition appeared in several different locations. The sightings went on for at least six weeks, long enough to generate considerable publicity.

While the apparitions appear to have slowed down in La Loma, other locations would soon become active.

Mojave Desert
Visitations

Just north of California City in the Mojave Desert, the Virgin Mary is reportedly making regular appearances. Starting in 1989, on the thirteenth of every month, thousands of people flock to the small valley in hopes of a vision. Amazingly, many people claim to have had encounters.

Says Leticia Alva, "In August we came, I didn't see anything, but my children saw the Virgin Mary and they cried. And then we came back again in September, and we saw the Virgin Mary. I saw her myself. I saw her today. She was really small. She was looking at everybody from the sky."

The miracle began in 1989 to Maria Paula, a Mexican Catholic. At the time, her three-year-old daughter was suffering from Leukemia. Paula prayed to God for a healing. Her daughter told her mother to look for a sign in the desert mountains.

Queen of Peace

Paula took her advice and ventured out into the Mojave Desert near their home. As she says, "I started climbing the mountain and saw a rock. I was going to step on the rock. I wasn't wearing shoes since I wanted to climb quickly. But this rock wasn't a rock. It was a snake. I heard a very nice sound, like a fine fabric. Birds were singing. And when I was going to turn around, I heard a voice say, 'No, don't look back, only look at me, and you are going to be saved. I am the lady of the rock, the queen of peace of southern California.' She came on a cloud when I saw her. When I looked over there, the sun was so beautiful. Behind her a bright ray of light. I could see her face so clearly, her eyes, brown hair and rosy cheeks. Her nose and mouth were the most perfect things you could see…she appeared to be very beautiful. She looked to be about sixteen years old…the voice of the Virgin Mother is very smooth, like singing or weeping."

Prepare an Army

The message to Paula was that she was supposed to "prepare an army for Christ on Earth."

Paula has taken the message very seriously and is now a prominent southern California spiritual leader. She can't explain why she has been selected for this mission. As she says, "I don't know, she chose me."

"The second time I was able to stand. Maria Paula prayed on me. She touched me and I felt heat. And after that I started getting better slowly."

Healings

People have since flocked to the site for spiritual fulfillment and even miraculous healings. Maria DeMesa, a registered nurse, claims to have been cured of Lupus. Says DeMesa, "Maria Paula prayed over me. And then after that I told Maria Paula, 'Oh, you know I have lupus.' And then she told me, 'No lupus. No lupus.' I said, 'Momma Paula, I have lupus.' And she kept on insisting that I don't have the lupus'." According to DeMesa, since that time, her symptoms have disappeared.

Another believer in the healing powers of Paula is Frances Pando. As she says, "After I got out of the hospital, and I was strong enough to come, I came. And they brought me by wheelchair and I came three times. And after that I've been coming."

Pando's healing occurred on her second visit. As she says, "The second time I was able to stand. Maria Paula prayed on me. She touched me and I felt heat. And after that I started getting better slowly."

No Official Sanction

"Our Lady of the Rock" has not been officially sanctioned by the church as a miracle. However, this makes no difference to the faithful who continue to flock to the location as they have done for years. Sister Maria Paula says she continues to have visions about three times per day. During the public meetings she gives spiritual wisdom, which she says the Virgin Mary has given to her. She also administers healings to the sick, who line up according to their illness. Reverend John Santillan, a Los Angeles priest, acts as Maria Paula's spiritual advisor and attends the meetings monthly. As he says, "I don't completely accept it, but my tendency is to say, 'Yes, something is happening.'"

Monthly Visions

A bulletin board set up at the site contains more than a dozen photographs of unusual light phenomenon. Many of the attendees claim to see visions of the Virgin Mary on a monthly basis.

Message: Love and Pray More

The crowd usually gathers hours before Maria Paula arrives. She comes in a white van with several close associates. Dressed in a simple white robe, she comes in a procession of her devotees with a large cross being carried in front of her. She then goes up on a stage and gives a lecture. A common theme is to "Love one another and pray more frequently." Paula warns that devastating consequences await those who fail to heed her advice.

The meetings continue today. Maria Paula lectures in Spanish to the crowd of several hundred believers, and then performs several hands-on healings. Whether a true religious miracle or not, Paula's lectures are becoming increasingly popular. (Unsolved Mysteries, ABC)

Madonna in Southern California

Numerous other cases of divine intervention have occurred in California. In 1991, Carmelo Cortez of southern California claimed to have experienced a series of visitations of the Madonna. Following these visits, he found himself gifted with the rare and bizarre ability to manifest detailed images of Jesus Christ, Mother Mary, and other religious figures onto rose petals. Some of the witnesses to this phenomenon have also reported miraculous healings. His story appeared in several newspapers and appeared on television programs. Some feel that it is all a clever hoax. The followers of Cortez, however, remain loyal.

Christ in the Window

In 1992, the Orozco family of Long Beach gained widespread media attention when seventeen-year-old Guadalupe Orozco noticed an unusual looking image in the window of their small apartment. Says Guadalupe, "We were parking the car and one of my friends felt something telling him to look toward the window. That's when we noticed the image of Christ."

Word spread quickly and before long, residents and neighbors were lining up to see the image. An altar with candle and flowers was set up below the window. Says one building resident, Carmelo Contreras, "We just want people to feel comfortable here coming and looking."

Virgin Mary on the Roof

The cases continued. In 1996, a church in the city of San Francisco became the location of a Virgin Mary apparition. The Immaculate Conception Church in San Francisco attracted crowds upwards of a hundred people to observe what appeared to be an image of the Virgin Mary on the church's gabled roof.

The image appeared shortly after the murder of two teenagers in a nearby park. Since then, numerous people have observed the image, which appears only after dark and disappears at sunrise. The crowd gathers each evening to observe the image, pray, and sing religious songs. Some people have reported other manifestations, including the unexplained scent of roses and even miraculous healings. Says one visitor, Taren Sapienza, "The presence of Her was quite overwhelming. It was quite a spiritual experience...From my abdomen to my neck it was like this overwhelming spiritual sense."

When the image persisted and its popularity began to grow, numerous news stations converged to report on the story, including CNN. Father Guglielmo Lauriola is the priest of the Immaculate Conception Church, and has been favorably impressed by the phenomenon and peoples' reactions to it. As he told CNN reporters, "We have a sign that is pulling our attention toward something supernatural...I've seen lots of young people come here and many people who have not been to the church in years."

English researcher Benjamin Crème has studied similar religious apparitions across the world. After visiting the Immaculate Conception Church to see for himself, Crème came away a believer. As he says, "This is part of the signs of an extraordinary event, which to my certain knowledge is taking place in the world." (www.themiraclespage.org)

"The presence of Her was quite overwhelming. It was quite a spiritual experience...From my abdomen to my neck it was like this overwhelming spiritual sense."

Part Four

Local Legends

Numerous places on our planet are steeped in mysterious legends. Myths and legends often take root in places that are themselves unknown. In the depths of the unexplored seas we have legends of mermaids and sea serpents. In the remote forests we have tales of wildmen, fairies, and Bigfoot. Legends of dwarves, kobalds, and various denizens are said to roam the deepest recesses of underground caverns, while the farthest reaches of our skies are the home to extraterrestrials of various types. It seems that when science is able to reach so far, myths and legends take the speculative leap deep into the heart of the unknown.

Each legend is unique to its particular geographic location, and California being uniquely mysterious, it has a few of its own uniquely Californian legends.

Death Valley. There are several legends and stories of underground cities, rivers, and golden caverns somewhere beneath the vast Death Valley National Park.

1. Underground Cities

Some of the strangest and most persistent legends about California are the existence of underground cities. We have already examined the legends of a secret civilization under Mount Shasta. However, there are numerous locations were other hidden subterraneous cities are supposedly located.

Living Beneath

Death Valley

Other than Mount Shasta, the most famous legendary underground city is probably the one located beneath Death Valley. The legend actually began with the local Cahroc Indians who claimed that a race of short, white-skinned people lived in giant underground caverns. Some early explorers reportedly found some of these caverns, which were illuminated by an unknown green light.

Remains of Giants

Then comes the enigmatic figure of Dr. F. Bruce Russell. In 1931, Russell announced his discovery of a giant cavern near Wingate Pass, which contained the skeletons of two eight-foot-tall giants and numerous artifacts.

Discoverer's Disappearance

Over the next fifteen years, Russell claimed to have uncovered no less than thirty-two similar caverns, all in the Wingate Pass area. Russell's claims were not taken seriously, mainly because he failed to bring back any physical evidence. In 1947, he promised to return to the caverns and show the world his incredible discovery. He returned to the area and was never seen again.

Elusive Caverns

Since then, numerous people have tried and failed to find the fabled caverns. Not surprisingly, today the United States government has taken over much of the area and built the super secret China Lake Naval Weapons area. Interestingly, employees at this base and at nearby Edwards report that the facilities themselves go underground as deep as forty stories, with numerous wide tunnels that crisscross the desert, leading under mountains to the various bases. If there is an underground city in Death Valley, it would seem that our government may be aware of it. Location: Death Valley National Park. Highway 190, Death Valley, CA 92328. Phone: 760-786-2331.

The City

Beneath the City

In 1934, mining engineer W. Warren Shufelt announce his discovery of a secret underground city beneath downtown Los Angeles. Shufelt had heard of Hopi Indian legends of a city built by lizard-people. Using radio waves, Shufelt detected what he believed were numerous large caverns. He later excavated a 350 shaft under North Hill Street. His research showed that numerous caverns existed, stretching from what is now Dodger Stadium all the way to the Pacific Ocean.

Shufelts claims were ignored and he faded into oblivion. More recently, in the mid-1990s, construction workers have in fact found tunnels and caverns in the areas where Shufelt first claimed to have detected them. The most popular explanation for the existence of these tunnels is that they were constructed and used by smugglers during the 1800s. Location: Beneath downtown Los Angeles.

> More recently, in the mid-1990s, construction workers have in fact found tunnels and caverns in the areas where Shufelt first claimed to have detected them.

2. Buried Treasures In California

If there is one thing California is known for, it is gold. It's called the Golden State for a good reason. Countless billions worth of this precious metal have been extracted from the ore-rich mountains, rivers, and valleys. The California gold rush changed the face of history and helped to propel the United States into becoming a major world super-power.

The gold rush era was also a time of complete chaos. It was the Wild West. Law and order took a low priority as gold fever swept the nation. California was a place of cops and robbers, cowboys and Indians, hopeful prospectors and zealous Spanish missionaries, desperate pioneers and enterprising entrepreneurs. The 1847 gold rush changed everything. Unfortunately, while hundreds of thousands of people converged on the state hoping to find their fortune, very few actually struck it rich.

On the other hand, a very few did. And not all of them were successful in guarding their claims. Some guarded their secrets to their death, leaving only small clues to the whereabouts of vast fortunes in hidden treasure.

W. C. Jameson is one of the world's leading researchers on lost treasure in the United States and has written several books on the subject. Not surprisingly, he has found that California is a literal treasure-trove of such cases. Writes Jameson, "California is an extraordinary place...[It has] an incredible legacy of folktales, legends, and mythology of lost mines and buried treasures.... The Golden State has, over the past couple of centuries, contributed impressive quantities of colorful tradition, lore, and contemporary mythology to the nation's store of tales and legends of lost mines and buried treasures." (Jameson, 9-16)

The truth is that there are actually *hundreds* of accounts of lost or buried treasures in California. What follows are some of the more famous and better-verified accounts. Fantastic treasures are out there just waiting for the right person to find them. Could that person be you?

Barter's Hidden Gold

Like thousands of other entrepreneurs, Richard Barter moved to California during the Gold Rush, hoping to strike it rich. And like most people, he failed miserably. Circumstances eventually turned against him and Barter turned to a life of crime. Ironically, he found that a career as a bandit was extremely profitable. He became quite wealthy robbing travelers in Shasta County. He soon had several other bandits working for him, and the robberies expanded to include farmers, settlers, and even churches.

Barter's home base was a small cabin outside of Folsom. Somewhere near his cabin, he buried most of the gold that he stole. He took another large cache and buried it somewhere in the Trinity Mountains in Shasta County. The only problem is, nobody knows where the treasure is. A bandit's life is dangerous. And it was only a matter of time before Barter and his gang ran into trouble. One by one, members of the gang were caught and imprisoned or killed. Before long, Barter's number came up. During another robbery attempt, Barter was shot twice in the chest and died instantly. With his death, nobody knew the location of the lost gold. All that is known is that millions of dollars worth of gold are buried somewhere outside of Folsom, and somewhere in a remote canyon in the Trinity Mountains.

Buried Treasure in Cahuenga Pass

In 1866, three former aides to Mexican Emperor Maximilian escaped into California with a large quantity of stolen treasure. Although they tried to hide it, the treasure was stolen from them by a sheepherder who had watched them bury it. The sheepherder himself loaded the treasure onto some mules and planned to take it to Mexico to feed his poor family. He got as far as Los Angeles. As he headed over the Cahuenga Pass, in what is now Santa Monica, he decided to bury his treasure in six large holes next to a grove of trees.

Shortly after doing so, the sheepherder fell ill. His condition worsened quickly until it was clear he wasn't going to recover. On his deathbed, he revealed the existence of the treasure to his caretaker. The caretaker at first didn't believe the shepherd's story. But as he followed his instructions, he found all the landmarks mentioned by the man. He searched the area, but was unable to find the exact location. Others have searched, but the grove of trees where the treasure was buried was cut down. To this date it has never been found. The treasure includes an incalculable fortune in gold coins, gold and silver jewelry, diamonds, pearls, rubies, and emeralds. The area where the treasure is buried has been built over and developed. The approximate location is the Cahuenga Pass, near the Hollywood Bowl.

> All that is known is that millions of dollars worth of gold are buried somewhere outside of Folsom, and somewhere in a remote canyon in the Trinity Mountains.

The Calaveras Coin Cache

By the 1860s, the gold rush was winding to an end. Most of the mines that still consistently produced had been taken over by large companies. Few individual miners were left. One miner who had resisted the large companies was Harry Oversem. About three miles east of the city of Mokelumne Hill, Oversem worked a small gold mine with his friend, Slava Tyroff. Unfortunately, however, gold sometimes has a way of affecting people's minds, making them do things they wouldn't normally do. In this case, Oversem took more than his fair share of the gold and buried it in three large chests under a large boulder near the mine. One day, Tyroff discovered the deception and became furious. Armed with a sledgehammer, Tyroff approached Oversem as he slept and murdered him, hitting Oversem over the head.

Tyroff then panicked, left the scene, and returned to San Francisco. While there, he was stabbed in the chest. Believing he was going to die, he revealed the location of the gold to his physician, Dr. Berlin. Although Tyroff survived the stabbing, he was murdered shortly thereafter. Dr. Berlin followed Tyroff's instructions and was able to locate the mine. However, he was never able to find the boulder or the treasure, which remains lost to this day.

The treasure is reportedly located only a few miles east of Mokelumne Hill. According to Tyroff, the mine is located beyond a wide mesa, in a range of mountains that has three large canyons. It is near a small spring, about a quarter of a mile below the crest of the center canyon. The treasure itself is supposed to be hidden under a large rock, a short distance from the mine down the canyon.

Coronado's Buried Gold

Coronado Island as seen from San Diego. Within a few miles of this location is a large cache of buried gold coins that has never been found.

In 1802, Captain Henry Brown maneuvered his sailing vessel, *The Determined*, northwards off Coronado, just north of the Mexican border. At the time, numerous pirate ships preyed upon ships, ruthlessly killing everybody and stealing all possessions. Onboard, Captain Brown had $60,000 dollars worth of gold coins in a small metal chest.

As they moved towards Coronado and San Diego, the ship's lookout spotted a suspicious vessel heading directly towards them. Captain Brown took immediate action to secure his gold. He loaded the gold onto a rowboat and landed at Russian Springs. Not far from the then well-known spring, Brown buried the treasure chest in a small pit and returned to the ship.

> Not far from the then well-known spring, Brown buried the treasure chest in a small pit and returned to the ship.

They then continued on. The ship turned out to be friendly, but with schedules to keep, Captain Brown headed up the coast, intending to pick up the gold on his return trip. However, in San Francisco he fell ill. His ship was then stolen by pirates. Captain Brown never recovered and died two years later.

Today Russian Springs has dried up and the area has been heavily developed. However, the treasure chest remains buried somewhere above the beach, just south of Coronado. Several people have searched for it, but it has never been found.

Death Valley's Lost Gold Mines

One of the strangest places in California is undoubtedly Death Valley. This vast and remote corner of the Mojave Desert has produced a surprisingly large number of local legends. Among the most popular of these are the legends of Death Valley's lost gold mines. While many areas in California are rumored to have buried gold, literally dozens of accounts come from Death Valley and the surrounding areas.

The Death Valley area is extremely rich in gold and has made many miners very wealthy. Unfortunately for some, the vastness and harshness of the desert has resulted in many lost treasures.

Death Valley. Violent volcanic activity in the distant past has made this area a prime spot for mining gold.

Numerous miners and prospectors have died in the harsh weather conditions in search of gold. Others, however, made vast fortunes. Reportedly the secrets to several of these locations are held by the local Native Americans, who know of hidden entrances to caverns literally filled with gold. Still following the old ways, they take only what they need to survive.

Hot, Dry, and Rich

Death Valley is not only the hottest and driest location in California, it may also be the richest. Throughout the vast desert region, numerous gold mines, gold-laced caverns, and even an underground river have been discovered, mined, and then lost. Some have been re-discovered. Some are still waiting to be found.

Coe's Lost Mine

Way back in 1872, miner Al Coe became lost while traveling through the Panamint Mountains of Death Valley. There he met an old miner who was working a quartz-gold mine that he had hidden beneath a small garbage dump. The miner was well known in the area, and had extracted a large amount of gold from his mine. Unfortunately, the old miner died shortly thereafter. But, before he expired, he revealed the location of the mine to Coe, who himself worked the mine for several years, becoming quite wealthy. However, the Death Valley environment is harsh, and Coe became deathly ill. He was cared for by Bert Topping. Coe revealed the location of the mine to Topping before he died. Afterwards, Topping went to find the mine but was unable to locate it. To this day, it has never been found. Today, somewhere just east of Death Valley, in the upper reaches of the Panamints, on the west side of the range, lies an old garbage dump which conceals a small hole in the ground filled with quartz and gold.

Repeatedly Lost and Found Mine

Another Death Valley mine has been repeatedly lost and found. It was originally mined by an unknown miner somewhere about a half-mile up the south fork of the Kings River in northwest Death Valley, near Kearsarge Pass. In 1862, German immigrant John Schipe re-discovered the mine, and called it the Golden Eagle mine. After easily pulling a fortune in gold out of the mine, he returned to nearby Visalia and cashed in his fortune. He announced his amazing discovery and bought drinks for everybody in several local bars. Unfortunately, he became so inebriated that police were called. Things then went from bad to worse. Schipe resisted arrest and the police shot him in the chest, killing him instantly. The exact location of the mine died along with him. Schipe's discovery became instantly famous and many people returned to the area to search for the Golden Eagle mine. Then in 1890, Mexican prospector Hilario Gomez claimed to have accidentally discovered it – nothing more than a twenty-foot deep shaft into the side of a hill. He pulled out as much gold as he could carry and returned with his discovery. Gomez's discovery was undeniable as he had the gold to prove it. He immediately organized a group of eleven people and returned to the mine. At this point, however, the party was attacked by hostile Indians. Everyone was killed except for Gomez, who barely managed to escape alive.

Two years later he returned and mined several thousand dollars worth of gold ore. Upon his return to San Francisco, however, he contracted pneumonia and died in his sleep. A few days before he died, he revealed to his caregiver that he had re-discovered the mine and that a huge quantity of pure gold was just waiting there for anyone to take it. He gave precise directions to Mr. Sharpe, the rancher who was taking care of him. However, when Sharpe went to find the mine, he tragically drowned while crossing the San Joaquin River. Since then, the exact location of the mine has again become a mystery. Numerous people have searched, but nobody has yet been able to find it.

Lost to a Series of Unfortunate Events

Still another lost fortune of gold lies just beneath a streambed in a small canyon on the eastern flank of the Cottonwood Mountains in north Death Valley, near Ubehebe Peak. In the late 1800s, just before the turn of the century, a group of three men were camping in this area. They took shelter in the small canyon. As they gathered water from the streambed, they noticed something shiny. A little digging revealed dozens of shiny pure gold nuggets. The men filled their pockets with the nuggets and left the area. They planned to return later, but a series of unfortunate events kept them from returning to the area.

Years later, in 1904, one of the men hired two additional men to finally locate the canyon and retrieve the gold. Unfortunately, the expedition ended in disaster. The men had difficulty finding the location and separated to search for the canyon. They became lost and one of the men died. However, the searchers who discovered his body also found that his pockets were packed with gold nuggets. He had apparently found the canyon, but became lost and died of thirst on the return journey. Since then, many people have searched, but nobody has been able to locate the canyon, which by a trick of the landscape remains hidden from the eye.

Ramie's Last Chance

Around the same time as the above account, another prospector, Alex Ramie, continued his years-long search for gold in the mountains north of Death Valley. One day, he became lost in the Last Chance Mountain Range in Northwestern Death Valley. He found himself in an unknown canyon between Ubehebe Peak and Dry Mountain. Literally dying of thirst, he dug down into a dry streambed hoping to find water. Instead, he found gold – millions of dollars worth of pure gold nuggets just three feet beneath the surface. His amazing discovery revived him. He somehow found the strength to fill his pack with a pile of gold nuggets, and then traveled a few more miles, before collapsing and falling unconscious.

He woke up hours later to find several Native American women who gave him water and turned him over to a local sheepherder. Unfortunately, by this time he was too far gone. Realizing he was about to die, he revealed the location of the canyon to Alfred Giraud, the sheepherder who was taking care of him. Following Ramie's death, Giraud later tried to find the hidden canyon. Despite several attempts he was never able to locate it. It remains undiscovered to this day.

Alkali Jones's Lost Vein

In the early 1900s, an old prospector named Alkali Jones decided to search the Death Valley area for gold. For the last twenty years he had tried unsuccessfully to pan gold from local rivers. Finally, his luck was about to change. As he traveled along the eastern flanks of the Panamint Range, he became lost in a sandstorm. He took shelter next to a low hill consisting of a flat-topped granite outcropping. It was here that he made his discovery – a three-foot-thick and hundreds-yard-long vein of quartz thickly laced with pure gold. He chipped off enough gold to fill his packs and returned to Searchlight, Nevada, to cash it in.

Jones bragged about his discovery and returned to obtain more gold. Somehow, however, things went wrong. Jones was never seen alive again. Years later, his pack was found by two Shoshone Indians, and human bones were found nearby. It appeared that Jones had died while searching for his lost vein of gold, which remains lost to this day.

Many Lost Troves

Several other incredible spots are just waiting to be found. There is a ledge of quartz and gold somewhere in the eastern foothills of Brown Mountain. It was discovered by Charlie Wilson in 1906. He made a fortune from the discovery, but he died shortly thereafter. Although dozens have searched for it, its location remains a mystery.

Back in 1852, another quartz ledge was discovered somewhere on the west side of Folly's Pass in the Panamint Mountains. This ledge, however, was speckled heavily with silver. The three men who discovered it, Cadwallader, Towne, and Farley, had all been miners and were amazed by the richness and purity of the find. Each broke off as much as they could carry. They later tried to return to the mine, but tragedy struck. Farley was shot to death during an argument. Towne died a short while later of food poisoning.

Investors then converged upon Cadwallader. An expedition was organized, but Cadwallader died of alcohol poisoning en route. Since then, the story about the lost silver ledge grew and numerous people have searched for it. At least two people have died in their quest. In 1857, a miner named Bailey collected $75,000 from investors to search for the mine. He was later found scalped and mutilated by hostile Indians. In 1858, another prospector by the name of Buel searched for the ledge and apparently found it. He returned with his packs filled with silver. Shortly thereafter, he died of unknown causes. Since then, many people believe the ledge is cursed. It remains once again lost.

In 1850, two German immigrants, John Goler and John Graff, became lost in the Panamint Mountains. In a lower canyon that opened to the west, they made camp and dug for water in a dry streambed. After scooping out a shallow hole, they were shocked to see numerous pure gold nuggets. They pulled out way more than they could carry. They stashed a large portion of gold into the crevice of a nearby ledge and carried the rest out of the Panamints. Not long afterwards, Graff was killed. Goler later returned to the area but was unable to locate the canyon.

In his old age, Goler revealed his story to Grant Cuddeback. In 1917, Cuddeback followed Goler's directions and actually located the canyon. Although he couldn't find the rock crevice filled with gold, he did find the dry streambed. Over the next two years, Cuddeback

and his employees mined over one million dollars in gold nuggets from what is today known as Goler's Wash. As recently as 1972, one anonymous prospector located Goler's Wash and found more than a dozen pure gold nuggets weighing about five ounces each.

Judging from the many accounts coming out of Death Valley and the local mountains, there must be countless tons of gold just waiting to be discovered.

The Donner Party's Lost Fortune

In 1847, one year before the California gold rush, a group of eighty-seven settlers banded together to make the thousands-mile-long trek across the United States to the land of opportunity known as California. The group was composed of several families including, among others, the Breens, the Murphys, the Reeds, the Donners, and other smaller family groups.

The trip westward was full of dangers including everything from wild animals and hostile Indians to getting lost, falling prey to disease or being robbed by bandits. While most pioneers made the trip successfully, the Donner party was particularly unlucky. What happened to the Donner party was so tragic that although more than 150 years have passed, the events are still remembered today.

Deadly Shortcut

Although things went well at first, the Donners made the mistake of following the advice of an unreliable guide named Hastings. The shortcut he recommended took three times longer than expected. As a result, the group was delayed a crucial month. They were then attacked by Indians who stole many of their horses. When they reached the foothills of the Sierras, it was already late October. By another twist of fate, an early snowstorm arrived, and when the settlers tried to cross what is now called Donner Pass, they were forced to turn back.

Snowed in, unable to go forward or return back, the Donner party spent the entire winter in the mountains. They soon ran out of food and, as a result, many died of starvation. Some of the survivors resorted to cannabalism in order to live.

Desperate Families, Hidden Caches

Of all the families, the Donners were hit hardest, losing more than half their members, including both mother and father. The Donners were also one of the wealthiest families. When the settlers realized that they were snowed in for the winter, several of them buried their money in secret caches. The Donners and the Graves were known to have buried a large amount of gold coins (up to $14,000 dollars worth), which were never recovered.

While some of the settlers were able to recover their possessions, the locations of some of the other caches were lost forever with the death of the responsible family members. Both George and Tamsen Donner perished, leaving the location of their money a mystery.

One Cache Found...

Years after the tragedy, the area was searched, and in 1891, a searcher found a large cache of coins, none dating after 1845. An investigation revealed the identity of the rightful owners of the money. The discoverer graciously returned this cache to the descendents of the Graves family. The strong possibility exists that more treasure lies buried somewhere in the area around Donner Lake, Donner Pass or Alder Creek. Today, the area is a park memorializing the tragedy. There are also some claims of ghostly activity. Location: Donner Memorial State Park, near Lake Tahoe.

The Elysian Park Treasure

In the heart of downtown Los Angeles lies several hundred acres of State protected land called Elysian Park. Although pathways wind through the park, it remains surprisingly wild and remote.

Elysian Park is most famous for one reason: it may contain buried treasure. Back in 1846, the Mexican-American War began. At the time, Los Angeles was occupied by many Mexicans who were forced to leave their residences as a result of the war. Back then, instead of banks, many people were forced to bury their possessions in secret locations.

For years, it has been known that many families hiked up into nearby Elysian Park and buried their money and valuables. These rumors are not without some historical documentation. Some descendents have firsthand accounts from their relatives, and have unsuccessfully tried to locate their family's property. In 1984, one expedition funded by relatives followed mysterious markings on some rocks such as initials and scoop-marks. Using these clues, they were led to a treasure-tunnel. Unfortunately, the tunnel had already been looted. While nothing was found, it verified the many accounts that the area was used to bury treasure.

Following this expedition, another city-approved search was undertaken, one involving complex equipment such as radar to look underground. Unfortunately, nothing was found.

Many people believe that much of the treasure in Elysian Park was never recovered because the families were killed or forced out of their homes. One of the searchers, Roy Roche, estimates that the unfound treasure in the park is easily worth millions.

Today Elysian Park is open to the public; however, digging without a proper permit is strictly prohibited. Some have continued to search the area with simple metal detectors. Who knows, you could be the first person to locate the buried treasure of Elysian Park.

The Donners were also one of the wealthiest families. When the settlers realized that they were snowed in for the winter, several of them buried their money in secret caches. The Donners and the Graves were known to have buried a large amount of gold coins (up to $14,000 dollars worth), which were never recovered.

Los Angeles Harbor's Sunken Gold Bullion

On April 27, 1863, the ferry *Ada Hancock* was loading passengers from the dock to transport them to another ship anchored two miles out to sea. Unfortunately, tragedy was about to strike. Onboard the ferry was Wells Fargo employee, William Ritchie. Locked in the safe onboard the boat was $100,000 in gold bullion. Ritchie had made an agreement with the owner of the gold, Louis Schlesinger, to transport the gold to San Francisco. However, Ritchie apparently caught gold fever and planned to steal the gold and live in luxury on one of the many islands in the South Pacific. Somehow Schlesinger caught word of the plan. Just as the ferry was departing, Schlesinger slipped onboard. Witnesses saw him with his pistol in hand, searching for Ritchie, who had himself taken refuge in the ship's engine room. This was apparently the wrong place to hide. Schlesinger found Ritchie and opened fire. At this time the ship was about five minutes offshore, halfway out of the harbor. Witnesses heard several shots. Then, suddenly, there was an enormous explosion and the entire ship blew up.

Of the fifty-six passengers, twenty-six were killed in the disaster, including both Schlesinger and Ritchie. Although it was never proven, the main theory accounting for the explosion is that a bullet struck and ignited a case of gunpowder – a known cargo of the *Ada Hancock*.

To this day, the wreck of the ship and the gold bullions inside of it remain somewhere in the shallow and very busy waters of old Los Angeles Harbor. If recovered today, the $125,000 in gold bullion would be worth millions.

Onboard the ferry was Wells Fargo employee, William Ritchie. Locked in the safe onboard the boat was $100,000 in gold bullion. Ritchie had made an agreement with the owner of the gold, Louis Schlesinger, to transport the gold to San Francisco. However, Ritchie apparently caught gold fever and planned to steal the gold and live in luxury on one of the many islands in the South Pacific.

Mission San Miguel's Buried Treasure

This mission is actually haunted by several ghosts. (See: Haunted Missions section.) Built in 1797, the mission was later purchased by businessman John Reed who converted it into a ranch home and profitable hotel.

Reed didn't trust banks and, furthermore, there were no banks in the area, so he resorted to burying his profits on the property grounds. For more than five years, Reed continued to deposit gold coins in his secret location.

One day, several travelers came to stay at the hotel. Somehow the men learned that Reed didn't use a bank and buried his profits somewhere on the property. Later that evening, Reed was accosted by the men who were actually bandits. One of them held a knife to Reed's throat and demanded that he give the location of the money. When Reed refused, the bandit slashed his throat, killing him instantly. The family and servants were then rounded up and when they too professed no knowledge of the location of the money, all thirteen of them were brutally slaughtered.

The murderers dug several holes looking for the treasure, but were forced to flee when more people arrived. Three of the murderers were later found and hung to death. The others escaped. The Reed family and servants were buried in a mass grave in the backyard.

Reed's estate was eventually acquired by the Catholic Church in 1859. Today, the mission is open to the public. Despite several searches, the treasure has never been found. Researchers believe the treasure is not very deep or very distant as Reed was known to only take about ten minutes to hide it. The amount of the treasure is believed to exceed $200,000 in gold coins.

San Francisco's Buried Gold Bullion

When the gold rush began in 1847, con-artist Harry Meigs left his home in New York City and headed out west in the hopes of striking it rich. He committed arson, burning down his holdings and collecting the insurance funds to finance his trip. Arriving in California and seeing the fierce competition, he changed his tactics and decided to build a sawmill at North Beach in San Francisco. With so many mining towns being constructed at a prodigious rate, Meigs' sawmill immediately prospered. Within a few years, he was rich.

Then, in 1854, numerous banks in California began to fail. Fearing the loss of his wealth, Meigs went to the bank and withdrew two million dollars in gold bullion. It turns out, however, that he was up to his old tricks. The bank documents turned out to be forgeries, and a warrant was placed for Meigs' arrest.

Meigs immediately packed up and left. However, before he left, he took half the gold bars and buried them in a secret location in the woods above North Beach in San Francisco. The treasure was hidden very quickly and could not have been buried more than a few feet deep.

Since then, Meigs tried to retrieve his buried treasure, but legal problems kept him from the area. He died on September 29, 1877, only a few days before he planned to return to the area.

As of yet, the exact location of the treasure remains a mystery. Writes W. C. Jameson, "Should anyone ever locate an 1856 map of San Francisco that showed the location of the old California Lumber Company, Broadway Wharf, and the road that connected the two, they would probably be in an excellent position to undertake a search for the lost million dollars buried by Harry Meigs." (Jameson, 22)

San Miguel
Island's Treasure

In October 1542, Juan Rodriguez Cabrillo landed on the island of San Miguel, the westernmost island of what is now known as the Channel Islands. Cabrillo had already been credited with the discovery of California. This would be Cabrillo's last exploration. While on San Miguel, he injured his arm. His wound became infected and turned gangrenous. A few days later, he was dead. Cabrillo was allegedly buried on the island in a lead coffin. He was placed in his armor and his invaluable jewel-encrusted sword was laid by his side. Despite several modern-day expeditions to locate the gravesite and coffin, it has never been found.

Sunken Treasure Off Point Bennett

San Miguel Island also holds another secret treasure. At some point in history, a Spanish Galleon struck the rocks off Point Bennett and sank with a reported two million dollars in Spanish gold coins. The waves and ocean currents at this particularly area are deadly. Since then, numerous salvagers have attempted unsuccessfully to locate the shipwreck. A few have lost their lives in the attempt. Today the treasure remains unfound and unclaimed.

See for Yourself

Location: Channel Islands State Park, off the coast of Santa Cruz.

Silver Boulder
in the Vasquez Hills

Throughout the 1870s, a band of Mexican bandits headed by Tiburcio Vasquez preyed upon numerous travelers – mostly miners – stealing their possessions and ruthlessly killing anyone who stood in their way.

However, as everybody knows, thieves never prosper. Sooner or later, Vasquez would have to pay for his crimes. That day came in 1872.

On that fateful day Vasquez and his gang attempted to rob a silver mine owned by the very successful businessman, William Stewart, who would later become a Senator in Nevada. Unfortunately for Vasquez, Stewart had prior knowledge of the planned robbery and had devised his own ingenious plan to protect his profit.

Vasquez had intended to take the silver while it was being transported from the mine in the Panamint mountains to Los Angeles. Stewart therefore simply delayed the transport of the silver.

However, this only worked for a little while before Vasquez decided to attack the mine itself and take the silver by force. Stewart then began his next plan to protect his treasure. He took all the silver and smelted it into two gigantic ingots, each weighing 500 pounds. This, Stewart cleverly reasoned, would make the silver impossible for Vasquez and his gang to transport.

Vasquez Rocks. This area outside of Los Angeles was the local hideout for the infamous Valdez Gang of robbers. They reportedly stashed and buried a large quantity of silver at the site, though the treasure has not yet been found.

As it turned out, Stewart was right, and wrong. As he had predicted, the gang attacked the mine and were unable to transport the ingots, and they departed the area. However, when Stewart later had the silver transported, Vasquez and his gang attacked.

This time the gang was prepared and had a horse-driven wagon. They took only one of the silver boulders and loaded it onto the wagon. Vasquez drove off with the silver while other bandits remained for twenty minutes, detaining Stewart's men, and then followed.

When a sheriff arrived with Stewart the next day, they found Vasquez's wagon only a few hundred yards away, abandoned and empty.

One month later, Vasquez was caught in another robbery attempt. Right before he was hung to death, he revealed a secret: the silver ingot that he had stolen from Stewart was hidden in a hole in the rocks only a few hundred yards from where his wagon had been found.

The robbery occurred in the center of Vasquez Hills, just north of Los Angeles. Vasquez Rocks is today a popular location for movie film locations and has appeared in numerous movies and television programs.

Warner Mountain Treasure

In March of 1881, Pit River Indian Dick Holden put his plan in action and robbed a freight wagon of hundreds of pounds of gold. Angered by the white people who took over the lands and pushed him into poverty, he decided to get vengeance. He murdered the two drivers of the wagon and allowed the other two to escape. He then took the wagon with the hundreds of pounds of gold nuggets and hid the ore in a small cave in a canyon somewhere below Eagle Peak, on the western slope of the southern section of the Warner Mountains near Susanville. Holden lived off the gold for years. Because he had hidden his face during the crime, nobody knew at first how he had come into possession of the gold. And because he was frugal with his gold, everyone assumed he was working an old used-up gold mine.

However, Holden grew braver and began to bring larger quantities of gold into town, even buying drinks for everyone in the local bar. On one such occasion, a group of men heard Holden bragging about his riches and observed his backpacks and its pockets bulging with pure gold nuggets. Greed took over and the men decided to follow him to his cache. Holden realized what was happening and, during the chase, shot one of his pursuers dead. As a result, Holden was arrested for murder. The whole story of the robbery came out and Holden was prepared for execution. He refused, however, to give the location of the gold.

Before Holden could be hanged, a group of men broke into his cell and threatened to kill him unless he told them where he hid the gold. Knowing he would be killed the next day anyway, Holden still refused. The men savagely beat and tortured Holden to death. His cache of gold has never been found and still remains hidden in a small cave in the Warner Mountains. Location: Warner Mountains, Susanville.

See for Yourself

Location: Vasquez Rocks, off 14 Freeway north of Los Angeles at Agua Dulce exit.

3. The California Hum

The California Hum. Originally reported around Taos, New Mexico, many Californians are now also claiming to hear a low frequency humming noise that never goes away.

Science Blames ELF

Starting in the early 1990s, residents of Taos, New Mexico, reported a strange and unique phenomenon called the *"Taos Hum."* This peculiar phenomenon is a very low frequency humming or buzzing noise that is heard emanating from the ground or surrounding area. The first "hearers" or "hummers" were thought to be imagining things, making it up or were perhaps sufferers of tinitis (a chronic ringing in one's ears). Then the phenomenon began to spread. Soon there were hundreds of people who were suffering from the unexplained hum. People began to complain of various symptoms including headaches, insomnia, and anxiety. The Taos Hum became front-page news. Scientists stepped in and tried to measure it. Incredibly, the hum has been repeatedly measured and verified by numerous scientists, who have concluded that the hum is connected to ELF (Extremely-Low-Frequency) or ULF (Ultra-Low-Frequency) waves.

All Pervasive Hum

The hum is heard indoors and outdoors, in rural areas and in urban centers. The sound is not caused by appliances as it can be heard during total power failures or in remote wilderness locations.

While the Taos hum was first heard in New Mexico, today it has been reported across the United States and around the world. Today, many cases are turning up in California.

Early Report

One of the earliest reports comes from John Kerliker of Cameron Park, California. Writes Kerliker, "I've been a hummer since 1985, when I decided to work out of my house in the foothills of the Sierras of Northern California. When I realized the sound was not easy to locate I called in a sound consultant, Brown and Associates of Sacramento. They brought out a hand-held electronic ear that isolated and amplified the component I was hearing at about 80 hertz. Even though they couldn't hear it, the $5000 mechanical ear could. They thought the phenomenon was so intriguing that they didn't charge for the call. Their speculation on what it might be – a large, distant generator or large mine shaft fans – didn't pan out, so I placed an ad in my local newspaper with my phone number and started to receive dozens of calls from fellow hummers. By comparing our experiences we at least figured out what it wasn't."

Kerliker, like some other "hummers," speculates that the phenomenon can be heard anywhere. As he says, "These 'hum' sites attract too many crackpots who can't seem to grasp the facts."

While he doesn't pretend to have the solution to the mystery, he writes, "Please, before anyone comes up with another theory, at least have the answer as to why the hum randomly starts and stops."

Hum Experiences

One of the hum hotspots is the San Francisco Bay area. Michael Theroux, editor of *Borderlands Magazine*, has researched the phenomenon since 1994. Says Theroux, "We have also recently developed a means for recording the 'HUM' phenomenon as it is quite active in the early morning hours here. I have several tapes of the HUM which we are currently analyzing using bioacoustic and spectrographic software."

Military Hum?

Another hearer is an anonymous Sacramento resident who writes, "I too have heard the 'hum' most of my life in Sacramento. Since we had two military bases in the area, Mather (now closed) and McClellan, I always assumed it was something the military was doing. One time in particular though was very strange. I was sitting at my desk using my computer, when all of a sudden a strange wave went through me like a Doppler effect. It nearly knocked me out of my chair."

Multi-year Hum

Marty Goddard of San Francisco is another hearer. Starting in 1993, he began to hear a low humming vibration coming from an unknown source. Like most hearers, he thought it was caused by electrical appliances. When further experiments proved that to be false, he assumed it was tinitis. Says Goddard, "Now I want to set up a sensitive microphone to attempt to capture the sound to see if it really is happening or whether it's psychological." Goddard has heard the hum continuously for more than five years.

Life Changing Hum

Jim Shannon's life has been forever changed by his exposure to the hum in his Placerville home. Writes Shannon, "For me it started on December 21, 1995, at 3:00 pm…it sounded like a diesel locomotive two miles away, pulling hard but running rough…At that time I had never heard of the Taos Hum. I started taking notes at that time and I still am…it has been with me ever since…this has been going on for three years now."

Shannon did the usual experiments to determine the source of the noise, but was unsuccessful. He is certain, however, that it is not his appliances, and that it is not coming from his own head. As he says, "It was not affected at all during two total power outages. My wife began hearing it three weeks after I did."

Shannon reports that the hum varies in intensity. Sometimes it is undetectable, and other times the hum gets so loud that it sounds like a "big engine idling." On one occasion, it stayed loud for two weeks and was strongest in the west end of the house. When it is very intense, the neighborhood dogs appear to sense it and start to howl low and mournfully. Says Shannon, "The HUM can be as loud as a 747 over your house."

Shannon has noticed what he believes is a correlation to variations in intensity of the hum and the occurrence of earthquakes, large airline crashes, and other disasters. He has heard the hum in other places and

speculates that "hearers" may be able to hear the hum in any location. He continues to hear the hum today.

Laguna Niguel Hum

Throughout 1997, Mary Allam has been hearing the hum on and off from her home in Laguna Niguel. On the night of September 15, 1997, the hum reached a "greater intensity" than it had on previous occasions.

Something Evil This Way Hums

Dean Blackburn of Santa Clara is also now a believer. In 1997, he began hearing the hum from his home. As he says, "It was after midnight. The house was quiet, except for this soft low hum. I felt almost intruded upon this time of night. I toyed with the idea of calling the police. Who in their right mind would be doing construction or using a blower right now? Even though the noise was soft, it kept boring itself into my head uninvited! I really thought I was going crazy."

A few days later, Blackburn visited a friend's house in Redwood City. Early in the morning, the hum woke him up again. Blackburn has no idea what is causing it, only that it is real. As he says, "All I know is I don't like it. I feel it's something evil."

Electronic Harassment?

Retired electronics engineer Edgar Gillham of Willits, California, began to hear the hum around the same time as Dean Blackburn. Says Gillham, "My wife and I have heard an annoying buzz for about two years. This differs from reports of the Taos hum only in frequency. Ours is near-ultra sound, very high-pitched. I would estimate it to be near the frequency emitted by a television set, near 17,000 cps. It is everywhere we go, even miles from any electrical lines. And it's extremely bothersome, sometimes maddening. We don't always hear it at the same time. Sometimes only one of us hears it, sometimes both."

Gillham speculates that because of his work on classified military projects involving microwaves that the cause may be electronic harassment or electronic detection devices being trained upon him by his former employers.

Elusive Hum

In November 1998, Mr. B. Brown of Simi Valley began to hear the hum. Despite extensive investigations, he hasn't been able to locate the source. As he writes, "It was/is loud in the middle of the afternoon, and I can never get a fix on where it's coming from. I even borrowed a stethoscope to listen to the walls of my house, but that wasn't it. At night, same thing. I thought maybe I was hearing (off in the distance) parking lot vacuum trucks. I even drove where I thought it might have been coming from…nope. It doesn't have to be that quiet and I can still hear it." Brown says that recently the humming oscillates in intensity, and that at times he also hears "various blips, buzzes and whirrs."

Like-a-Fan-Distant-Motor-Driving-Me-Batty Hum!

Nancy Kiang of Berkeley, California, started hearing the hum in 1999. As she says, "This is a noisy city, so the hum would be drowned out for most people. But at night and in the morning, I can hear the like-a-fan-distant-motor-driving-me-batty hum when I am in North Berkeley. I went through the whole series of turning off appliances and electricity, checking with doctors, wandering around checking at night for the last three years, but trips away from Berkeley confirm that its not tinitis."

Kiang also hears the hum outside. She speculates that the hum may be coming from the Department of Nuclear Engineering or Lawrence Berkeley National Labs near her home. Whatever the cause, Kiang only finds peace when she leaves the area.

Hear for Yourself

The reported California hum locations include both southern and northern California. For those who would like to hear the hum, the San Francisco Bay area appears to have the most activity. But be warned, I tried to hear the hum myself and ended up realizing that the condominium building that I live in actually vibrates and hums constantly. I didn't sleep for two days until I learned to ignore it. Hmmmmm…?

Theories Abound

The speculations about causes of the hum run wild. Some believe it might be a natural earth vibration. In 2004, two scientists from the University of California Berkeley, Junkee Rhie and Barbara Romanowicz, measured the hum. They found that the entire planet vibrates at a very low frequency, which Rhie and Romanowicz say is too low for human ears but sensitive to seismic instruments. Interestingly, the hum was loudest on days with no seismic activity, indicating that the vibration was close to the surface.

Other explanations have been raised. A few have tried to correlate the hum to natural disasters. UFOs have been mentioned. But the most popular theory is underground construction, or bizarre secret government experiments using ELF and ULF frequencies to remotely conduct mind control experiments. Some say the hum is confined to geographically specific sites, while others feel that "hearers" can detect the hum wherever they are.

Whatever the case, causes such as electrical appliances or tinitis can be easily ruled out. The phenomenon has spread across the entire world and seems to be increasing. No cause has yet been determined. (Note: the direct quotes in this chapter were researched from www.taoshum.com. See Taos Hum Page: Hum Reports, 1-31 & www.paranetinfo.com/UFO_Files/UFO/hum.txt)

4. Will California Fall into the Sea?

If you have lived for any length of time in California, you have probably experienced an earthquake. The city of Parkfield in southern California experiences earthquakes up to 6.0 on the Richter scale on a regular basis. Seismologists from around the world have converged upon the tiny town in an attempt to understand the mechanics of earthquakes.

Giant Turtles and *el Diablo*

As with many natural disasters, a number of uniquely Californian legends have been generated to explain the devastating destructive power of a widespread earthquake. The mythology of the early Gabrielano Native Americans in California states that the land itself rests on the backs of giant turtles, and the shaking ground is caused when the turtles fight. During the same era, Mexican settlers brought a new mythology, explaining earthquakes as being caused by the anger of "*el Diablo.*"

Today modern science has replaced these beliefs with the explanation that earthquakes are caused by the shifting continental plates and the gradual settling of the earth's crust. Despite our advanced knowledge of earthquakes, however, science has not been able to make accurate predictions of seismic events. Nor have scientists been able to extinguish or explain away the numerous other modern myths and legends that continue to circulate even today.

Earthquake Weather

Probably the most popular myth surrounding earthquakes is the uniquely Californian saying known as "*earthquake weather.*" Practically every time there's an earthquake, seismologists are interviewed on the evening news, trying to dispel the myth that the weather has any effect on temblors. Statistically, earthquakes occur most often in the early morning. There is no known correlation involving the weather.

Earthquake Lights

Another earthquake legend is known as *earthquake lights*. Although very rare, during a powerful earthquake, a plasma-like substance may be emitted from the ground in the form of powerful illumination.

During the 1994 Northridge earthquake, at least one person claims to have observed powerful earthquake lights. According to his anonymous testimony: "I live in the San Fernando Valley, only a few miles from the epicenter of the 6.8 quake. When it hit, I ran out onto my balcony, which looks north towards the mountains. I watched the electricity go out and many transformers explode. Then I saw a huge sheet of light come up from the base of the mountains. It lasted only seconds, but it was a thousand times brighter than all the exploding transformers. I later learned that I had seen a rare scientific phenomenon of earth-lights that are caused by the friction of earthquakes." (personal interview)

Today, seismologists have verified the presence of these lights by placing granite boulders under extreme pressure. They crushed the boulders and produced numerous short-lived earthquake lights, which they photographed with high-speed photography. Repeated experiments have brought the same results, forever proving that, while rare, earthquake lights are real.

Animal Forecasters

Another interesting earthquake legend is that animals can predict earthquakes. This has actually been an accepted belief for centuries and has been used successfully in many cultures to predict earthquakes. In California, one man discovered a unique method to predict earthquakes. Knowing of the ability of animals to sense upcoming earth movement, he scanned the newspapers, keeping a careful record of the number of ads involving lost pets. He figured that prior to an earthquake, there would be a corresponding rise in ads. He claims to have predicted at least one earthquake using this method.

The Big One

There are many other earthquake myths, but the most powerful and persistent earthquake myth of all, at least for California, is that an earthquake called "the Big One" will strike and plummet California into the ocean.

Scientists Deny California Slated for Watery Grave

This prophecy or prediction is well known among Californians, and seismologists have tried their best to dispel it. It is impossible, they claim, because the ocean is only about two miles deep at most, but the state of California is well over twenty-five miles thick. Furthermore, the fault lines show that the California land mass is slowly moving northwards, not up or down, and that the massive continental shelf off the coast would make it impossible for California to fall into the sea.

And Yet...

Despite this, the legend of California's shaky foundation has persisted. These stories can be traced back to at least 1931, when the world-famous psychic Edgar Cayce began making prophecies of upcoming earth changes. Cayce, the Sleeping Prophet, is probably best known for his ability to go into a sleep-like trance during which time he displayed a paranormal ability to diagnose and prescribe cures for illness, and give all kinds of psychic readings and predictions. During his decades long career as a professional spiritual advisor, he gave thousands of readings, many of which were recorded. Even today, a museum is devoted solely to his material.

However, way back in 1931 and again in 1936, Cayce stated during a reading that the land of California would become "flooded and inundated." During this reading, he also explained that many other areas around the world would experience massive earth changes, which would begin around the turn of the century. None of these predictions have yet occurred.

Another possible influence on this peculiar myth is the novel, *The Last Days of the Late Great State of California* by Curt Gentry. Written in 1967, this novel tells the story of a massive earthquake which rips California apart from the United States and sends it plunging into the ocean. While this is a fictional story, the details are strikingly familiar to other accounts.

Visions and That Sinking Feeling

In 1974, San Jose resident Clarisa Bernhardt began having "visions" of upcoming earthquakes. The first was a prediction of a 5.2 earthquake that would hit the city of Hollister at 3:00 p.m. on Thanksgiving Day. Incredibly, Bernhardt was only one minute off. After a series of accurate predictions, her fame grew quickly. She was soon able to get her own radio show as a live psychic. On her show, "Exploration," she stated that in 1976, she was taken onboard a UFO craft. She said that the ETs told her that they were interested in her ability to predict earthquakes, and recommended that she warn the scientists of the two biggest earthquakes for that year.

Bernhardt took the advice seriously and contacted Dr John Derr, geophysicists and coordinator of the U.S. National Earthquake Information Service in Denver, and seismologist Dr. David Stewart, director of the MacCarthy Geophysics Laboratory at the University of North Carolina. She told them her prediction that there would be a 7.0-sized earthquake on June 26, 1976, somewhere in the western Pacific.

To the amazement of the scientists, the earthquake occurred exactly as predicted. Says Dr. Derr, "Mrs. Bernhardt's accuracy was remarkable. It was far beyond the possibility of chance...the vast majority of psychics are whistling in the dark, but Clarisa has had some damn close hits that are hard to ignore."

Dr. David Stewart was equally persuaded. As he says, "I'm convinced psychics can predict earthquakes. Clarisa Bernhardt has proved that. Current technology could not have achieved anywhere near the accuracy she accomplished."

Clarisa Explains It All

Bernhardt has made numerous other public predictions that have come true including the assassination attempt on President Ford, the apprehension of Patty Hearst, and danger for King Faisal of Saudia Arabia. By this time, she was regularly consulted by both local and federal law enforcement agencies.

Clarisa has also foreseen that much of California will eventually fall into the sea. According to her visions, she saw that the changes would occur very gradually, starting in 1978. Says Clarisa, "Yes, the poles will shift, but very gradually, no sudden slips. And the new polar alignment will be more harmonious for the Earth...I do not see a great loss of life however. The tremors and the shifts and changes will be gradual enough to permit evacuation of the areas affected."

Bernhardt says that after these earthquakes, all of southern California and most of northern California will be completely submerged. San Francisco Bay will be a large inland sea. All that will remain of the rest of California is a chain of large islands, including areas in San Diego, Los Angeles, Santa Barbara, and other mountainous locations. Says Clarisa, "The Imperial Valley will go back into the sea. A new bay will open up, and there will be a waterway clear up to Arizona. And Phoenix will be known as the Port City of the West. A beautiful Riviera, a marvelous marina will stretch across the southwestern United States." (Steiger, 184-196)

Bernhardt predicted that these events would begin in 1978 and span about ten years. Fortunately for Californians, Bernhardt was wrong on this one. Or maybe the events just haven't happened yet.

More Psychics Predict Watery Future

By this time, numerous psychics were predicting California's eventual watery demise. Probably the most famous among these is Gordon Michael Scallion. In 1979, Scallion stunned the new-age community with his claims of angelic visitations and monumental visions of the future of a very different United States. While in a trance state, he observed a huge disaster occurring that caused the earth to tilt on its axis. As a result, the coastlines of the United States and the world were completely changed. In his many visions, he observed that the west coast of the United States would be completely inundated by the ocean, with California being reduced to a few large islands. He had numerous visions during which he viewed most of the globe. He has written about his prophecies and published future maps of the United States in at least two books and numerous private letters. As of yet, his predictions have also thankfully failed to come true.

More prophecies about California come from the highly respected Chippewa medicine man, Sun Bear, whose 1990 book *Black Dawn, Bright Day* details his many visions of upcoming massive earth changes across the world. Writes Sun Bear of California's fate, "There will be a major earthquake that will affect the coast of California from San Francisco south. I expect major destruction along the coast, and for a distance inland in the southern part of the state. The Sierra Nevada Mountain areas, north of Bishop and north of Sacramento will be good places to be in this state. Stay away from all the large cities."

Sun Bear has had other visions pertaining to California, some of which have already come true. Writes Sun Bear, "A few years back I had dreams – two in a row – about California. I dreamt that I was in southern California and there was snow on the ground." The next day, Sun Bear was not surprised when he encountered snowfall in Palm Springs. His second vision, however, was more foreboding. "I also saw another thing that hasn't happened yet, but spirit tells me it's going to come. I saw 150-foot waves hitting the California coast; they went way up the sides of the cliffs there."

In more general terms, Sun Bear writes, "What I do see overall is a lot of coastal flooding caused by the greenhouse effect, severe hurricanes, and other storms that will affect many of the world's coasts, as well as inland areas; and increasing climactic changes. I do see some coastal areas being hit by large tidal waves that will completely submerge them." (Sun Bear, 97, 189, 202)

While none of the above prophecies have come true, even today similar predictions are being publicized. California Psychic Jorge Villasana has written about his fu-ture California visions in his on-line e-book, *My Weird Feelings*. Writes Villasana, "One vision that I know will happen is when a big chunk of the California coastline drops into the sea." Villasana is not sure exactly when this event will occur, but he predicts it will be no later than 2030.

Another California psychic, Joseph David, is equally dismal in his prospects for the Golden State. Writes David, "When I was in San Luis Obispo one day, I had a deep impression that the ocean could so easily spill over from Morro Bay on the coast of the Pacific, about fifteen to seventeen miles down the valley from San Luis Obispo – and that the ocean could cover San Luis Obispo." (David, Joseph, calif psychic)

Apparently, these predictions are very popular. During my own visit to a channeler in 1995, I was told that at some undetermined point in the future, there would be a very long-lasting earthquake in Los Angeles. Although it would register only five or six points on the Richter scale, it would last for many minutes and cause huge inland floods up and down the coast.

Obviously, all these predictions have failed to materialize, at least so far, and California thankfully remains above sea level. California is still waiting for the "Big One" that will transform the state into the newly formed *Islands of California*.

> **California Psychic Jorge Villasana has written about his future California visions in his on-line e-book, *My Weird Feelings*. Writes Villasana, "One vision that I know will happen is when a big chunk of the California coastline drops into the sea." Villasana is not sure exactly when this event will occur, but he predicts it will be no later than 2030.**

Part Five
Ghosts and Hauntings

California's Ghostly Crowds

If there is one thing California is well known for, it is ghosts. There has been an incredible amount of extensive research done on haunted places in California. My own book, *California Ghosts* (Schiffer, 2004), presents twenty-six previously unknown Golden State hauntings. Other researchers, like Antoinette May, Richard Senate, Hans Holzer, Dennis William Hauck, Barbara Smith, and Mike Marinacci, have also made significant and extensive explorations of the many haunted spots in California. Literally scores of books have been written about the crowds of California ghosts.

With several ghost books to his name, Richard Senate is probably the leading authority on California ghosts. Writes Senate, "California is a haunted land. Here the ghosts of Native Peoples mingle with the restless shades of robed padres and booted miners…All such things are part of the story that is California, from the Spanish conquest to the gang-ridden headlines that dominate today's newspapers." (Senate, i)

Prominent researcher Antoinette May writes, "In the past eighteen years of investigating alleged hauntings, I've discovered that psychically speaking California is loaded and apparently always has been…That California with its riotous history and unresolved conflicts would inspire a legion of restless spirits is not surprising." (May, 11)

Public Access

For this book, we shall focus *only* on locations that are available to the public. Only cases with sufficient information establishing the credibility of the haunting as well as the location of the haunting are included. For those who can't get enough of ghosts, they are strongly encouraged to seek out the books and research of the above prominent California ghost hunters.

While many of the hauntings we shall explore are famous, some public hauntings are revealed here for the first time. No private haunted houses here. Private business offices have also been excluded. All of the following locations are places that you can visit and maybe see the ghosts for yourself.

Because there are literally *hundreds* of public hauntings in California, I have organized them into separate groups, including hotels, cemeteries, missions, businesses, theaters, roadways, museums, ghost towns, parks, and general haunted spots.

Why Ghosts Haunt

Ghosts are ghosts for a reason. In many cases, they are suicides or the victims of murder or violent death. It seems that these people do not realize they have died. Some appear to be searching for their killers or reliving the tragedy that placed them in their state of purgatory.

Another common reason someone may become a ghosts is because of an earthly attachment to a former residence. It seems that some people just love their homes so much that they cannot bear to leave them. Or they are simply attached to earthly life itself. Ghostly activity can actually be ignited when new living people move into a departed resident's home and start moving furniture or remodeling.

Personal Experience

I have visited several of the following locations and have personally sensed some of the lost spirits who remain sadly tied to their locations. It is incredibly thrilling to wander through ancient courtyards, rooms, and hallways knowing that ghosts are all around you. More than once I could feel the hair on my arms stand-up and sense the ghostly stare of somebody I couldn't see. I have also interviewed many firsthand witnesses to supernatural activity at these locations. There is plenty of evidence that ghosts are alive and well in California. Below are more than 140 haunted places that you can visit and perhaps meet a ghost.

In this first section, we shall focus on a very popular type of public haunting location: haunted hotels.

1. Haunted Hotels

Hotels are particularly attractive to ghosts for many reasons. Probably the main reason is their age. Many of the haunted hotels in California are upwards of a century old, giving ghosts plenty of time to be created. Another apparent reason is that hotels have been used by many people for many purposes for many decades. The majority of them have functioned at one time or another as a private home, a ranch, a bar, a dance-hall, a restaurant, a church, a school, a hospital, a brothel, or some other type of business. With so many people conducting so many types of activities, it is only a matter of time before these structures become haunted.

What follows are twenty-four of the most famous haunted hotels in California. In most cases, I was able to obtain firsthand confirmation from the hotel officials that these locations are, in fact, truly haunted.

American River Inn

This hotel was actually the location of an old mine, which collapsed and killed an undetermined number of miners. It wasn't until the hotel was later built, however, that the ghosts came to haunt. One of the ghosts is known as Oscar, who was murdered on the hotel doorsteps after an argument about a prostitute. A few days later, the prostitute herself committed suicide by leaping from the hotel balcony.

Today, Oscar's former residence, room 5, is still haunted by his spirit. In 1986, more than a dozen guests witnessed his full-color apparition stride across the room and out the closed door. When I called the hotel, the lady at the desk denied having ever seen the ghost (nor did she want to!), but she did confirm the above accounts and said that several researchers have investigated the area and reported activity.

See for Yourself

Location: Highway 193, Georgetown, CA 95634. Phone: 530-333-4499.

Bella Maggiore Inn

Many hotels are haunted because of the tragic fate of the people who stayed there. Sylvia Michaels was a prostitute who in 1947 – no longer able to withstand her suffering – committed suicide by hanging herself in the hotel closet. Since then, sporadic poltergeist-like activity has been reported. Famed ghost hunter Richard Senate investigated the case, and in 1994 held a séance to try and free the ghost. Unfortunately, the séance was not successful and the activity continues. According to the front desk clerk, several recent guests reported smelling a rose-scented perfume, and others have felt a strange presence.

See for Yourself

Location: 67 South California Street, Ventura CA 93001. Phone: 805-652-0277.

Brookdale Lodge

In northern California, among the Santa Cruz mountains, is the famously haunted Brookdale Lodge, rebuilt in 1923 over an old hotel built in 1880. A former favorite hideaway for entertaining celebrities, politicians, and mobsters, the hotel is now most famous for its ghosts.

The ghostly activity first attracted attention in 1990. At that time, the hotel was closed down. It was then purchased by new owners, Bill and LeeAnn Gilbert. They remodeled the hotel and opened it for business. A short time later, the ghosts appeared *en masse*.

One ghost is a little girl in a formal dress. Many others have heard ghostly voices coming from various empty rooms. Phantom footsteps are often heard accompanied by bizarre cold spots.

More than two dozen hotels across California proudly claim to be haunted. Among the most haunted of these is the Brookdale Lodge. A wide variety of ghostly phenomena continue to occur here.

There are also slamming doors and then there's the jukebox that comes on by itself. Hotel rooms 26, 31, 32, 33, and 46 are all reportedly haunted by various ghosts. Writes one visitor, "After one night's stay in room 26 of the lodge's motel wing, I can definitely assure you I am a firm believer in ghosts…Drawers were opening and closing by themselves, a faucet in the bathroom turned on by itself, and after my shower, a ghost wrote her name, 'Kristie,' on the foggy bathroom mirror. I could tell it was a child's handwriting, and she had drawn little stars around her name. I slept with all the lights on." (www.brookdalelodge.com)

Other ghosts include an unidentified woman, a lumberjack, and more than forty other separate disembodied entities! I called the front desk and the attendant confirmed the accounts. Although she is a new employee and hasn't yet had any encounters, she has heard of several recent cases. One guest was lying in bed watching television when suddenly an invisible person lay down next to him, causing the bed to wiggle. Another couple was staying in room 46 when they saw a misty apparition hovering at the corner of the bed. They quickly snapped a photograph. A third incident occurred when a kitchen worker was giving a guest a tour of the kitchen. Suddenly, one of the doors flung open and slammed shut.

Del Coronado Hotel

Known simply as "the Del" to locals, this massive hotel (built in 1888) has its own special ghost. The history of the haunting has been traced to the murder of a woman named Kate Morgan on Thanksgiving Day in 1892. Kate was a con artist who worked with her husband to swindle people using card games. When her husband failed to show up for a job, things went from bad to worse. Kate was staying at the Del in room 3312. Nobody knows exactly what happened. What is not disputed is that Kate was found dead in her hotel room, the victim of a gunshot wound to the head.

While her death was ruled a suicide, some researchers feel that she was murdered by her husband. In either case, since that day, numerous guests have seen her ghost in Room 3312. One researcher learned that the light bulb above the steps where Kate was killed constantly burns out. Other reputedly haunted rooms are 3505 and 3502.

I was able to talk with a firsthand witness who stayed at the hotel in June of 2005. She and her husband woke up at around 2:00 a.m. to the sound of young children running down the hotel corridor and laughing. They both wondered who would allow such young children to be up that late at night. The next day, they discovered that other people also heard the children. They asked about it and learned that the children were actually ghosts. One of the hotel employees told them that numerous visitors have experienced the same phenomenon.

I was able to visit the hotel myself and wander through its long corridors. As with all old haunted buildings, it was like stepping back in time. After spending some time in there and soaking up the energy, you can definitely see why many people believe it's haunted.

Dorrington Hotel

Built in the 1860s, this northern California hotel is haunted by the wife of the original owner. In 1870, Rebecca Dorrington died tragically. Her ghost has since been seen wandering the hallways. Employees and guests have also heard her sorrowful cries echoing through the building.

See for Yourself

Location: Dorrington Hotel and Restaurant. 3431 Highway 4, Campconnell/ Dorrington, CA 95223. Phone: 209-795-5800.

Website: www.dorringtonhotel.com.

Faculty Club Hotel

Professor Henry Stephens lived in Room 219 of the Faculty Club Hotel for no less than twenty years. After he died in 1919, people began to see his ghost. Witnesses reported seeing his apparition sitting down at his desk. Others have heard him reciting poetry. In 1974, visitor Noriyuko Tokuda saw several apparitions in the room.

See for Yourself

The hotel is actually located on the campus of University of California in Berkley, which incidentally has more than one ghost. (*See below:* haunted schools.) Phone: 510-540-5678.

Durgan Flat Inn

This small hotel is allegedly haunted by the wife of the owner. After falling or being pushed to her death more than a century ago, Gertrude Peckwith still haunts the area. She has been seen by guests and workers in the basement laundry room and most often in the bedroom where she used to reside. I spoke with the new owner and he confirmed the story and the identity of the ghost, but reports that he is skeptical, and has not yet experienced any encounters with the ghost.

See for Yourself

Location: 121 River Street, Downieville, CA 95936. Phone: 530-289-3308.

Georgetown Hotel

This hotel was built in 1897. While the identity of the ghost who haunts this hotel is not known, guests and employees certainly know what he looks like. His tall, dark-haired figure with a pipe in his mouth has been seen by many witnesses, who often mistake him for a member of the staff. His favorite haunts are the kitchen and room 13. At least two other ghosts have also been reported on the premises.

When I called up the hotel, I spoke with an employee of the establishment who confirmed the above accounts and revealed that she has had several encounters herself. On the first occasion, she smelled the strong odor of cigar smoke when nobody in the hotel was smoking. She attributed it to the male ghost. On another occasion, she heard a small child laughing and running down the hallway, bouncing a ball. Again, there was nobody there, at least not that she could see! She reports that several other visitors have also had the same experience. Probably her most dramatic encounter involved the ghost of a prostitute who was killed back in the mid-1800s. While at work, she observed the silhouette of the ghost gliding silently up the staircase. She reports that the haunting is still very active, with most reports occurring during the winter months. Today many other visitors and employees continue to encounter the various ghosts.

keeper both observed a "lady in white" appear and disappear before their eyes. On another occasion, the same apparition walked out of a wall, across the room, and disappeared into the opposite wall. Other people have seen the ghost of a small boy. One employee told me that he had only been working there less than a year and has already felt a strange presence and felt like he has been followed. He hasn't seen the ghost yet, and says that if he does, he will probably stop working there. However, he does admit that the haunting is still active and that numerous people have visited the hotel just to see the ghost.

See for Yourself

Location: 18767 Main Street, Groveland.
Phone: 209-962-4000 or 1-800-273-3314.

See for Yourself

Location: 6260 Main Street, Georgetown, CA 95643. Phone: 530-333-2848.

See for Yourself

Location: 134 North Mill Street, Santa Paula, CA. Phone: 805-933-5550. Website: www.glentavern.com.

Holbrooke Hotel

This 150-year-old hotel located in Grass Valley has two known ghosts. The first is a blond woman who appears in the upstairs corridor. The second is a cowboy whose apparition appears in the basement dining room. Hotel officials confirmed the haunting to me and said that many guests have reported a wide variety of phenomena, including apparitions, electromagnetic effects, and odd noises. The haunting is currently still active.

Glen Tavern Inn

Built in 1911, this hotel reportedly has at least one room that is haunted. Room 307 (a.k.a. the Rin-Tin-Tin Room) is haunted by the ghost of an unknown actor of old western movies. The haunting allegedly began when the actor was caught cheating at a poker game. Things went from bad to worse and he was shot and killed. Ever since then, the room has been haunted. According to the former owners, several visitors have reported supernatural activity in the room, and one visitor managed to take a photograph of an apparition. In 2005, a professional group of ghost hunters visited the area and obtained unusual photographs of glowing orbs.

The hotel is now under new management and is being refurbished. However, according to employees, the ghost is still active. The former manager and house-

Groveland Hotel

This quaint bed and breakfast inn is haunted – say the owners – by the ghost of a miner named Lyle. Although he died back in the 1920s, Lyle still makes his presence known by opening and closing doors, turning lights on and off, turning showers on, and even making unlocked doors impossible to open. His favorite room is reportedly room 15. I called up the hotel and spoke with staff members who were well aware of the haunting. One employee reported that Lyle has often made his presence known to the various women visitors in the room. On one occasion, a guest reported that her cosmetics and make-up were thrown off the bathroom sink by the ghost. Another guest observed a chair move by itself. And yet another reported that her alarm clock was turned off. Some of these incidents were recent, so the ghost is definitely still active.

See for Yourself

Location: 212 West Main Street, Grass Valley, CA 95945. Phone: 530-273-1353.

Horton Grand Hotel

While this hotel was originally built in 1886, one hundred years later in 1986 it was torn down and moved brick by brick to a new location. The entire hotel was rebuilt as an exact replica of the original. Apparently, the replica was so good that the ghosts that haunted the hotel for years moved along to the new location.

The story actually reaches back to 1843, when Roger Whittacker was shot to death by his fiancée's father, who apparently objected to the union of his daughter to a professional gambler. It was then that Whittacker's ghost began to appear. Room 309 seems to be the ghost's favorite hangout.

Surprisingly, moving the hotel only seemed to make the haunting stronger. In 1987, hotel maid Martha Mays was cleaning Room 309 when she felt the bed start to shake. As she continued, the lights turned on and off and the armoire door opened and closed. Says Mays, "There are lots of things that happen in there. A lot of times when I'm in there, I get the feeling someone else is in there with me, looking over my shoulder." Most of the other maids refused to clean the room.

Then hotel guests began to complain. Says concierge Nancy Titus, "We've had guests checking out at 2:00 a.m., saying they won't stay in that room…other times, it's been cold outside, but really hot in that room. We turn on the air-conditioning, but half an hour later, it's still just as hot in there…so many people have had things happen in there, you really have to wonder."

Hotel officials finally had enough and decided to call in two professional ghost hunters/psychics, Shelly Deegan and Jacqueline Williams, to investigate. The psychics claimed to have made contact with the ghost of Roger Whittacker, who was not happy about people being in his room. The two investigators recorded unusual activity, including a picture that moved by itself and a light turning off and on. Says Deegan, "It was incredible. We weren't sure what he was going to do next."

Deegan reports that she was able to sense numerous other ghosts. As she says, "There are ghosts all over the place here…this is a good place for them. We're planning on coming back to find out more."

More than a dozen employees and guests have seen Whittacker's solid-looking apparition. However, there are also many other ghosts. According to history, Michael McKeever, the previous hotel owner, revealed that the hotel was haunted by several ghosts. Several people have seen apparitions of men, women, and children dressed in old-fashioned clothes walking up and down the old grand staircase. Another common complaint is voices coming from various empty rooms. As can be seen, this hotel is definitely haunted. In fact, hotel officials know all about the hauntings and keep a history of the activity, which they freely distribute to guests and visitors.

See for Yourself

After an article about the haunting appeared in the San Diego Tribune, Room 309 became the preferred room for many guests and was booked solid for three years! So be sure to make reservations early. Location: 311 Island Avenue, San Diego, CA 92101. Phone: 619-544-1886.

Jamestown National Hotel & Restaurant

Founded way back in 1859, this 150-year-old hotel is haunted by a friendly ghost nicknamed Flo. The actual identity of the ghost remains a mystery. There is no question, however, that Flo is an active ghost. Her apparition has been repeatedly seen in various hotel rooms as well as floating through walls, into the dining room, through the lobby, and across the front of the hotel. She has been blamed for turning lights on and off, slamming doors, and even disturbing the luggage of various hotel visitors. The concierge on duty verified the existence of the ghost and told me that many visitors have reported all kinds of encounters. The hotel actually displays a short history of the ghost for interested visitors.

See for Yourself

If you want to have your own encounter with Flo, the Jamestown National Hotel is located at: 18183 Main Street, Jamestown, CA. Phone: 209-984-3446.

Julian Hotel

The town of Julian was founded in the mid-1800s during the California gold rush. In 1897, freed slaves Albert and Margaret Robinson purchased a tavern/bakery and transformed it into "the Hotel Robinson." Unfortunately, prejudice against black people was still strong. When Albert Robinson died, he was initially supposed to be buried in the cemetery along with all the other white people. However, some of the townspeople protested and Albert's body was buried in the local black cemetery.

This act is what apparently caused the haunting. Ever since then, people have reported haunting activity. In 1921, the hotel was sold and renamed the Julian Hotel. This, however, had no effect on the haunting, which continued strong. A wide range of supernatural activity has been reported. Maids complain of neat beds being mysteriously messed up. Phantom pipe smoke is often detected. Most of the activity occurs in Room 10, Albert's old room. People have reported seeing his apparition there. Other manifestations include cold spots, footsteps, slamming doors, opening and closing windows, and moving objects, including furniture. I spoke with an employee who has worked there for twelve years. She says that she doesn't really believe in ghosts and hasn't experienced anything herself. But she did admit that throughout the years, several guests have reported "strange activity," particularly in Room 10.

See for Yourself

Location: 2032 Main Street, Julian, CA. Phone: 760-765-0201 or 1-800-734-5854.

Leger Hotel

Room 7 of this very old hotel is haunted by the former owner, George Leger, whose portrait still hangs on the dining room wall. The employees of the hotel attest to hearing sounds of activity coming from the empty room. Some guests have also seen his apparition floating in the hallways. The ghost has been encountered so many times that the staff has become used to his sudden appearances and disappearances. According to the hotel staff, numerous manifestations occur each year. A constant stream of professional ghost hunters and enthusiasts visit the hotel seeking an encounter.

See for Yourself

Location: 8304 Main Street, Mokelumne Hill, CA 95245. Phone: 209-286-1401.

Mansions Hotel

Unlike some hotels, this one actually advertises its haunted history in a public gallery. Throughout the years, haunted activity has occurred on a regular basis, including unexplained noises, shadowy apparitions, cold spots, moving objects, and more. Numerous séances have been held. During one such séance, a ghost actually materialized and was photographed. The photo is currently in the gallery.

Psychic medium Sylvia Brown has confirmed the presence of several spirits. Owner Bob Pritikin admits candidly that there are "…ghosts in the hotel. We get all kinds of weird things happening here."

See for Yourself

Location: 2220 Sacramento Street, San Francisco CA 94115.

Mendocino Hotel

This hotel was built in 1878, and has been haunted for many years by a variety of male and female ghosts. Guests at the restaurant have reported ghostly apparitions in the mirrors on the walls. Rooms 10 and 307 are also apparently haunted by other unidentified ghosts who leave impressions of their bodies lying on the hotel beds.

See for Yourself

Location: 45080 Main Street, Mendocino, CA 95460. Phone: 707-937-0511.

Murphys Hotel

Built in 1856, this is one of the oldest hotels – not only in California, but in the entire United States. It boasts several famous guests, including Mark Twain, J.P. Morgan, Ulysses S. Grant, Daniel Webster, and others. Not surprisingly, it is haunted by at least one ghost, which has been most often seen roaming the second floor hallways. The hotel has been declared a historic landmark.

See for Yourself

Location: 459 Main Street, Murphys, CA 95247. Phone: 209-728-3444.

Roosevelt Hotel

The Roosevelt Hotel in Hollywood is listed in many books as being haunted by several ghosts, one of whom is Marilyn Monroe. A mirror in the lobby formally used by the actress when she stayed in Room 1200 has been said to still reflect her image. In room 928, the ghost of actor Montgomery Cliff has made his presence known with phantom footsteps, sounds of bugle-playing, weird cold-spots, and invisible hands tugging at random guests.

Says cocktail waitress Teryl Valazza, "I was getting off the ninth floor elevator, and I was walking down the hall, and I heard footsteps behind me. I turned around to see if there was anybody following me, and there was nobody there. And as I was continuing to walk, I felt a cold breeze walk right by me. And I went down in the elevator and never went back up."

See for Yourself

Location: 7000 Hollywood Boulevard, Los Angeles, CA. Phone: 323-466-7000. or 323-469-4169.

Santa Maria Inn

The ghost of Rudolph Valentino has been reported in this 1917 hotel, especially in Room 210, where he used to stay. According to the staff, several guests who stayed in that room have felt a strange presence and heard unexplained knocking noises. But that is only the beginning of the strangeness at this hotel. Two ghosts who have made their presences known are the "Sea Captain" and his mistress. According to the hotel's own official history, room 221 is haunted by the mistress's spirit: "We have had several testimonies from guests who claim they would wake up in the middle of the night and see her eerie figure floating at the foot of their bed." One housekeeper was cleaning the room when she felt somebody touch her shoulder. At the same time, a cold chill filled the room. She immediately fled the premises.

The Patio Suites Room is also haunted. One guest was in bed when a light bulb flew out of the socket and hit the pillow. Other guests have reported full color apparitions. As the hotel history reads: "Even more weird is the guest who thought she was dreaming, and awoke to laughter and watched silhouettes of several people who were seemingly at a party in her room! The host of the gala affair was next to her bed staring down at her and was costumed in mid-1800's style clothing." As she watched, the images disappeared into thin air.

There are many other ghostly encounters that have occurred here. As the hotel history reads, "Housekeepers on their regular inspections of the second floor rooms in the original section have opened locked doors to find furniture mysteriously stacked in a corner…. One housekeeper had a balloon follow her while she cleaned the second floor. When she went down the staircase to clean the rooms on the first floor, the balloon followed her downstairs. Our Executive Housekeeper personally witnessed this incident."

The staff of the hotel graciously supplied me with the above stories, and assured me of their authenticity.

See for Yourself

Location: 801 South Broadway, Santa Maria, CA 93454. Phone: 800-462-4276.

Sutter Creek Inn

Built in the late 1800s, this mansion was later converted into a hotel. In 1966, Jane Way purchased the property. She learned it was haunted a few weeks later when she was confronted by the apparition of a man. Delving into the structure's history, she was able to identify the ghost as former state Senator Edward Voorhies, who lived there in the 1880s. Since then, Way and others have encountered several other spirits. On one occasion, the apparition of a young man appeared in front of a group of old ladies and promptly dropped his pants!

See for Yourself

Location: 75 Main Street, Sutter Creek, CA 95685.

Wynham Hotel

Room 538 in this hotel is reportedly haunted by the ghost of a suicide victim. Ever since a depressed salesman killed himself in the room, other occupants have seen his apparition dressed in a dark suit.

See for Yourself

Location: 1350 North First Street, San Jose, CA 95112.

Zaballa House

While the owner of Zaballa House bed & breakfast hotel is skeptical that his hotel is haunted, researcher Dennis William Hauck reports that visitors to Room 6 have experienced a wide variety of poltergeist-like activity, including rattling windows, electromagnetic disturbances, and difficulty with the doors. When I spoke with the desk clerk, he too was skeptical, but admitted that guests have written various accounts of their weird experiences in the hotel journal registry.

See for Yourself

Location: 324 Main Street, Half Moon Bay, CA 94019. Phone: 650-726-9123.

2. Haunted Parks

Haunted parks are particularly interesting because they are so easily accessible to the public. And unlike hotels, the fees are nominal or nonexistent. In each case, it again appears that the ghosts are the result of some type of tragic death. What follows are fourteen California parks that various ghost researchers have confirmed to be haunted.

Alvarado Park

A well-known local haunting, this case involves a ghost known as the White Witch. She is an old woman who reportedly has a vendetta against young blond men. According to local legend, the haunting began more than a century ago. At the time, the woman dabbled in black magic. She also had a young daughter of dating age who longed for male companionship. One evening the daughter brought home a young, blond sailor. That evening, a fire broke out in the house and the only survivor was the young, blond sailor. Ever since then, people have seen the ghost of the old woman, looking for the blond sailor who left her and her daughter to die. She appears in flowing white garments and floats a few feet above the ground.

White Witch Paces Horses

Today the ghost is known as the White Witch. Many people claim to have seen her. One case involves two ladies who were riding horseback when they heard a noise behind them. They turned around and saw the tall, glowing form of the ghost behind them. They took off galloping but the ghost was easily able to keep up with them.

Really Trippy

In 1990, five young men, all members of a heavy metal band, went to the area hoping to have an encounter and were incredibly successful. They drove up to the area late at night and waited for the ghost to appear. To their surprise, the ghost *did* appear. Says one of the witnesses, Tom X., "She was white and she was pretty tall. She was almost six feet, and she kind of hovered above the ground. There were no feet, just her and her dress following behind her. Really trippy. I was kind of worried about getting out of there…You could kind of see through her, especially the end of her dress. She put off a pretty bright glow."

Says John X, another member of the band, "All I really saw was a big, white flash because I turned, looked, and ran…she was just a white woman with a long white dress. I didn't really look at her very well." (Dennett 2004, 65-69)

The five boys returned later that evening and actually had a repeat encounter with the ghost.

See for Yourself

For those who would like to see this ghost, she haunts the areas in and around Alvarado Park, located in El Sobrante, California.

Camp Comfort County Park

This park south of Ojai is allegedly haunted by no less than five ghosts, including the hostile ghost of a Spanish man who became a vampire and was buried in a sarcophagus in the park, an apparition of a black dog that guards the sarcophagus, a ghostly horsewoman, a headless motorcyclist, and a phantom hitchhiker – a woman in a wedding dress.

> "She was white and she was pretty tall. She was almost six feet, and she kind of hovered above the ground. There were no feet, just her and her dress following behind her. Really trippy."

See for Yourself

Location: 11969 Creek Road, Ojai, California.

Channel Islands National Park

This small cluster of islands off the coast above Santa Barbara attracts thousands of tourists every year. The islands are breathtakingly beautiful with more than 150 species of plants and animals that are found nowhere else in the world. A few of the islands are also inhabited by ghosts.

Famous Ghost

San Miguel Island is home to the ghost of Spanish Explorer Juan Rodriguez Cabrillo, credited with the actual discovery of California. Cabrillo had injured himself while exploring San Miguel Island and his wound became gangrenous, causing his death. His ghost, and at least one other ghost have been seen wandering over the small island.

Chinese Fisherman

Santa Cruz Island is the largest of the group of islands. The northeast shore is haunted by the ghost of a Chinese fisherman. As the story goes, in the late 1800s, the fisherman was hunting for mollusks when his hand became pinned between two boulders. Unable to free himself, he grabbed his knife and sawed off his hand. He scrambled to the beach, where he lay down and bled to death. Ever since then, his ghost has been seen along the beach, searching mournfully for his hand.

Murderer's Wife

Another area on the island – Christy Ranch – is reportedly haunted by the ghost of Mary Morrison Reese, the wife of the infamous Daniel Reese who was responsible for the murder of hundreds of Chinese immigrants.

Suicidal Wife

Santa Rosa Island also has its own ghost – the wife of a sheepherder who committed suicide. Today her glowing apparition has been seen floating above the ground, moving among the various remote valleys of the island.

See for Yourself

Location: Channel Islands National Park, Santa Barbara, California. Phone: 805-658-5700.

Clear Lake Wildlife Refuge

Numerous California parks are haunted, including Clear Lake Wildlife Refuge. This refuge is haunted by a glowing "lady in white."

tlers. One young daughter escaped the massacre. Tragically, the next day she returned to bury her parents and was found by the natives, who kidnapped and killed her. Since then, her glowing white apparition has appeared on numerous occasions. Some witnesses also report hearing her wailing mournfully, especially in the late night hours.

See for Yourself

Location: Near the Oregon border, sixteen miles south of Newell on Highway 139 at the Clear Lake Road exit, off the north shore of the coast.

Off the coast of the city of Clear Lake lies a small island locally known as Bloody Island. The area received its name because it is the location of a tragic incident in 1850, when a group of Modoc Native Americans attacked a wagon train, killing nearly all the white set-

Elfin Forest Park

Nobody knows the identity of the ghost which haunts this small southern California park. Known only as the *White Lady*, her apparition is surprisingly solid. Many visitors have thought she was a living person when approached by her in broad daylight. Only as she moves closer do they realize that she is floating through the air.

Fernwood Campgrounds

Ghost researcher Dennis Hauck investigated this case, which involves the ghost of a Native American man. His apparition appears only between 2:00 and 3:00 am, in a particular location near the cabins. The area of the campground is known to have been sacred to the Esalen Indians, who used it for spiritual visions and various ceremonies.

Fort Tejon State Park

A sad chapter of American history occurred here when thousands of Native Americans were imprisoned at Fort Tejon from 1854 to 1864. However, the main haunting activity comes from an earlier tragedy.

Bear Confusion

On October 17, 1837, French trapper Peter Le Beck was killed by either a bear or a Native American named Chief Black Bear. Le Beck was buried and an oak tree was planted over his grave. Today, the old oak tree is called Le Beck Tree. It still holds Le Beck's gravestone, and apparently his ghost, which has often been seen lingering around the tree.

Bear Hung!

Chief Black Bear was hanged from another nearby oak tree, and his ghost too has been seen in the area.

Gaviota State Park

The history of this particularly spot of land has left it badly haunted. Back in the early 1800s, it was the location of a bloody battle between the Native Americans and the Spanish. It then became a Native American burial ground. Wooden crosses were erected to mark the graves and the graveyard was blessed as sacred land by local priests. Later, the crosses were removed and a stagecoach stop was built directly over the graveyard. This structure was later rebuilt into Las Crucas Adobe, which was used as a hotel, gambling hall, and brothel.

The haunting actually began after two prostitutes were murdered and a third committed suicide by hanging herself in her room in the hotel. Since then, the three women have haunted what are now the abandoned ruins of the structure.

Gold Discovery State Park

The California gold rush of 1847 had a huge effect on the state. At the time, the population of the state was only 15,000. A little more than ten years later, after the gold rush was over, the population was 380,000!

The Famous Dead

The gold rush actually began when James Marshall found two gold nuggets at the logging mill he operated with his partner, John Sutter, in what is now the city of Coloma.

Marshall became instantly famous. His discovery electrified the world and hundreds of thousands of people converged on the scene. Marshall was followed wherever he went, hoping that he would reveal his secret for finding gold. Marshall died on August 10, 1885, totally destitute. Later *Marshall Monument* was erected in his honor. Since then, tourists at the location of the monument have seen his ghost.

Phantom Bells

A few other locations in the park are also haunted. The remains of Bell's General Store – an old brick building once frequented by the hoards of gold miners – lies north of town. Reportedly witnesses still hear the phantom doorbell ringing.

Disembodied Voices

Also, in the Wah Lee Store, now a museum, ghostly voices can be heard.

Grover Hot Springs State Park

This haunting dates back to the 1870s, when stagecoach drivers reported the apparition of a Union Civil War Soldier dressed in uniform, wandering the various backroads outside of Markleeville in northern California. The apparition has been seen numerous times since then. When confronted, the ghost simply fades away.

Robinson-Rose House

This 1853 building is now the visitor center for Old Town San Diego State Park. Numerous employees and visitors have seen ghosts in the structure. The apparitions have appeared as cloudy white forms and full-colored apparitions.

Shadow Ranch Park. This old ranch house in Canoga Park is allegedly haunted by the original owner, whose glowing apparition has been seen by numerous witnesses.

Shadow Ranch Park

Formerly a ranch estate, this area is now a small public park. In the center of the park stands a two-story brick and wood ranch house that is reportedly haunted by the original owner, Albert Workman. Numerous witnesses have observed his apparition floating through the structure. An employee of the park told me that there are other ghosts. Reportedly, back in the 1930s, five members of the Paul family all died within one week of each other. Ever since then, visitors and employees have seen their spirits. I was able to visit the building and walk through several of the rooms. While there were other people with me at the time, I still had the familiar feeling of an unseen presence staring from the dark corners. It was the same muffled, timeless feeling I have felt in several of the other haunted structures and places I visited.

This area is haunted by the local Chumash Native Americans who used to inhabit the area. In the Trippet ranch area up Entrada Road, several homes are built adjacent to and on an Indian burial ground. Several of them have reported haunting activity. One home had phantom footsteps that moved through the home. Another experienced both objects that would move by themselves in full view of the stunned witnesses and unexplained noises. Several hikers in the park have seen or sensed the ghosts of Indian spirits, who seem angry or sad that their sacred land is being misused. One lady was meditating in the park when she sensed the spirit of a small Native American girl in full native dress peering at her. According to the witness, the girl seemed sad and lost. Another witness was a jogger who sensed that he was being stalked by the angry spirits of several young braves.

Trippett Ranch in Topanga State Park. At least four homes adjacent to the park have reported ghostly activity. Several other reports come from visitors to the park. In each case, the encounters involve Native American ghosts who are apparently angry about the mistreatment of the land, including homes being built on sacred burial grounds.

Topanga State Park

Vallecito Station County Park

Built in 1858, this park was once a stagecoach station. It was abandoned in 1888, but restored in 1934 as a historic site. Since then, many visitors to the area have reported extensive haunting activity. At least five different ghosts have been seen, including cowboys, gunfighters, and "the White Lady of Vallecito," a young bride who died and was buried at the station.

The moving stones present another mystery. Numerous rocks appear to move by themselves, ending up in the strangest places, including on picnic tables and in high tree branches. Nobody has seen the rocks move, and nobody can explain it. The most popular theory is that spirits are moving the rocks.

3. Haunted Cemeteries

What more likely place for a ghost than a cemetery? In fact, I would be surprised if a cemetery wasn't haunted. Below are a dozen of the most well-known and actively haunted graveyards in California.

El Campo Santo Cemetery

This cemetery is more than 150 years old and badly haunted. A variety of ghosts and apparitions have appeared in the area, most often along an old brick wall that intersects the graveyard. Over the years, the outer edges of the graveyard have been built up with homes and businesses, several of which have reported poltergeist-like phenomena.

See for Yourself

Location: Center of Old Town San Diego at the 2400 block.

Forest Lawn Cemetery

This huge cemetery is haunted by an angry ghost that resides in one of the mausoleums. In the early 1970s, a skeptical trucker reported that he had been led by a friend to the area specifically to see the ghost. Not believing in ghosts, he panicked when the ghost actually appeared and chased him out of the cemetery. He was so traumatized by the experience that he vowed never to return.

See for Yourself

Location: Forest Lawn Drive, off 134 Freeway in Los Angeles.

Greenwood Cemetery

The earthbound spirit of a tall man has been seen wandering through this cemetery as if searching for someone. Unlike many ghosts, this spirit is apparently aware of visitors and has reportedly chased several people out of the graveyard, including a group of teenagers who were vandalizing the grave markers.

Also, a tree in front of the Old Mortuary Building was used repeatedly for hangings. It is now a haunted tree. Numerous witnesses have seen the ghostly form of a man hanging from a noose tied to one of the branches. Other ghostly forms have been seen, apparently family members of those who had been hanged.

See for Yourself

Location: In the town of Greenwood on Highway 193, ten miles west of Georgetown. The tree in front of the old Mortuary Building is located at 300 Main Street, Greenwood, CA 95635.

It should come as no surprise that many graveyards are haunted. The Greenwood Cemetery in Greenwood, California, became actively haunted after teenagers vandalized various headstones. This is just one of many cases that prove it's not a good idea to disturb the dead.

Hollywood Memorial Park

If you want to see the ghost of a famous celebrity, your best bet is probably in Hollywood Memorial Park, which holds the remains of dozens of well-known Hollywood stars. The ghost of actor Clifton Webb is said to haunt the Abbey of the Psalms mausoleum. This is also the location of other ghosts. The apparition of an unknown woman dressed in black has been repeatedly seen knelling in front of crypt number 1205.

See for Yourself

Location: 6000 Santa Monica Boulevard, Hollywood CA 90028.

Los Angeles Pet Cemetery

Los Angeles Pet Cemetery holds the remains of the pets of numerous famous stars. Kabar, the Great Dane of Rudolph Valentino, was buried here back in 1929. However, people have reportedly heard panting or felt phantom dog-licks near his gravesite. There are also several other famous animals buried here, including Hopalong Cassidy's horse and Mary Pickford's dog.

See for Yourself

Location: 5068 Old Scandia Lane, Calabasas, CA 91302.

Mission San Juan Capistrano Cemetery

A very old cemetery, dating back to 1778, is reputedly haunted by several ghosts, including the legendary Llorona. The origins of this famous Latino myth remain unknown. As the story goes, years ago a young mother betrayed her husband and drowned her two children. Ever since then, her evil spirit has been condemned to wander the earth, forever searching for her two children. Seeing the ghost is a sign of ill omen, and the story is still used by mothers to scare their young children and keep them indoors at night. The cemetery contains numerous Native Americans and original residents of San Juan Capistrano. The graveyard is locked up, but can still be viewed from the outside.

See for Yourself

Location: Ortega Highway, San Juan Capistrano. Directions: Take 5 Freeway to Ortega Highway. Turn left, go past gas station to the right. Cemetery is at the top of the hill.

Mission Santa Barbara Graveyard

Located behind the Mission Santa Barbara built in 1786, the graveyard contains the bodies of thousands of Indians and early pioneers. Today their ghosts continue to be seen in the walled-in cemetery.

See for Yourself

Location: 2201 Laguna Street, Santa Barbara CA 93101.

Old Yorba Linda Cemetery

This cemetery is allegedly haunted by Alvina De Los Reyes, a young high society woman killed in 1900 in a tragic carriage accident. Since then her ghost – nicknamed the Pink Lady – has been seen kneeling in the graveyard, weeping. Legend has it that she appears yearly on June 15.

See for Yourself

Location: In the town center of Yorba Linda.

Old City Cemetery

More than 40,000 people are currently buried in this 150-year-old graveyard. Not surprisingly, it is haunted by several ghosts. Among them are engineer William Brown, who died in 1880 in a tragic train wreck, and twelve-year-old May Woolsey, who died in 1879 of encephalitis.

See for Yourself

Location: 10th and Broadway, Sacramento.

Pioneer Cemetery

Located across the street from the haunted Vineyard House Hotel in Coloma, this graveyard is reportedly haunted by the ghost of a woman who was buried there in the late 1800s. She apparently watches over the Schieffer family plot, signaling passersby to visit the gravesite with her.

See for Yourself

Location: see Vineyard House Hotel (above).

Rose Hill Cemetery

One of the most well-known haunted cemeteries, more than a hundred formal and informal exorcisms have been held here to try and appease the restless spirits. The graveyard has been abandoned for years. Since its abandonment, it has been repeatedly vandalized, which might explain the unhappiness of its permanent occupants. In any case, the cemetery is known to produce a wide range of supernatural activity, including ghostly screams, shouts, cries, laughter, and the sound of ringing bells.

See for Yourself

Location: Black Diamond Preserve in Concord. Take Highway 4 east to Loveridge exit. Go east on Buchanan and south at Somersville.

Westwood Cemetery

Westwood Cemetery in Westwood is reportedly haunted by the spirit of Marilyn Monroe. Her apparition was seen and photographed near her tomb. The photograph has appeared in several books.

See for Yourself

Location: 1218 Glendon Avenue, Westwood, CA 90024.

4. Haunted Roadways

There are numerous accounts of haunted stretches of road. This is not very surprising when you consider that many modern streets are actually extremely old, built over long existing pathways and wagon-train roads. Furthermore, as many roadside crosses reveal, roadways have often been the scenes of traumatic deaths – a leading cause of ghostly activity.

Another unique facet about haunted highways is that they are very easy to locate. You don't even need to get out of your car.

There is something particularly sad about these hauntings. To die on the road, far away from home, is tragic. Many lonesome travelers have perished on the way to their destinations. A few of these unhappy travelers are still trying to make it home.

What follows are thirteen of the most famous haunted roadways in California.

California Street

This street located in the Nob Hill district of San Francisco has been haunted for many years by the ghost of a woman who appears from her dress to be from the Victorian era. Researchers believe that the ghost is Flora Sommerton, who ran away from her home in 1876 rather than imprison herself in an arranged marriage. While she died in Butte, Montana, her body was returned to her family plot, where she now appears as a ghost along California Street.

See for Yourself

Location: California Street, San Francisco, between Jones and Powell.

Creek Road Bridge

This small span of bridge in Ojai became haunted after an unidentified man died in a horrible car accident in the 1950s. He escaped from the wreckage of his automobile and ran away and burned to death. His body was never found. Since then, his ghost, called the "Charman," has been seen by numerous witnesses on the bridge. Reportedly, his apparition appears in full ghastly color, with his horrible wounds bleeding profusely. Witnesses even report smelling his burned flesh and clothes. The ghost is also hostile, and at least one person claims to have been attacked by the apparition.

See for Yourself

Location: Creek Road Bridge on Creek Road off Highway 33, south of Ojai.

Hollywood Boulevard

Formerly the location of Native American settlements, the intersection of Hollywood Boulevard and Sierra Bonita Boulevard in Hollywood is one very haunted spot. Numerous witnesses have observed ghostly Indians riding horses, running on foot, shooting arrows, and throwing tomahawks. Others have heard loud Indian drumming music. One motorist claims to have been driven off the road by a ghostly pioneer wagon that suddenly materialized in the intersection. Reportedly, the reason for so much activity is because it was at this location that hostile Native Americans would attack passing stagecoaches. Therefore, many people have died at this location.

Phantom Beats

I was actually able to interview a firsthand witness who lived near the location and was woken up on several occasions by the sound of phantom drums. Says the witness, "I moved into this new house and I kept waking up in the middle of the night because somebody was playing this loud music." She asked her neighbors and then learned that the location was haunted, and the music was actually coming from ghostly Native Americans. When asked to describe the music, she said it sounded like "nothing I've ever heard, like 'woo-woo-woo-woo.' At first I thought it was rap-ghetto music. There were drums." As can be seen, this particular stretch of road is still very actively haunted.

See for Yourself

Location: Hollywood Boulevard and Sierra Bonita in Hollywood, CA.

Jersey Bridge

Like most haunted places, this bridge has a gruesome history. On July 5, 1851, a twenty-four-year-old woman known as Juanita was hung from the bridge by a lynch mob after it was discovered she had murdered a popular man in the then small town of Downieville. However, the crime didn't stop there. Later, Juanita's corpse was unburied and her skull stolen for use in gruesome secret ceremonies and rituals. Apparently that was enough to bring Juanita's ghost back. Her apparition is still seen on the southeast corner of the bridge, beckoning sadly to passersby.

See for Yourself

Location: Jersey Bridge over Yuba River in Downieville, CA.

Laurel Canyon Boulevard

The intersection of Laurel Canyon and Lookout Mountain: a ghostly carriage pulled by speeding horses has been seen here on numerous occasions.

In West Hollywood there is a street called Laurel Canyon. Narrow and winding, it climbs over a mountain pass that separates the cities of West Hollywood and North Hollywood. One of the longest streets in LA County, Laurel Canyon is also reportedly haunted.

The location of the haunt is one particular intersection at Lookout Mountain. About a mile down the south side of the pass, there is an intersection that now contains a traffic light. There are numerous reports of witnesses who, driving through the intersection at precisely midnight, have observed an old carriage being pulled by white horses. In each case, the horses are galloping wildly, pulling the carriage roughly onto Laurel Canyon. Sec-

onds later, the carriage and horses promptly disappear. On a few occasions, witnesses have been so startled that they crashed their cars.

See for Yourself

Location: Intersection of Laurel Canyon Boulevard and Lookout Mountain in West Hollywood.

Los Rios Street

"The White Lady of Capistrano." This famous ghostly apparition appears regularly along the railroad tracks on Los Rios Street in the center of San Juan Capistrano's historic district.

San Juan Capistrano has a number of public hauntings. One of the most public is a stretch of road along Rios Street, along the railroad tracks in the center of the Historic District. According to local legend, the area is haunted by "the White Lady of Capistrano."

Other variations call the apparition "the Phantom of Del Obispo" and say that she was a witch or "bruja." The hostile ghost is reportedly seen walking along the railroad tracks, sometimes with a phantom black dog.

See for Yourself

Location: Historic district, Los Rios Street, San Juan Capistrano.

Ortega Road

A particularly poignant haunting has been occurring for more than a hundred years along a stretch of road in Montecito, near Santa Barbara. A century ago, three nuns were tortured and killed by local Indians. Ever since then, the "tres hermanas" (three sisters), dressed up in their habits, have been seen by numerous drivers standing by the side of the road with arms folded.

See for Yourself

Location: Ortega Road, Montecito. (Off Highway 192.)

Old Butterfield Road

Way back in 1860, a four-mule stagecoach traveled along Old Butterfield Road. Suddenly, the driver was shot and killed. The mules panicked and pulled the stagecoach off into the desert. Ever since then, numerous people have claimed to see this ghostly stagecoach. Others have not seen anything, but have *heard* the sound of the stagecoach and mules as they gallop by.

See for Yourself

Location: Highway S2, sixteen miles north of the city of Ocotillo, at Sweeney Pass.

Pacheco Pass

Says California psychic Sylvia Brown, "This pass is actually the most horrifying place." Right outside of Gilroy, Sylvia Brown psychically observed the many horrendous tragedies that have occurred along this mountain overpass. It turns out, however, that she was not the only one. She had gone to the area to investigate a few reports from other witnesses. After her own experience, she went to the media and was surprised to find that she was not alone. Says Sylvia, "The calls and letters poured in. We have a file like this," she raises her hands several inches high. People have seen Indians, Spanish, covered wagons, soldiers…It's almost a Bermuda Triangle on land."

The television program, "The Other Side," took video footage at the location. Incredibly, much of the camera equipment stopped working for no apparent reason. Says cameraman John Hessler, "As we went up into the pass, I noticed, slowly by slowly, things were developing. And at one point when we were in the heart of the pass, we had multiple malfunctions which I've never seen before…I was very concerned from a professional standpoint, but I was certainly relieved when I got down out of the pass." Hessler came away convinced that the pass is, in fact, haunted.

See for Yourself

Location: The five mile stretch of Highway 152 at Pacheco Pass just west of the Santa Clara County Line.

Portal Road

This location was the area of frequent battles between the Paiute tribes and the United States army during the 1860s. Numerous residents along Portal Road report that they still see ghostly Indians fighting with old-style rifles. The apparitions have lasted for fifteen minutes and are apparently still occurring. Portal Road appears to be, like other haunted locations, a portal to the other side.

See for Yourself

Location: Portal Road, three miles west of the city of Lone Pine, near Mount Whitney.

Westlake On-ramp Highway 101

The Westlake On-ramp to the 101 Freeway in Ventura. At least four people have reported a ghostly hitchhiker in this location.

Prospector's Road

This road got its name from the many gold prospectors who laid their claims there during the California Gold Rush 150 years earlier. While most of the prospectors are long gone, there is one miner who remains to this day. His angry ghost has been seen along the seven-mile stretch of Prospector's Road, confronting travelers, apparently saying, "Get off my claim!"

See for Yourself

Location: Prospector's Road, between the cities of Georgetown and Lotus.

Solvang Road

This stretch of road in Santa Ynez is haunted by a phantom stagecoach. Well-known locally, the ghostly stagecoach has been seen on several back roads in the area, but mostly along Solvang Road. The stagecoach is pulled by four black horses and driven by a man in a tall black hat. One witness saw the apparition very clearly and described lanterns on the sides of the coach and a female passenger sitting inside. Why the stagecoach appears or what happened to it remains a mystery.

See for Yourself

Location: Solvang Road, between Santa Ynez and Solvang.

According to ghost hunter Richard Senate, the Westlake on-ramp to Highway 101 has its own phantom hitchhiker. In 1981, Senate received four independent reports from drivers who observed an old man waving frantically at them, screaming, "Christ is coming." One driver stopped, picked the man up, and drove for several miles down the freeway when the hitchhiker suddenly disappeared. Each of the stunned witnesses reported their experience to the California Highway Patrol.

See for Yourself

Location: Westlake on-ramp to Highway 101 in Westlake Village, California.

5. Haunted Museums

It is not unusual for museums to be haunted. The many antique items housed in these locations attract the attentions of numerous ghosts. Also many museums are converted from large, important institutions where many people have experienced profound or tragic events. Below are fifteen of California's most famous haunted museums.

Alcatraz Island

Today a museum, Alcatraz (a.k.a. The Rock) was once a high-security prison housing only the very worst of California's hardened criminals. A more desolate, depressing location could hardly be imagined. The gray cement structure exudes awful feelings of loneliness and despair. The area is literally saturated with negativity.

Intense Misery

It is also one of the most famous haunted locations in California, if not the world. As presented in countless books, Alcatraz Island is infested with countless ghosts. Some researchers have speculated that the intense misery and negative emotions have been somehow psychically recorded into the environment, so that the haunting is more an echo of past events than caused by active spirit activity. Many research groups have conducted studies and come away convinced.

Spooky Activity

The employees of the museum are unanimous in their belief of spooky activity. Sounds of men screaming and crying, footsteps, cold-spots, lights going on and off, cell doors shaking, apparitions, cameras failing to function – all of these and more have been reported.

Major Attraction

Despite its depressing nature, or perhaps because of it, Alcatraz Island is a major tourist attraction, bringing in over one million visitors every year! If you want to get spooked by a truly haunted location, this is one experience you will never forget.

See for Yourself

Location: Alcatraz Island, San Francisco Bay, San Francisco.

Castle AFB Museum

This museum is devoted to vintage military equipment, such as a World War II B-29 bomber. This particular plane, called *Raisin' Hell*, however, is reportedly haunted. Employees have seen dark apparitions and observed hatches that open and close by themselves. On at least one occasion, the plane's lights came on, even though there was no power source or even a light bulb!

See for Yourself

The plane is located at: Castle Air Force Base Museum on Buhach Road of Highway 99 in Atwater. Phone: 209-723-2178.

Firehouse Museum

Many hauntings are not caused by the structures, but by items contained within the structures. An old 1861 firehouse was converted into a museum in 1948. Shortly thereafter, haunting activity began, including full-blown apparitions. Perhaps this ghostly activity revolves around the museum's antique piano or the sacred Taoist shrine?

See for Yourself

Location: 214 Main Street, Nevada City, CA 95959. Phone: 530-265-5468.

Hollywood Entertainment Museum

With their large collections of old artifacts, museums are well equipped to provoke the appearance of ghosts. The Hollywood Entertainment Museum is a perfect example. Originally called the Warner Pacific Theater, the building is allegedly haunted by the ghost of the man who helped to build it: Sam Warner. Numerous people have reported seeing his full-color apparition pacing the lobby or sitting in his former office. Strange noises that sound like furniture moving have also been heard. And finally, the ghost seems to enjoy playing mischief with the elevator.

See for Yourself

Location: 7021 Hollywood Blvd, Los Angeles, CA. Phone: 323-465-7900.

Kern County Museum

Some cases of paranormal activity seem to be the result of residual hauntings as opposed to active spirits. In other words, some places seem to echo and replay past events. Instead of being inhabited by ghosts, some areas leave such strong psychic impressions that the energy causes ghostly activity to occur. A good example is Pioneer Village, operated by the Kern County Museum in Bakersfield. Ghostly activity has been reported in the Weill House, in front of the Norris School building, and in the basement storage room where ancient Native American artifacts are kept.

See for Yourself

Location: 3801 Chester Ave, Bakersfield, CA 93301.

La Casa De Estudillo Museum

This structure was built way back in 1829 and has served countless functions, including Army fort, government office, hotel, church, and orphanage. Today it is a museum haunted by several ghosts. Employees and visitors have seen apparitions, faces in mirrors, unexplained lights, and more. They have also heard ghostly music.

See for Yourself

Location: 4002 Wallace Avenue, San Diego CA 92110. Phone: 619-220-5426 or 5422

Leonis Adobe

Leonis Adobe in Calabasas. Placed right in the middle of a bustling city, this haunted ranch house stands like a lone beacon, showing what life used to be like more than one hundred years earlier.

The original owners of this structure, Miguel and Espiritu Leonis, died a century ago, but continue to haunt the area. Miguel Leonis was apparently a difficult man and was involved in numerous property disputes with his neighbors. He was known to shoot at anyone who trespassed upon his land. Today, the apparitions of both Miguel and Espiritu have been seen on the property, still on guard against unwary trespassers. The employees verified the haunting, and said that many visitors have heard voices and other strange noises, and have seen strange shadows moving around the property. In fact, an entire book (*Spirits of Leonis* by Rob Wlodarksi) has been written about the activity. I visited the location myself. Although I didn't see their ghosts physically, I could almost sense the sadness of the couple. The whole structure feels like it is lost in time, locked in a bubble of ghostly silence. After being there, it doesn't surprise me at all that ghosts still haunt the antique structure.

See for Yourself

Location: 23537 Calabasas Road, Calabasas CA 91302. Phone: 818-222-6511.

The *Queen Mary*

A haunted stateroom aboard the *Queen Mary*. After several maids and guests complained of paranormal activity, this stateroom was converted to an office. When the activity still continued, the room was vacated and permanently locked up. It is now used only for the *Queen Mary* Ghost Tour.

The *Queen Mary*. This enormous ship, now a museum, is one of the most haunted places in California, with literally hundreds of ghost encounters on record. The haunting is still very active.

The *Queen Mary's* haunted pool room. One of the most severely haunted places onboard the ship, ghostly manifestations occur here on a regular basis.

Located in Long Beach, the *Queen Mary* is probably California's most famous public haunting. The activity there has been documented by numerous prominent researchers and has been presented on countless television programs. Literally dozens of testimonies have been collected from staff workers and visitors. The entire range of phenomenon is present, with the majority of activity involving unexplained noises: footsteps, voices, laughter, crying, singing…the list goes on. Certain areas, like the pool, seem to be more haunted than others. Today, the *Queen Mary* is actually a hotel and tourist attraction. Ghostly tours are given daily.

Ghostly Tour

In 2005, as part of research for this book, I traveled down to Long Beach and signed up for the ghostly tour. Twenty-eight dollars later, I found myself with about fifteen other people gathered in a theater room in the stern of the ship, ready to begin the tour.

The tour actually began with a short film hosted by psychic and ghost hunter Peter James, the leading paranormal investigator on the *Queen Mary*. The film re-enacted several of the most famous hauntings on the ship: An apparition of a lady appearing in the bar; two guests woken up by their faucets and lights being turned on and their bed-cover being torn away by unseen hands; an apparition of a small girl in the pool room.

Then the official tour began. Our tour guide, Yolanda, said that she was a skeptic when she started working on the *Queen Mary* eight months earlier. She was assigned to conduct the haunted ghost tours. Only a few weeks after she began, Yolanda had her first experience. She saw a cloudy apparition of a lady in a dress. A few weeks later, she felt her hair pulled. On another occasion, she heard strange noises. Since conducting the tours, Yolanda has counted four major encounters and dozens of smaller ones. She then explained that the theater room we were in had actually been the location of several apparitions.

We left the theater and descended deep into the bowels of the ship. Our first stop was where a sailor had been cut in two by the watertight doors. We all stopped in the doorway and tried to feel the energy of the ghost.

The next stop was the boiler room, where several apparitions have been seen. One visitor reportedly took a photograph that showed the figure of a young girl.

Our next adventure was in the haunted pool room. It was here that a young girl named Jackie had drowned. Her apparition has been seen numerous times. Psychic Peter James attempted to make contact and succeeded in making an actual audio recording of the haunting.

We then moved up to another room that had been converted into a banquet room. Here staff and employees observed the solid-looking apparition of a lady that remained for ten minutes, then promptly disappeared in full view of witnesses.

The tour continued with one haunted place after another. We next explored a haunted stateroom. The small room had been recently opened for the ghost tours and had actually been locked up for more than two years because of constant complaints from guests and employees of all kinds of haunting activity. All attempts to stop the activity failed, including turning the bedroom into an office. The room today remains unused, except for the ghost tour.

Signs of Spirits

Numerous other places throughout the ship have been the locations of haunted activity. The staff of the museum is very serious about their ghosts. In fact, numerous plaques throughout the ship mark the actual locations of haunted activity.

So Many Ghosts

Investigators and staff have kept careful records of the paranormal reports and have counted more than 600 separate ghosts, about 100 of whom they have identified. Why the *Queen Mary* is so haunted is no mystery. In its long history, countless people have died tragic deaths on the ship. On one occasion during World War II, the ship evacuated more than 16,000 soldiers in dangerously overcrowded conditions. On that voyage, doctors recorded one death on the ship every seven minutes! It's not too surprising that this ship is haunted.

After taking the ghost tour, then taking a self-guided tour and exploring the ship itself, I can honestly say that I believe the reports of ghosts. As we walked through the haunted locations, you could feel the history of the place. There were numerous cold spots and strong musty odors in the allegedly haunted spots. There were also definitely odd noises like distant, muffled talking or laughter. In the pool room in particular, I encountered the odd feeling of timelessness and silence that I've come to recognize in other haunted spots. For those who want to wander into the past and walk among the ghosts of yesterday, the *Queen Mary* is a doorway into another time and definitely worth the trip.

The Stagecoach Inn Museum

A former hotel, this structure is now actually a museum. According to the staff, all kinds of strange things happen here, including an apparition of a tall, high-society lady who leaves behind her perfumed scent, poltergeist-like activity, phantom voices, and more. The ghosts of a man and a young boy have also been seen. Famed English psychic medium Sybil Leek visited the hotel and, during a séance, allegedly made contact with one of the ghosts.

The Stevenson House

Like most truly haunted locations, the Stevenson House, formerly inhabited by Robert Louis Stevenson, has a long, tragic history. The two-story adobe structure is 150 years old and was first used as a hotel. Writer Robert Louis Stevenson reportedly stayed there back in 1879. The haunting activity seems to have started as the result of a Typhoid epidemic that killed off the entire Girardin family, who originally owned the hotel. Many people have seen the apparition of Manuela Girardin. Other phenomena include a rocking chair that moves by itself and unexplained odors of antiseptic. Today, the Stevenson House is a museum open to the public.

See for Yourself

Location: Monterey State Park, Monterey.

Phone: 831-649-7118.

The USS *Hornet* Museum

Located on Pier 3 on the coast of Alameda Point, Alameda, the USS *Hornet* remains permanently docked, a museum devoted to Naval history. Interestingly, the ship has become just as well known for its haunting activity. The staff and visitors attest to seeing apparitions of WWII guards and other strangers. Also common are doors that slam by themselves and unexplained cold gusts of wind.

See for Yourself

Easy to visit, interesting, spooky, and open to the public. Alameda, CA. Phone: 510-521-8448. www.us-hornet.org.

Villa Montezuma

Well-known opera singer Jesse Shepard built this Victorian mansion in 1887. Shepard was known to be a little eccentric and actually had a séance room built in the house where regular séances were held. He later moved to Europe after being rejected by the local high society. Today, the mansion is a museum run by the San Diego Historical Society. It is reportedly haunted by Shepard and the ghost of one of his servants, a victim of suicide.

See for Yourself

Location: 1925 K Street, San Diego, CA 92102. Phone: 619-232-6203.

The Whaley House Museum

Another of California's most famous haunts, this location is said to be infested by no less than eight ghosts! The ghosts include the entire Whaley family, even their dog! Another ghost is "Yankee Jim Robinson," who was hanged on the property after being caught for petty thievery. Unfortunately, things did not go well for Robinson. He was a very tall man and the hangman had overestimated the length of rope needed to hang him. When the trapdoor was released, he was just able to stand erect on his tiptoes. Because of this, it took Robinson forty-five minutes to slowly strangle to death. Not surprisingly, his phantom still appears in the spot where he was hung. The full range of paranormal phenomena has been reported, including ghostly voices and footsteps, odd cold spots, weird phantom lights, organ music coming from nowhere, and other strange occurrences. The place is so haunted that it was actually declared an official haunted site by the United States Chamber of Commerce, an honor bestowed upon only twenty-nine other locations.

Eyewitness

When I called them up, the man who answered the phone verified that the museum is believed by many to be one of the most haunted places in the United States. He has only been working there for a few months and has already had at least two ghostly encounters. On one occasion, he heard mysterious footsteps in an empty hallway. Later, he was walking down the corridor when he saw a man on the staircase. He thought the man was flesh and blood until, suddenly, he just disappeared. As can be seen, this haunting is still very active.

See for Yourself

Location: 2482 San Diego Ave, San Diego, CA. Phone: 619-297-7511.

William Hart Park and Museum

For those who want to see a famous ghost, the ghosts of cowboy actor William Hart has been observed in his former home, now a museum. His wife has been seen as well.

See for Yourself

Location: 24151 San Fernando Road, Newhall, CA 91321. Phone: 805-254-4584.

The Winchester Mystery House

One of the strangest and saddest stories in American history is that of Sarah Winchester, heiress to the Winchester Rifle fortune. Following the death of her husband and infant child, Sarah Winchester became a haunted woman. She became convinced that her misfortune was caused by the spirits of those people who had been killed by Winchester rifles. She eventually sought out a psychic who gave her some advice: build a house for the spirits and you will be left in peace. The only thing was, the construction must never stop, or Sarah would suffer the same fate as her dear departed husband and child.

Bizarre Construction

Winchester took the advice. In 1884, she bought an eight-room farmhouse and began construction of what is now one of the weirdest houses in human history. Sarah Winchester was deeply affected by the paranormal. She attended séances on a nightly basis in a special room in the house. She asked the spirits what to build and the messages that came through were bizarre. The house seems to be specifically designed for spirits. Doors and windows open into solid walls. Staircases lead nowhere and end. A cupboard has only one half inch of space inside. There's a miniature balcony and a chimney with no fireplace. There are 160 rooms, 2,000 doors, 10,000 windows, fifty-two skylights, forty-seven fireplaces, and six kitchens. Many of the rooms reflect Sarah's fascination with the numbers 13, 7, and 11. For example, a sink with thirteen drain holes, thirteen palm trees lining the driveway, and staircases with thirteen steps. One staircase goes seven steps down, then eleven steps up, and ends.

Other bizarre features include doorways that are a foot or two shorter than normal, forcing anyone over five feet tall to duck. Another is a staircase that has forty-four miniature steps, rising only nine feet. Another mystery is the bell tower. The tower could only be entered from outside, using a ladder! And the bell itself could only be rung from a rope that hung down to a secret underground tunnel built beneath the home. Nevertheless, the bell was rung every night at midnight to summon the spirits.

The house is a literal maze of winding passageways and oddly placed rooms. As one visitor wryly commented, "Guided tours are required. Without them, you might not ever get out."

Evidence of Angry Spirits

In 1906, a large earthquake struck and Sarah Winchester was trapped in the house for several hours. She interpreted the event as anger from the spirits about the building of the house. She had the front thirty rooms boarded up and closed to all entry. Construction continued for decades. Sarah employed dozens of construction workers who built the strange rooms and structures without asking questions. When she died in 1922, construction ceased so quickly that there are still nails that remain only halfway hammered into the wall!

Winchester's belongings were auctioned off and the home was sold, and later restored and open to the public.

Spirits in Residence?

But is the house actually haunted? According to the staff, the answer is yes. A wide variety of paranormal phenomena have been reported, including phantom footsteps in the hallways, unidentified voices in the kitchens, doors that open and close by themselves, lights that go on and off … and more. The identities of the ghosts are presumably the victims of Winchester guns, though there has been some indication that some of the original builders also haunt the many rooms and hallways.

See for Yourself

Today, anyone can visit the sprawling Victorian mansion. Open daily, they also hold special spooky events such as Friday the 13th tours or Halloween flashlight tours. Location: 525 South Winchester Boulevard, San Jose, CA. Phone: 408-247-2000.

Website: www.winchestermysteryhouse.com

6. Haunted Businesses

Hauntings can occur in the most unlikely places, including at your place of employment. In fact, a surprising number of hauntings take place in offices, stores, restaurants, and other public places. However, unlike haunted hotels, most of these businesses are not happy to be haunted and do not advertise their ghosts. Below are twenty-one well-known haunted businesses, though surely there are many more.

Aetna Springs

Golf Course

Numerous visitors to this golf course have observed ghostly monks dressed in white robes. Witnesses report that the monks have fixed expressions of pain on their faces. The theory is that the monks are actually Dominican friars from the 1500s who were tortured and killed by other monks. One visitor was reportedly able to capture a photograph of the ghostly monks.

See for Yourself

Location: Aetna Springs Golf Course. 1600 Aetna Springs Lane, Aetna Springs, CA 94567. Phone: 707-965-2115.

Charlene's

Country Treasures

Antique stores regularly attract ghosts. It appears that ghosts become deeply attached to certain items. A good example is a little toy/gift shop in Bodega, owned by Charlene Weber.

Almost every ghost story starts with a tragedy. This haunting had its origins in the 1800s, when a young couple gave birth to a brain damaged child. The child was confined to a crib and soon died. The grief-stricken father was unable to part with his dearly departed daughter, and in order to preserve her memory, he had a doll made in her likeness. To strengthen the connection, the doll was actually made with the hair, eyebrows, and eye lashes of the dead child.

Recognizing that the doll was unique, and probably quite valuable, owner Charlene Weber purchased it and placed it in a crib in her store. Soon afterwards, customers started to come forward and tell her that they saw a tall man with a beard examining the child. After several such reports, Weber decided to investigate. A psychic medium told her that the identity of the ghost was the father of the sick child. This turned out to be Captain McCuen, who matched the description of the spirit.

See for Yourself

Weber's incredible story has been featured in several books and on television. Location: Off Highway 1 in Bodega, near the Salmon Creek Bridge.

Banta Inn

Restaurant

Tony Gukan loved his hotel and, although he died of heart attack while working behind the bar in 1968, his spirit continues to be encountered. Following his death, numerous objects around the now restaurant/bar began to move by themselves, including glasses, coins, ashtrays, and more. The only logical explanation witnesses could come up with was that Tony Gukan was back. The owner and front desk clerk confirmed the account, and say that, yes, the restaurant is definitely haunted.

Bakersfield Californian Newspaper

Ghost hunter Dennis William Hauck uncovered an interesting public haunting in a newspaper office. He interviewed firsthand witnesses who observed the ghost of a German shepherd dog that sits quietly on the sidewalk outside the *Bakersfield Californian* newspaper office. There are a few ghosts inside, including former publisher Alfred Harrel, and the apparition of an unknown elderly man who appears near the first floor elevator and in the lunchroom.

See for Yourself

Location: 1707 Eye Street, Bakersfield, CA 93310. Phone: 661-395-7258.

Big Yellow House Restaurant

This old house was converted into a restaurant in 1973. Previously, the owners used to conduct séances. Today, the spirits continue to parade through the structure. One ghost, called Hector, is blamed for breaking dishware, banging on doors, and tugging at people's clothes. The hostess confirmed that the stories are true and that a lot of people visit the restaurant just to see the ghost. The story has also garnered considerable media attention. While the hostess hasn't seen the ghost herself, several of the waiters and waitresses have. One waiter saw Hector's apparition. Another waiter heard disembodied voices. And one of the waitresses had experiences on both the second floor and in the basement – which she refused to venture into now. For those who desire more information, a full-length book has been written about the events, appropriately titled, *Spirits of the Big Yellow House.*

El Adobe Restaurant

This structure was built way back in 1778 and was designed as a personal residence. However, times change and the building later served a number of other functions, including a justice court, a jail, and a wine cellar. Today, the adobe structure is a restaurant, with a ghost. The ghost of a headless monk has been seen wandering the premises. Many of the waiters have also reported strong feelings of being watched. I confirmed some of the above accounts, and also learned that some of the employees have experienced the unexplained opening and closing of doors.

El Fandango Restaurant

This restaurant was built over an old mansion owned by the Machado family. It seems that one member of the family – a lady in white – still haunts the location. Her glowing white apparition has been seen in the dining room, sitting in the shady corners of the restaurant. I spoke with the current caretaker, and she confirmed the haunting and said she had one very dramatic sighting of the ghost a few years ago. Another employee, she said, used to work nights. But after a series of scary encounters, he refused to work evenings, and won't even stay there at night.

Many public businesses are haunted, such as the El Fandango Restaurant in San Diego, which is inhabited by a female ghost who periodically appears as a white glowing apparition sitting at the corner tables.

Far West Tavern

This former hotel is now a steak-house. In the 1930s, a one-legged man by the name of Franconeti (or maybe Oscar Ferrari) died in a fire in an upstairs room. Today, his ghost can be heard noisily thumping around on his wooden leg in his room, which is located directly above the dining room. His ghost has also been seen in the room. His presence can be detected as a defined cold spot. I spoke with an employee who has worked there for thirty years, and she says that she hasn't had any personal experiences. However, she says that several employees "swear up and down" that they've had objects disappear, have been grabbed when nobody was there, or have seen apparitions flying around the room. Again, most of the activity is confined to the upstairs floor.

See for Yourself

Location: Off Highway 1, 899 Guadalupe Street, Guadalupe, CA 93434. Phone: 805-343-2211.

Four Oaks Restaurant

Built in 1880 as a stopping point for travelers between Los Angeles and the San Fernando Valley, this restaurant has served many functions over the years including hotel, restaurant, bar, and brothel. The structure is haunted by at least one ghost, who appears as a brightly glowing apparition. The ghost's identity remains unknown.

See for Yourself

Location: 2181 North Beverly Glenn Boulevard, Los Angeles, CA 90077. Phone: 310-470-2265.

La Casa Bodega Liquor Store

Researcher Mike Marinacci uncovered this public haunting, which is the result of a tragic murder. A young male store-clerk was shot to death during a robbery. Since then his ghost has been seen by employees and customers, usually between the hours of 7:30 and 9:30 pm.

See for Yourself

Location: 500 Del Monte Street, Monterey, CA 93940.

Los Angeles County Arboretum

In 1932, Chief Buffalo Child Long Lance committed suicide in his home in Arcadia. Long Lance gained fame with his claims of being raised by Native Americans in the old west. He wrote an extremely popular book about his experiences and became a celebrity. Then it was discovered that he had hoaxed the entire story. He was really an African American and had never lived with the Indians. Devastated, Long Lance shot himself in the head.

Later, the estate was purchased and transformed into the Los Angeles Arboretum. Since the suicide, numerous people have seen his ghost. The estate was actually used during the filming of the television series "Fantasy Island." Numerous people in the television crew, including producer Aaron Spelling and actor John Anderson, observed Long Lance's apparition.

See for Yourself

Today, the Arboretum is open to the public. Location: San Luis Obispo County Crystal Rose Inn, 789 Valley Road, Arroyo Grande, CA 93420.

Moss Beach Distillery

Sometime in the 1920s, a young woman was stabbed to death by a jealous lover. The murder occurred in front of the Moss Beach Distillery restaurant, which is now haunted by her ghost. According to the owners, her ghost has appeared nearly one hundred times, at least once or twice a year for fifty years. She has been seen by the owners, the managers, the cooks, the waiters and waitresses, and customers. She has not only been seen, but also moves objects and furniture. The restaurant has been featured in numerous articles and television programs. When I called them up and asked about the supernatural occurrences, the front desk clerk confirmed that the haunting is still very active, and said that she herself has experienced some strange paranormal activity – in her case, ghostly footsteps when no one was present.

See for Yourself

Location: At the intersection of Ocean Street and Beach Street in Moss Beach, CA 94038, just south of San Francisco. Phone: 650-728-5595. Website: www.moss beachdistillery.com.

New Castle

Inn Restaurant

This establishment is allegedly haunted by Gary the ghost, as the employees call him, who makes his presence known by either turning lights on and off or flinging glasses and bottles from their shelves.

See for Yourself

Location: 525 Main Street, Newcastle, CA 95658.

Richard

Nixon Library

The only presidential ghost in California is that of Richard Nixon. The library devoted to the former commander-in-chief has been the location of ghostly manifestations, including unexplained tapping noises, machines that mysteriously break down, and a luminous apparition that was seen floating over Nixon's gravesite.

See for Yourself

Location: 18001 Yorba Linda Blvd, Yorba Linda, CA 92686. Phone: 714-993-3393.

Santa Clara

House Restaurant

Many years ago, when this restaurant was a private Victorian mansion, a young woman named Rosa who lived in the house committed the sin of adultery and became pregnant. The strict moral ethics of Victorian society apparently drove her to the extremes of suicide. Rather than live with what she had done,

The library devoted to the former commander-in-chief has been the location of ghostly manifestations, including unexplained tapping noises, machines that mysteriously break down, and a luminous apparition that was seen floating over Nixon's gravesite.

Rosa went to the attic of the home and hung herself. Ever since then, her apparition has been seen peering down from the second-floor window.

See for Yourself

Location: Santa Clara Street, Santa Clara.

Stokes Adobe

Restaurant

Built in 1838 as a private Victorian mansion, this structure has now been converted into a restaurant. According to manager Paul Johnson, the former owner was forced to close down his business because an invisible ghost kept harassing the guests by tugging at their clothing. Furthermore, on many evenings the kitchen would be thrown into disarray by the ghost. I spoke with a couple of the employees and both agreed that the place is haunted. Not only have many reported activity, at least one employee has felt a "presence" around when nobody was visible. According to the employees, the haunting is still active.

See for Yourself

Location: 500 Hartnell Street, Monterey, CA 93940. Phone: 831-373-1110.

Sweet Lady Jane's Bakery and Restaurant

One of the most famous ghosts of California is none other than Orson Welles. One of his favorite places to sit down, relax, and have a bite to eat was Sweet Lady Jane's Bakery and Restaurant. Following his death, Welles apparently still frequents the establishment. His ghost has been seen sitting at his favorite table. Others have smelled his signature cigar smoke and fine brandy.

See for Yourself

Location: 8360 Melrose Ave, Los Angeles, CA 90069. Phone: 323-653-7145.

Toys R Us

Probably the only known haunted toy store in existence, the Toys R Us haunting was thoroughly documented by researchers Antoinette May and Sylvia Brown. The ghost, named John, died back in the 1880s of a blood infection after wounding his leg. Since then, his spirit has haunted the area. When the original ranch was torn down and a Toys R Us store was erected, the haunting continued. Numerous employees have seen his spirit. John also makes his presence known by turning water faucets on and off and by moving toys around.

Medium Sylvia Brown made contact with the ghost during a séance, and a photograph was obtained which clearly shows John's dark silhouette leaning up against the wall. It is one of the most impressive ghost photographs in existence.

See for Yourself

Location: 130 East El Camino Real, Sunnyvale, CA.

Valley of the Moon Saloon

Carolina Ceelena is the proud owner of this haunted bar, which is more than a century old. She has seen the ghost herself, as have her employees and many customers. Although nobody knows the identity of the ghost, the spirit is very fussy, often rearranging the furniture and turning off lights.

See for Yourself

Location: 17154 Sonoma Highway, Sonoma, CA 95476.

Willow Steakhouse

In the early 1840s, this location was actually a gold mine. After it collapsed and killed twenty-three men, the mine was closed down. Later, in 1862, a hotel was built on the site. Then in 1896, the town went up in flames. In order to save the hotel, the surrounding buildings were blown up with dynamite. Incredibly, however, the buildings were not fully evacuated. Ever since then, the hotel has been cursed with ghostly activity. In 1975, a mysterious fire started in the hotel and witnesses reported seeing apparitions surrounding the fire. Ten years later, the entire hotel burned down. Only the restaurant and bar were rebuilt. Today at least three different ghosts have been seen on the premises.

I spoke with one of the waitresses and she confirmed that many of the employees have had experiences. The cooks, especially, have reported a lot of encounters. The waitress who spoke with me said that the ghost is definitely still very active. Each morning, when she unlocks the back dining room, one of the tables is always messed up. In particular, the sugar packets or Sweet-n-Low™ packets are always thrown across the room. Each time it happens to a different table; otherwise, it's always the same thing. The only explanation they can come up with is a ghost.

See for Yourself

Location: 18723 Main Street, Jamestown, CA 95327. Phone: 209-984-3998.

Zander Building

This structure today houses several commercial businesses and at least one ghost. The apparition of a tall man wearing a gray suit has been seen in various stores, including *Eddie's Treasures* and *The Cat's Meow*. Others have seen the apparition on the rear stairwell to the parking lot.

See for Yourself

Location: 427 E. Main Street, Ventura, CA 93001.

7. Haunted Theaters

A great many theaters are haunted. Why exactly they are so attractive to ghosts remains a mystery. Could it be because, even in death, actors continue to crave attention from their audiences? What follows are eight of the most famous haunted theaters in California.

The Comedy Store

Ghosts are no laughing matter at the Comedy Store in Los Angeles. A more unlikely place for a haunting can hardly be envisioned, and yet the activity has been so strong it cannot be ignored.

The building was formally called Ciro's and was a known hangout for gangsters and mobsters. Murders and other violent acts have taken place on the premises.

Now that the building has been refurbished, the haunting activity seems to have escalated. As reported by the staff, working comics, and the occasional visitor, a variety of ghostly activities continue on a regular basis, including moving objects, strange cold spots, phantom voices, weird crashing noises, and more. As featured in books and on television programs, the activities show no sign of slowing down. So, whether you want a good laugh or to have your hair pulled by a ghost, the Comedy Store might be a good place to check out.

See for Yourself

Location: 8433 West Sunset Boulevard, Los Angeles, CA. Phone: 323-650-6268.

Conejo Players

This small community theater is haunted by a ghost named Alfred who apparently remains a theater critic even after his death. According to several actors, Alfred has stomped loudly down the aisle during performances and has even moved stage props. Numerous items around the theater disappear and then are found again in different locations.

See for Yourself

Location: 351 South Moorpark Road, Thousand Oaks, CA 91362. Phone: 805-495-3715.

Mann's Chinese Theatre

The sidewalk outside Mann's Chinese Theatre in Hollywood is reportedly haunted by the ghost of actor Victor Killian. In 1982, Killian was bludgeoned to death by a man he had met at a nearby bar. The killer was never found. Backstage, in the theater itself, an unidentified ghost pulls at the stage curtains and haunts the various dressing rooms.

See for Yourself

Location: 6925 Hollywood Boulevard, Hollywood, CA 90028. Phone: 323-464-8111.

The Palace Theater

A large number of theaters are haunted, apparently because of the emotionally-charged activity that takes place in such locations. The Palace Theater was used originally for stage plays and radio shows, but later was also used for television. The ghostly activity includes an apparition of a man in a tuxedo, an older couple, ghostly piano playing, lights turning on and off, objects moving by themselves, and more. The clerk at the desk not only confirmed the haunting, she said it's "very scary" and that "everybody here" has experienced activity. The events at the theater have been featured in numerous newspaper articles and on television. The haunting is still very active.

See for Yourself

Location: 1735 Vine Street, Los Angeles, CA. Phone: 323-467-4571.

Pantages Theatre

The Pantages Theater was originally used for stage plays but is today a movie theater. The location has experienced a good deal of haunting activity, which has also been documented by researchers. One researcher successfully recorded the sound of a ghostly singing woman. Most of the activities, however, are attributed to the alleged ghosts of the theatre's former owner, Howard Hughes, who purchased the place in 1949, or to its founder, Alexander Pantages. The manifestations include mostly unexplained cold spots and the occasional apparition.

See for Yourself

Location: 6233 Hollywood Blvd, Los Angeles, CA. Phone: 323-468-1770.

Sacramento

Theater Company

This theater is haunted by so many ghosts that several parapsychologists and psychics have conducted onsite investigations. A male ghost named Pinky appears regularly to employees. Other ghosts continue to appear in the upstairs, stage-left dressing room. In 1994, investigators were able to successfully record ghostly footsteps and photograph temperature anomalies.

See for Yourself

Location: 1419 H Street, Sacramento, CA 95814. Phone: 916-443-6722.

Ventura Theater

A tragic haunting is currently taking place in this theater. The ghost is that of a young lady who was crushed to death by falling stage lights. Since then, the ghost has relived the awful accident on several occasions, her death scream echoing each time. Her glowing apparition has also been seen dancing on the center of the stage where she died.

See for Yourself

Location: 26 South Chestnut Street, Ventura, CA 93001. Phone: 805-653-0721.

A male ghost named Pinky appears regularly to employees.

Woodland

Opera House

This 100-year-old theater is haunted by a ghost who frequents the upper balcony, making his presence known with the smell of cigar smoke. I spoke with one of the docents, who not only confirmed the haunting, she also admitted to several of her own encounters. As she says, "I have actually heard some bizarre noises up there, footsteps and these types of things, when nobody is there!" She admits that many of the other employees have also heard strange noises and that the basement area below the stage is also known to have some activity. Reportedly, the ghost may be that of a fireman who died in a fire in the structure. For those who would like to visit and maybe see the ghost for themselves, the Opera House gives public tours every Tuesday.

See for Yourself

Location: 340 Second Street, Woodland, CA 95965. Phone: 530-666-9617.

8. Haunted Missions

The Spanish Missions of California play a huge role in the state's colorful history. Some of them are more than three centuries old and are still in use today. Not surprisingly, several of them are also haunted. Below are eight of the many California missions that have earned the biggest reputation for ghostly activity.

Royal Presidio

Chapel and Rectory

Built in 1770, this building is one of the oldest structures in California that is still in active use. For more than 200 years, the location has been used as a place of worship. Today, the structure still contains the haunted vibrations of its long history. The most common manifestation is the apparition of a priest, who has been seen floating through the church carrying a lit candle. The activity also includes ghostly footsteps, lights turning on and off, strange noises, and, finally, the church bell ringing by itself! Also known as the San Carlos Cathedral, the structure is open to the public. I spoke with the information officer, and she confirmed that several of the staff members have reported "mischievous stuff," but only rarely and usually at night.

See for Yourself

Location: 550 Church Street, Monterey, CA 93940. Phone: 831-373-2628.

Mission La

Purismma Concepcion

Because they are so old, it is hard to find a mission that doesn't have some sort of haunting activity. Built in 1787, this mission first became haunted when a man named Don Vicente was murdered there in the mid-1800s. However, he is not the only ghost. When the mission was remodeled in the 1930s, workers were plagued by the apparitions of small children. It was learned that they were the victims of a smallpox epidemic and had been buried underneath the mission floor. Other ghosts include a phantom monk and a ghostly gardener.

See for Yourself

Location: In the La Purisima Mission State Historic Park at 2295 Purisima Road, Lompoc, CA 93436. Phone 805-733-3713/1303.

Website: lapurismamission.org.

Mission San

Antonio de Padua

Like many haunted locations, the Mission San Antonio de Padua is very old, built in 1771. The mission is said to be inhabited by ghostly monks. One of the witnesses is leading California ghost hunter, Richard Senate. While staying at the mission for his archaeological studies, Senate observed a monk walking towards him on a path. Writes Senate, "I had been observing him for well over a minute, and as he got closer, I could see that it was the figure of a monk in a cowl, carrying a candle...I got about twelve feet away from him, and he vanished. Gone! No trapdoor, no nothing. All of a sudden, it dawned on me – this was a ghost." It was this event that sparked Senate's interest in ghosts.

Several of the monks at the mission, including brother Timothy Arthur, have heard phantom footsteps. Several students also reported seeing an apparition. A headless horsewoman has been seen on more than twenty separate occasions. One time, four military policemen encountered the ghost and chased it for miles in their jeep, but the ghost easily eluded them.

The activity continues. I spoke to an employee of the gift shop who both confirmed the mission's haunted status and admitted to a few experiences of her own. It seems that the windows in the gift shop sometimes open and/or close by themselves, or will suddenly rattle when nobody is there. Also, the ceiling fan will sometimes turn on by itself.

See for Yourself

Location: Jolon Road Exit off Highway 101 in King City. Phone: 831-385-4478.

Mission San

Buenaventura

Built in 1782, this mission is haunted by a ghostly monk with gray hair and a gray robe. The ghost wanders widely, and has been seen inside the original adobe structure, in the garden, sitting along the banks of the Ventura River, and even walking along Main Street in Ventura. The staff member I spoke with told me that ghostly activity is allegedly a part of the history of the mission, but had no other information.

See for Yourself

Location: 211 East Main Street, Ventura CA 93001. Phone: 805-643-4318.

Mission San Carlos

Built in 1770 by the well-known Father Junipero Serra, this mission is haunted by a ghostly Spanish soldier riding a spectral horse. According to local legend, the man was killed by Indians. Never having reached his destination, this soldier continues to haunt the area where he was killed.

See for Yourself

Location: 3080 Rio Rd, Carmel CA 93921. Phone: 831-624-3600.

Mission San Fernando

Built in 1797, this mission is more than 300 years old and still retains most of its original construction. An unidentified apparition has been seen walking under the archway, especially late at night. I was personally able to visit this mission. As I walked along the haunted archway, I felt the same feeling I've felt in other haunted spots. There's a weird sort of timeless silence that pervades the atmosphere. Again, it feels like stepping backwards in time. In my mind's eye, I could imagine all the history of this place. Now surrounded by a dense city, the mission was once the only structure around. While I didn't see the ghost, I definitely felt a lost, lonely sensation that I've felt in other haunted spots. I took some photographs and sent a prayer that any unhappy ghosts would find their way home.

See for Yourself

Location: 15151 San Fernando Mission Boulevard, Mission Hills, CA 91345. Phone: 818-361-0186.

Mission San Juan Capistrano

Famed father Junipero Serra founded several missions that still survive today, including this one, the "jewel of the missions," which contains numerous ghosts, including a headless soldier, a faceless monk, and other earthbound spirits.

Numerous people have observed an unidentified apparition floating along this corridor outside of the 100-year-old Mission San Fernando, located in the San Fernando Valley.

See for Yourself

Location: 31882 Camino Capistrano #107, San Juan Capistrano, CA 92693. Phone: 949-234-1300. Website: www.missionsjc.com.

Mission San Miguel

This mission was built in 1797, but didn't become haunted until 1848, when a bloody murder took place, leaving it forever haunted by the victims. English pirates heard that the owner, John Reed, had a large volume of gold hidden on the property. The pirates invaded the home and killed Reed and thirteen others, including his entire family. The bodies were so badly torn apart that they had to be buried together in a common grave behind the mission. Today, several visitors have encountered their unhappy ghosts. The treasure itself has never been found (*See chapter: Buried Treasure in California*). Today the mission has been temporarily closed to the public because of earthquake damage. Fortunately, plans are being made to have it repaired and reopened to the public.

See for Yourself ... Eventually

Location: 775 Mission Street, San Miguel, CA 93451. Phone: 805-467-2131.

9. Haunted Ghost Towns

When the gold rush began in 1847, it changed the face of California forever. Literally overnight, hundreds of ramshackle towns were thrown together. Thousands of people converged to create one of the most unique periods of human history: the era of the "Wild West." Lawless towns were quickly populated with gunfighters, prostitutes, miners, Indians, saloon-owners, entrepreneurs, pioneers, and other adventuresome types.

And when the gold rush dried up as quickly as it had started, the towns were abandoned in the same manner that they had been built. California has scores of ghost towns. And given the lawless nature of these places, it should come as no surprise that many of them live up to their names as true ghost towns – complete with actual ghosts.

What follows are the six most haunted ghost towns of California.

Benton Hot Springs Ghost Town

This obscure little ghost town is reportedly haunted by its former inhabitants. The area's current residents report seeing a couple wearing clothes that appear to be dated around the 1890s. At night, the residents have also seen ghostly lanterns being carried across the town.

See for Yourself

Location: thirty-seven miles north of Bishop of Highway 6, and five miles west of Benton Station.

Bodie State Park Ghost Town

In central California is a remote ghost town now called Bodie State Historic Park. Once a thriving silver mine with 10,000 residents, the area is now most famous for the dozen ghosts that haunt the area. The John S. Cain house is haunted by the ghost of a Chinese maid, who causes various types of poltergeist activity. The maid doesn't like adults, but apparently loves children.

The Gregory House is haunted by the ghost of an old woman. Her apparition has been seen sitting in the rocking chair, which has also been seen to move by itself.

Other types of ghostly activities have occurred there, including ghostly smells of cooking, sounds of people talking and laughing, and other strange occurrences, including the appearance of a phantom white mule outside one of the collapsed mines. There is a graveyard that is also haunted. Several other ghosts have also appeared.

Largest of its Kind

More than 168 buildings remain standing, making this one of the largest ghost towns in the United States. Some of the structures are more than 150 years old.

Bodie Park is pretty severely haunted. Apparently this is what happens when a town sprouts up over night in the Wild West and then becomes abandoned by the living and inhabited by the dead.

See for Yourself

Located southeast of Bridgeport, California, near the Nevada border. Phone: 760-647-6445.

Calico Ghost Town

Calico was actually a silver mining town and the location of a controversial archaeological site. Reportedly, the local Playhouse is haunted by the ghost of a woman named Esmerelda. Wyatt Earp lived in Calico for a short time, and his ghost has also been seen in the area.

See for Yourself

Location: Calico Ghost Town, 36600 Ghost Town Road, Yermo, CA 92398. Phone: 760-254-2122. www.calico town.com.

Cerro Gordo

In 1865, towards the end of the gold rush, a rich silver mine brought a flood of thousands of hopefuls, creating what is now the ghost town of Cerro Gordo. In its day, this particular town was so violent and unlawful that it was nicknamed "the shooting gallery." Today local residents have reported seeing apparitions moving among the abandoned buildings. One of the ghosts in the area was an Indian guide. Now nicknamed "Rescue Jim," he has reportedly aided several lost and injured hikers.

See for Yourself

Location: Take Highway 395 to Owens Lake, off Highway 136 at the end of an eight mile dirt road in the Inyo Mountains.

Hornitas

Ghost Town

This ghost town, outside of Mariposa, was an unusually unlawful town. Death was so common among the outlaw gunfighters that bodies weren't even buried, but were simply dumped into a deep ditch outside of town appropriately named Dead Man's Gulch. Not surprisingly, the area is haunted. The identity of one ghost has been determined to be Joaquin Murrieta, a notorious bandit who was wanted dead or alive. He was killed by bounty hunters who decapitated him and chopped off his hand in order to collect their reward. Since then, Murrieta's ghost has been seen wandering the area, apparently searching for his missing body parts.

See for Yourself

Location: 5119 Jessie Street, Mariposa, CA 95338.

Skidoo

Ghost Town

Like most California ghost towns, Skidoo was built around the gold mining industry. And as we have seen, gold has a way of turning normal men into greedy killers. The main ghost in this town is reportedly that of bank robber Joe Simpson. After robbing the town's only bank and killing the banker, a lynch mob hunted Simpson down and hung him to death. When newspaper reporters arrived weeks later and wanted a photograph, Simpson's body was dug up and hung again! This apparently angered Simpson, whose ghost now haunts the area.

See for Yourself

Skidoo is located in Emigrant Canyon near Furnace Creek in Death Valley National Park. Phone: 760-786-2331.

> The identity of one ghost has been determined to be Joaquin Murrieta, a notorious bandit who was wanted dead or alive. He was killed by bounty hunters who decapitated him and chopped off his hand in order to collect their reward.

10. Haunted Schools

It may come as little surprise that several California schools are haunted. In most cases, the haunting can be linked to a traumatic event that occurred some time in the past. In other cases, the haunting could be better explained as a "residual haunting." In these cases, instead of active ghosts that haunt the structure, the activity could be better explained as a sort of psychic imprint, during which past events seem to come alive. In either case, the effect is very similar. Ordinary people suddenly find themselves confronted with the unknown. What follows are nine such cases. Note: While these are technically public buildings, please secure permission before attempting any explorations.

California State University, Camarillo

Some of the contributing factors to haunting activity are traumatic emotional events. So when a former mental hospital is remodeled into a university, it should come as no surprise when haunting activity occurs.

The hospital was actually haunted before it even became a school. In 1962, the night staff was blamed and fired for unexplained poltergeist activity that basically trashed the place. When the mysterious vandalism continued, former patients were blamed.

The hospital was eventually converted into a school, but the haunting activity continued, including the normal activity and actual apparitions.

See for Yourself...Students

Location: 1 University Drive, Camarillo, CA 93012.

California State University, Sacramento

During the construction of the university theater, a young man fell, was impaled upon steel girders, and died. Since then, his ghost has been seen in various locations, but not far from the area of his death.

See for Yourself...Alumni

Location: 6000 J Street, Sacramento, CA 95819.

Gorman Elementary School

Gorman is a very small desert-town located northeast of Los Angeles. According to Wesley Thomas, the superintendent of Gorman Elementary school, the building is haunted by the ghost of a child named Harriet. Thomas has heard doors slamming by themselves. As he says, "We had it locked up from the inside; nobody could have gotten in."

Mary Jane Fuller, a custodian at the school, has often heard phantom footsteps and doors slamming. On one occasion, the ghost followed her through the school, slamming doors both in front of and behind her. Says Fuller, "I was really getting the willies."

Teacher Joanne Yolton-Pouder confirms the accounts, and says that Harriet has often played tricks in her classroom, such as disturbing papers, locking doors, and moving objects.

Harriet became a ghost back in the 1930s, after being killed in a tragic tractor accident. The school was built on the property in 1938. Ever since then, Harriet's been a regular resident. She has also been viewed by several students and residents of Gorman.

See for Yourself...Faculty

Location: 49847 Gorman School Rd, Lebec, CA 93243.

Kohl Mansion

This old mansion is now converted into a high school on the grounds of the Sisters of Mercy Convent. Students have reportedly seen the ghost of the former owner, Frederick Kohl, walking up and down the main staircase.

See for Yourself...Scholars

Location: 2750 Adeline Dr., Burlingame, CA 94010.

Peninsula School

Suicide is a tragedy that sometimes causes its victim to become a ghost. In this case, it was apparently an accidental suicide that caused Carmelita Coleman to haunt the Peninsula school. After Coleman accidentally shot herself while packing her husband's gun, the husband refused to return to the mansion, which was eventually converted to a school. Since her death, numerous students and teachers have seen her apparition, which appears in a glowing green light. On one occasion, Coleman's apparition materialized for a period of five minutes in front of twenty amazed students and one teacher.

See for Yourself...Academics

Location: 920 Peninsula Way, Menlo Park, CA 94025.

San Francisco Art Institute

This school was actually built over an old cemetery, so it is not too surprising that it is haunted. The center tower is particularly haunted. Students, security guards, and janitors have all witnessed dramatic activity.

See for Yourself...Artists

Location: 800 Chestnut Street, San Francisco, CA 94132.

Santa Barbara Community College

Nobody seems to know the identity of this ghost, other than she is a woman wrapped in white shawl. She has been seen to follow the same route, floating a few inches above the campus lawn and over to the cliffs that look over the ocean. At this point, she is said to disappear in a flash of blue light.

See for Yourself... Professors

Location: 365 Loma Alta Dr, Santa Barbara CA 93109.

Sather Tower

Located in the center of the campus of the University of California, Berkeley, this six-story stone bell tower is reportedly haunted by the ghost of a student. Back in 1960, the student climbed up to the top of the tower and leaped off the edge to his death. In the years following the tragedy, students have reported seeing his apparition.

See for Yourself... Researchers

Location: University of California, Berkeley.

U.S. Naval Postgraduate School

This former hotel converted into a school is still haunted by one of the hotel's early founders, Charles Crocker, whose gray-suited apparition has been seen in various places in the building.

See for Yourself... Graduates

Location: University Circle, Monterey, CA 93943.

11. Haunted Places

This section is a catch-all category of nearly a dozen hauntings that are currently taking place in various specific locations across California. The following ten locations all have a reputation for having ghosts.

American River

The ghost of a young male has appeared along the shore of the American River on numerous occasions over the last fifty years. Residents do not know his identity but believe he drowned years ago in the cold, swift waters.

Location: Fair Oaks, at the Junction of the American River and Sunrise Boulevard in Sacramento.

Black Lake

According to local residents, a glowing, faceless apparition named Alice appears late at night, at half-past midnight. She is seen most often wandering back and forth among the sand dunes.

Location: Black Lake, south of Pismo Beach, off Highway 1, Oceano.

Fannette Island

In Emerald Bay of Lake Tahoe lies a tiny little spot of land called Fannette Island. In 1863, a man by the name of Dick Barter came to Emerald Bay to work as a caretaker for a local landowner. Barter loved the area so much, he lived a hermitic life there, rarely leaving the area. He often boated around the bay and one day was nearly killed in a storm. Following his near-death experience, he constructed his own elaborate stone tomb on Fannette Island in the middle of the bay.

Three years later, in 1873, Barter was caught in another storm. This time, however, he was not so lucky. He was drowned when his boat sunk. His body was never recovered. The empty tomb still remains, which is reportedly haunted by Barter's ghost. Location: Emerald Bay in Lake Tahoe, California.

Folsom Prison

Opened way back in 1880, this high security prison is still active, housing thousands of prisoners. According to the investigations of Dennis William Hauck, it is also haunted. He learned that numerous areas in the facility are haunted by various ghosts. The activity has taken place in Building 5, in Guard Tower 13, on the catwalk above the front gate, in the prison morgue, and especially in the thirteen cells that comprise death row. Reportedly, the haunting activity became so severe that prison officials were forced to call in Catholic priests to conduct exorcisms.

Location: 300 Prison Road, Represa, CA 95671.

Hell's Gate and the Slaughterhouse

Murder Most Foul

Located outside Antioch on Empire Mine Road, this location is truly spooky. Numerous cult-activities have occurred here, including several unsolved murders.

According to local legend, the property was originally owned by a man named Morgan. He owned a slaughterhouse for many years, until one night members of a Satanic cult killed him and several of his workers. The slaughterhouse then became the cult's favored location for human sacrifices and bizarre occult practices.

Today the area reportedly continues to attract groups of devil worshippers, white supremacists, and other unsavory characters.

> He was drowned when his boat sunk. His body was never recovered. The empty tomb still remains, which is reportedly haunted by Barter's ghost.

Witnesses Most Fearful

There are also a number of firsthand witnesses to ghostly activity. Says one gentleman, "In 2001 I went to personally investigate this barn house inside Hell's Gate. I will not go into details here so as to allow skeptics their right to believe what they will without contradiction. However, I can say that I received perhaps the most frightening and graphic experience I have witnessed, which seems to confirm the presence of past and present occult activity in the area. I am a generally prideful man, but the fact is that I sprinted all the way from the now burnt out shell of a barn house to my car in the dead of night, without slowing, stopping nor becoming tired, due to fear."

Says another witness, Andrea X., "When you go up there, you definitely get weird vibes...As soon as we got on the road, I started crying and shaking and I couldn't stop. My friend was trying to calm me down. We went by the slaughterhouse, and it was like 11:00 at night. I was so freaked out. Our friend who was driving usually isn't afraid of anything, but he was of that. He kept driving so fast, he was afraid to stop."

Says Wayne X., "The first time we went there was in the summer of 2000. We entered this place with weird feeling about it and [were] very scared. We didn't know what to expect. We entered the bottom of the slaughterhouse and we shined the flashlight on the far left side of it and we saw something that freaked us out. We saw these black-hooded people which were devil worshippers crowded around this table doing something. So what we did was, we took the flashlight and shined it to the right. We saw nothing so we went back to the right side again. But we didn't see them anymore in human form. We saw them there with a blue glow outline of them...then they disappeared...I heard in the distance an old engine and I looked and there was nothing there. About a couple minutes after that I heard these dogs running after us that sounded right behind us. So we ran fast back to the car and looked back, and there was nothing there...We went there other times and took other people, but nothing compares to the first night there. Other times we went I heard many things. Like you might hear babies crying, people mumbling or talking or screaming, or some lady saying, 'Help me!' which I heard."

There are numerous other reports of "white figures," "black figures," and other strange apparitions.

Located just beyond the Empire Mine gravity hill road in Antioch, take March Creek Road and turn left on Deer Valley Road. Take Deer Valley down to Empire Mine Road and turn left. The slaughterhouse is located on Empire Mine Road. Enter at your own risk! (www.angelfire.com/extreme/thrillseekers)

Lake Isabella

In the early 1900s, a young woman revealed that she had been raped by the Chinese cook of a logger's camp. A lynch mob composed of the loggers captured the cook, named Mr. Wong, and hanged him until dead. They then sat down and ate the meal he had just prepared for them.

Outraged by the murder of their fellow citizen, a group of Chinese immigrants used occult Taoist techniques to make contact with the spirit of Wong, who pointed out the identity of his murderers. The immigrants apparently got their revenge as all five loggers in the lynch mob disappeared. However, this apparently didn't appease the ghost of Mr. Wong, who today continues to be seen hovering over Lake Isabella, which was created when the area was purposely flooded.

Location: Lake Isabella, near Kernville.

Point Loma Lighthouse

Spanish explorer Rodrigo Cabrillo landed here in 1542, claiming the land for Spain. Centuries later, in 1851, a lighthouse was built over the area. However, because of the constant low cloud cover, the lighthouse was deemed useless and was abandoned in 1891. Today, it has been restored and is opened to the public. Visitors reportedly have heard the sounds of human moans echoing through the empty structure.

See for Yourself

Location: Cabrillo National Monument at end of Highway 209 on Point Loma. Phone: 619-557-5450.

We saw these black-hooded people which were devil worshippers crowded around this table doing something. So what we did was, we took the flashlight and shined it to the right. We saw nothing so we went back to the life side again. But we didn't see them anymore in human form. We saw them there with a blue glow outline of them...then they disappeared...

Point Vicente Lighthouse

Point Vicente Lighthouse: One of the few haunted lighthouses in California.

This is another of the few haunted lighthouses in California. A tall ghostly woman with tangled hair and a flowing gown has been seen by local residents walking around the tower. According to local legends, the ghost is the first wife of the lighthouse keeper, who became lost and fell to her death off the sheer coastal cliffs in the area. Today, her ghostly form continues to haunt the area.

See for Yourself

Location: 31501 Palos Verdes Dr, Palos Verdes, CA 90274.

Red, White, and Blue Beach

This small stretch of beach near Santa Cruz is haunted by a particularly active ghost who appears on the average of about once a month! The ghost is that of an old sea captain. His ghost has been seen throughout the campground, and is blamed for a variety of poltergeist effects, including malfunctioning lights, slamming doors, moving objects, and more.

See for Yourself...Matey

Location: Six miles north of Santa Cruz on Highway 1.

Wheeler Canyon

Located north of Ojai in southern California, this undeveloped canyon is home to a phantom French sheepherder. According to legend, the sheepherder was murdered by rival cattleman more than a century earlier. Today his ghost continues to wander the hills, tending to his herd of sheep, which have long since left.

Location: Wheeler Canyon, north of Ojai.

12. California Ghost Tours

Because there are so many ghosts in California, a few professional ghost tours have been organized by various researchers. So, if you prefer to do your ghost hunting with an experienced guide, one of the following tours may be just what you're looking for. It's also nice to have the safety of other people, just in case something supernatural does occur.

Ghosts and Gravestones Tour

This professional tour promises "a spine-tingling trolley and walking tour of some of San Diego's most haunted sites." Location: 410 Island Ave, San Diego, CA. Phone: 1-800-868-7482. Website: www.historictours.com.

Dearly Departed Tours

This is a professional ghost tour through Hollywood focusing on the death sites of numerous celebrities, or well-known suicide/murder locations. The route includes haunted houses, hotels (including the Roosevelt), cemeteries, and other spooky locations. Tours are conducted daily. Location: 5419 Hollywood Blvd #C404, Hollywood, CA 90027. Phone: 323-466-3696. Website: www.dearlydepartedtours.com.

San Francisco Ghost Hunt

According to this touring company, "In the San Francisco Ghost Hunt we walk to some of San Francisco's most notorious haunted places, and meet the enchanting ghosts that call them home. You hear ghost stories based on serious documented research, see and touch eerie haunted artifacts and learn how you can catch a ghost." The tour is three hours long and is done on foot through the neighborhood of Pacific Heights. Visitors are shown various haunted buildings and structures. Location: Queen Anne Hotel, 1590 Sutter Ave, San Francisco, CA. Open daily. Phone: 415-922-5590.

Part Six
Psychic California

Psychic California: California has always been a Mecca for fortune tellers, psychics, palm readers, channelers, mediums, and other spiritually-based professions.

California has often been called the "psychic state," and certainly there are a lot of people here who make their money this way. As you drive through the major cities of California, you will find an unbelievably large number of signs, notices, and banners advertising psychic readings.

Growing up in California, I had my first psychic reading as a teenager, and following that, they came pretty regularly. I have since seen channelers, palm readers, fortune-tellers, mediums, healers, psychics, astrologers, tarot-card readers, and more. I can confidently report that many of these unique people have provided at least some accurate psychic information. I am totally convinced of the reality of psychics because I have witnessed them firsthand.

There is something incredibly thrilling and at the same time unnerving when you realize that there are certain people who can see into your past, present, and future, telling you private information about your personality, love life, career, health, financial situation, and many other secrets you may be trying to keep hidden.

There is something incredibly thrilling and at the same time unnerving when you realize that there are certain people who can see into your past, present, and future, telling you private information about your personality, love life, career, health, financial situation, and many other secrets you may be trying to keep hidden.

This part of the book is somewhat personal, but I have been so impressed by my visits to psychics that I strongly encourage other people to open their minds and give it a try. You just may be surprised.

1. Vivian Grace, Psychic Advisor

It's not hard to find a professional psychic in California. Every other street corner blazes brightly with glowing neon signs advertising psychic readings.

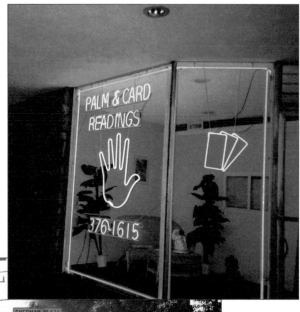

her quaint little home/office and sat behind a small table and began to look at my palms. She would not let me record the session.

She immediately told me what many psychics have told me, that I would have a long life and that I was an honest and sincere person. She said that I was the kind of person people depended on. This may have been true, but most people would say that this was true of themselves. Flattery can sometimes go a long way.

She then said that while I was happy with my job, it was also holding me back from doing what I really wanted to do. She said that I was working in another direction and that this thing that I was doing on the side was really beginning to take off. She was again correct on both accounts. While my accounting job pays the bills, my true passion is researching and writing about the supernatural. And, as Vivian saw, I had recently been doing very well in this area.

Vivian then touched on relationship and health issues, again surprising me with her accuracy. Then came something that gave me goose bumps. She said that spiritually she saw a female presence around me, someone that was very loving and very nurturing and protective. She said that there was a very strong bond between us and that she watches over me like an angel. She said that she is an older female whom I look up to.

This one gave me chills as it could only be my deceased mother, with whom I have had many incredible ghostly encounters.

Overall, I would give Vivian Grace a pretty high score. She never said anything that was way off, and she gave impressive specifics which convinced me of her psychic ability. I would definitely recommend her for those who are interested.

One of my first forays into psychic California was to a fortune-teller who lives near my home. Vivian Grace actually calls herself a psychic advisor. She reports that she is a sixth-generation psychic and has been doing readings since she was a teenager. With a $10.00 walk-in special, I figured I might as well take the plunge.

The $10.00 reading is a ten-minute long palm reading. Vivian also offers a $25.00 tarot card reading, a $40.00 past-life reading, and it goes up from there. I settled for the $10.00 reading. She invited me inside

See for Yourself

Contact Info: Vivian Grace, Canoga Park, CA.
Phone: 818-884-4818.

2. Ashley, Tarot Card & Palm Reader

As I drove along Sherman Way near my home, another glowing neon sign caught my attention: *Psychic Readings*. Sandwiched between an auto shop and an adult video store, I had never noticed the tiny office before. I pulled over and checked to see if I had any cash on hand. Thirty bucks ought to be enough, I figured. I got out and knocked on the door.

The door was answered by an attractive middle-aged woman of Latino ancestry who presented herself as Ashley. The charge for a reading was a reasonable twenty dollars.

Ashley led me to the next room. It was a small room, sparsely furnished with two comfortable easy-chairs and a little table. Various candles, new-age items, and pictures decorated the walls and a small shelf.

Ashley looked at me and said, "Have you been here before? You look familiar."

"No," I answered, though I had to admit she also looked very familiar to me. She tilted her head and asked, "Have you been to a psychic recently?"

I raised my eyebrows in surprise. "Yes, I have."

"How was it?"

"It was interesting."

"I see you're on a spiritual quest. You are seeking spiritual help."

I nodded. This was true, but pretty easy to conclude because, after all, I was seeing a psychic at that moment!

She asked what I did for a living. "I do accounting," I replied.

She nodded and asked me to shuffle the tarot cards. She then dealt them out and asked me what type of information I was seeking. I told her I wanted to know about relationships and career.

She started in with the standard lines. She told me I was a good person, friendly, honest, and giving. She said I was creative, hard-working, and easy-going. All perhaps true, but then again, doesn't everybody want to feel this way about themselves?

She then told me several correct and highly personal details about my current relationship. I was astounded by her accuracy. Like all good psychics, Ashley first touched on the past and present, and then predicted the future. As for her predictions, I am keeping those secret for now!

As far as career, this was the most exciting part of the reading. Ashley said that she saw that I have not had major financial problems, although I don't have a lot of money or expensive items. All true. Then she looked at me and said, "I'm getting that you are going to start your own business. I see this happening very soon. I see you actually being offered a partnership, and it's going to be very successful financially. I see no problems with money around you."

This part of the reading has not come true yet, but I can only wait and see.

The reading was winding to a close. Ashley told me that I would have to be spiritually strong to get through what might be a difficult year, with considerable obstacles to overcome. At this point, she tried to convince me of the necessity for further psychic consultations, but I politely declined.

Despite the hard sell at the end, I was still impressed by the reading.

See for Yourself

Contact information: Ashley. Canoga Park, CA.

She then told me several correct and highly personal details about my current relationship. I was astounded by her accuracy. Like all good psychics, Ashley first touched on the past and present, and then predicted the future. As for her predictions, I am keeping those secret for now!

3. Brian Hurst, Medium

For those who would like to meet their spirit guides or deceased loved ones, medium Brian Hurst of Reseda, California, is a Godsend. Born in England in 1938, Hurst had many early experiences with ghosts. As a child, he regularly saw apparitions and heard strange voices whispering messages in his head. At night, his bedroom would become crowded with ghosts.

As a young man, Hurst attended a series of séances and became deeply interested in spiritualism. At the same time, he continued having numerous mediumistic experiences. When he gave an impromptu reading for a friend, she was so impressed that she insisted Hurst could make a living as a professional medium.

Before long, Hurst was giving readings regularly. His reputation as an accurate and honest medium spread quickly and he became widely sought. In 1980 he moved to Reseda, California. Hurst's claim to fame is simple: he is incredibly accurate. With the help of his spirit guide, Doctor Grant, he is not only able to talk to the dead, but can also give psychic readings, health information, and future predictions. In fact, world famous medium James Van Praagh credits Hurst with predicting his own rise to fame as a medium.

Hurst holds meetings on the first Saturday of every month. The groups contain about forty people and are only available by reservation. I have attended the meetings on more than a dozen occasions, and have also attended two readings which are held with much smaller, private groups.

In the larger sessions, Hurst first gives an illuminating lecture on various aspects of mediumship, life after death, and ghosts. Then, after a short break and meditation, he begins to give readings. Each reading lasts about five to ten minutes. He picks various people out of the audience and basically bombards them with highly specific details regarding their lives or their deceased loved ones. Usually about one-third of the audience members receive a reading.

The second time I attended the group I got my first reading. Hurst turned to me and said, "I see books above your head. Do you have any connection with science fiction?"

"Yes," I answered. I used to be a huge fan.

"Because I see science-fiction books around you. Authors like Authur C. Clark, Robert Heinlein, Ray Bradbury."

"Yes," I replied. I had read all those authors. This guy was specific!

"Do you do writing?"

"Yes," I replied, shocked.

"Because the spirits are telling me that you do writing. You have a lot of creative ideas. They are telling me they like what you are doing and you will get published."

"I just found out yesterday I sold a piece!"

Everybody laughed and clapped. "See, I didn't know that. I don't know you. I see you writing many different things, maybe even something to do with this subject."

"Yes, that's true." I could only shake my head in awe. He had no idea that I had several books published about UFOs and the paranormal.

Hurst then moved away from me and began giving a reading to another person. I have since had four additional readings. On each occasion, Hurst gave details that he could not have possibly known. He told me that I had a tremendous interest in the paranormal. He saw a small Cessna-type plane over my head. My father is a pilot. He saw that a small shed had recently been built near my father's home. He knew that I and my family are interested in moving out of Los Angeles and to a more rural area in northern California. During one reading he said, "Who is Florence? Florence is here." That was my grandmother. He gave me many other personal details which no stranger should be able to know. I found the experience of being read by Hurst to be exhilarating, a little unnerving, but mostly incredibly interesting.

I have also heard Hurst give readings to dozens of other people, including my sister-in-law Christy, who was moved to tears by the accuracy of the details. As he gives his readings, one cannot help but be astonished by the specificity of the many unusual details.

For those who would like more information, they are highly advised to read Hurst's excellent autobiography, *Heaven Can Help*.

I was very impressed by Hurst and give him an extremely high rating. I am not only convinced of his honesty and integrity, but I am awe-struck by the incredible connection he has to the spirit world. Anybody who wants communication from a deceased loved one is highly recommended to reserve a meeting.

Hurst holds monthly group sessions in his home in Reseda. The price is ten dollars and is by reservation only. For those who would like to attend a smaller group with a higher chance of getting a reading, the price is a reasonable forty dollars and again is by reservation only.

See for Yourself

Location: Brian Edward Hurst. Reseda, CA. Phone: 818-345-2997. Please call only between 9:00-11:00 am on the 1st, 2nd or 3rd of each month.

4. Selacia, Channeler and Healer

Another phenomenon that has taken root in California is known as channeling. In these cases, people claim to be in communication with Enlightened Masters from the spirit realm who impart sage advice or give healing energies. Others claim to channel extraterrestrials. One prominent figure in the southern California New Age scene is an attractive blond woman by the name of Selacia. Selacia channels the "Council of Twelve" and performs "DNA healings." The price is $100.00 dollars for a fifty-minute session.

While I had seen several psychics, a healing channeler sounded like something a little different. So, using research for this book as an excuse, I plopped down the hundred bucks and scheduled a session.

I chose to get a "DNA healing and activation." Selacia called me on the phone (apparently distance is no obstacle to psychic healers) at the appointed time and explained what would happen. First she would go into a trance where she would be able to clairvoyantly see my energy field and DNA structure. Then, with my permission, she would activate my DNA. This would occur throughout my body and would cause a facilitation in healing and enlightenment. While in trance, she would receive channeled messages which she would relay to me. She asked me what issues were concerning me most.

Selacia says, "The activation – what it does is, it helps you become more connected to all parts of yourself, more aware, and through that process, also more aware of your gifts as well as what's in the way of what you want ... You become more immune and your health gets a boost. You can more easily fight off the stuff that's out there, the viruses and stuff. That's one of the benefits of the activation. But at the same time, becoming more aware also means having more conscious awareness of: 'Okay, this is what I do in relationships, maybe this is why this is not working.' The healing not only heals and raises awareness, it also makes it easier to connect to your past lives."

Selacia says that she is able to activate all the DNA in one session, but it takes awhile to integrate and show its effects. The activation only needs to be done once, and it remains permanent. Says Selacia, "I go into that deep state of Theta and a part of me basically connects with your space and I actually see in there."

Then the actual session began. Selacia instructed me to simply relax while she went into trance. I lay there and allowed Selacia to do her thing. When she next spoke several minutes later, she told me that she had entered into my bio-energetic field and had activated my DNA, which she said was actually already partially activated. I can't say that I felt anything other than a soothing relaxation.

Afterwards, Selacia explained that she went into my energy field and was able to successfully activate the DNA in all my cells. "I went through your whole body. What it looked like to me was like I would be in the head, the heart, the arms, and it would light up. Okay, it's done here, it's complete."

During the session, Selacia also obtained intuitive impressions. "Almost as soon as I went into your space I saw two angels that are right around you. They came forward. I don't know if you are aware of them, or if you talk to them. But these are maybe not the only two that are around you, but these are the two I saw today. And they're with you a lot, including when you do your out-of-body work, when you do inner work, when you do healing. And I got their functions. Basically the first one is helping you to synthesize and transmit information in the world, further developing your mind and your gift of mental focus and precision. And it's definitely helping with that. The second one is helping with matters of the heart. Interestingly, what I was shown is that you tend to pay more attention to the first one...and that sometimes you don't pick up on the messages or what the second one is trying to show you. That's very typical for us in these human forms. Because when we have spirit interacting with us, it can be all kinds of ways...we don't always pay attention to that kind of stuff. Speaking of synthesizing, they were saying that this is a lifetime where you are synthesizing teachings and universal truths, from many planes of existence, past, present, and future. And that was just for you to know or be reminded of."

Selacia returned back from her trance to state a few times to me surprisingly accurate information about my personal relationships and other issues. She would then go back into a trance state to conduct more activations and receive more impressions.

Selacia perceived that I had at least two major angels working with me. One was helping me with relationships, but I wasn't listening very well. Another, however, was helping me to bring together and organize information from a wide variety of sources, which would assist me in my writing endeavors.

This didn't surprise me because numerous times I have been seemingly magically guided to certain books, people or events that have helped me immensely in my research. Overall I found the session satisfying and very intriguing. While I can't verify the DNA aspect, I can say that the information she provided was positive, accurate, and helpful.

See for Yourself

Phone: 310-915-2884. www.Selacia.com

5. Sylvia Browne, Psychic Medium

One of the most famous psychics in California (if not the world) is Sylvia Browne. The author of more than a dozen books, and a consultant to the police, doctors, and countless private clients, Sylvia Browne has been providing incredibly accurate psychic readings for most of her life.

Browne gives thousands of readings per year. Her services are in such high demand that the waiting list can be up to a year. Although she is one of the more expensive psychics (readings start at $700.00), her reputation as a genuine psychic has guaranteed that she will be busy for a long time.

I got on the waiting list in 2003 and had my reading later that year. I had seen her on the "Montel Williams Show" many times and couldn't have been more excited.

To my delight, she called me at my home exactly at the appointed time. She politely introduced herself and told me that she would tell me whatever came to her, good or bad. She said that I should give her no information other than if the event she is describing has already happened or if it might be in the future. I requested to record the conversation and the session began.

Sylvia first said that she was sensing a problem with my back. "How have you been doing with your lower back and upper stomach area?"

I gulped, and said that yes, that I was having some problems in both those areas. I had been doing sit-ups to keep my back strong, but stopped out of laziness. So when Sylvia recommended doing sit-ups to strengthen my back, I realized that I had better get back on my old exercise routine. Incidentally, I didn't and I had a terrible pinched nerve about a month later. Needless to say, I now do my sit-ups regularly.

I had also recently been having problems with an overly acidic stomach. Sylvia said that my stomach problem was caused by too many caffeinated and carbonated drinks, which were also disturbing my sleep-cycle and making me tired. I laughed. She was right on all three accounts.

"What is this, a promotion your going to get? Because it looks like a job or career change."

When Sylvia said this, I was skeptical. But she insisted that she was correct. "Yeah, in March, somebody's going to come looking for you…somebody comes to you to be an administrator, human resourcer, and it comes in March. But that's good because it's more money too."

She then turned to another subject. "What's this about moving? Because it looks like you're going to be moving."

This comment made me skeptical, but also excited. I have lived in the same condominium for nearly fifteen years. On the other hand, I had recently been thinking about selling it and buying a house with a yard and a garden. Unfortunately, with my current salary, it was out of the question. Still, I really wanted to live on the ground again.

Sylvia again insisted that I was going to move. "You will next year. Wait until this whole thing starts developing with more money, and then you'll be able to buy a property. Probably around September or October of next year."

She then moved onto relationships. First she talked about my past relationships and then moved on to the present and future. I have to admit, she was pretty accurate and specific. As far as the future predictions, again I'll just have to wait and see.

Sylvia then said that the good news is that according to my "chart," a kind of psychic blueprint of my life, I was right on track. She said that two years ago was one of the worst times of my life, but that now things were falling into place.

I shook my head in disbelief. Again, she was right. I asked her about my UFO connection. Although I have no memories of any onboard UFO experience, I feel a strong connection to UFOs. Sylvia said flat out, "I think it came from when you were a kid…I think you had a visitation. I bet if you went under regression you could find it…It happened when you were four." Sylvia then asked me if I had any other questions. At this point, my mind was a little blown, and I wasn't really thinking clearly. I wanted to ask about my deceased mother, but I totally forgot! Instead, my mind's eye kept seeing Sylvia surrounded by this bright white light, which felt like it was also surrounding me. I couldn't think of any other questions, so Sylvia politely ended the call.

Although the reading was expensive and lasted only about fifteen minutes, I was impressed not only by Sylvia's accuracy, but by the physical feeling of the experience. It gave me a weird feeling of elation and timelessness. As far as her predictions, they haven't come true yet. The promotion part may be developing. I can only wait and see.

My only main regret is forgetting to ask for a communication from my deceased mother and not asking more questions. Also, the price is somewhat prohibitive for most people. I rationalized it by telling myself it was for this book, and put it on my credit card. Still, it was by far the most expensive reading I've ever paid for. However, it was also definitely among the best.

See for Yourself

Contact information: Sylvia Browne. 35 Dillon Ave. Campbell CA 95008. (408) 379-7070. Website: www. sylvia.org.

6. The International Academy of Consciousness

Flight
Instructions

Would you like to learn how to go out of your body? Are you ready to travel with your astral body into other dimensions beyond Earth? If the answer to these questions is yes, then the International Academy of Consciousness (IAC) is for you!

The IAC was founded in 2000 in Brazil, however today it has offices throughout the world, in Australia, England, Holland, Italy, Portugal, Spain, and the United States, including Los Angeles, California. It is a non-profit research and educational organization dedicated to the study of consciousness through the out-of-body experience.

The IAC offers seminars and classes to interested students. I first heard about the IAC while surfing the internet. Having studied and practiced astral travel for years (see my book *Out-of-Body Exploring: A Beginner's Approach*), I was delighted to discover that other people were as interested in the out-of-body experience as I was. I immediately signed up for their introductory seminar.

Don't
Believe Anything

The IAC is located in downtown Los Angeles in a modern office building. It seems somewhat out-of-place next to the other mainstream doctors' offices. The main office is a small classroom with about thirty seats. The walls are decorated with paintings showing people leaving their bodies and IAC slogans such as: "DON'T BELIEVE ANYTHING. EXPERIMENT. HAVE YOUR OWN EXPERIENCES."

The International Academy of Consciousness. This modern mystic school teaches the ancient phenomenon of out-of-body travel. *Photo credit: IAC.*

I sat down in the front row and looked around at the other attendees. There was about ten other people: two young couples, an older gentleman, a middle-aged man, and a few others: all normal-looking people.

Our instructor this evening was Luis Minero, an astral traveler, researcher, teacher, and a chemist by profession. He began by introducing himself and the subject of out-of-body experiences. He explained that we all have an astral body, our "soul," and that we all have out-of-body experiences each night, we just don't remember. He said that the ability to travel consciously out of the body can be learned by anybody through simple exercises.

Once out-of-body, the astral traveler can fly, move through solid objects, travel into other dimensions, visit deceased loved ones, learn about their past lives and their current life mission, and much more. By going out of body, one loses the all-pervasive fear of death.

Recovering Thirty
Lost Years!

Most people sleep about eight hours every day. That means, if you live to age ninety, you will have slept a total of thirty years! By going out-of-body, one is able to be conscious during the sleep state, and essentially extend their life experience by one third.

Minero explained that dreams and OBEs, while connected, are different phenomena, and that the out-of-body state represents a superior state of consciousness. The IAC is composed of several hundred scientists who use the OBE as a tool to study consciousness. They have conducted numerous laboratory experiments in which they have obtained veridical (truthful) information confirming the validity of the out-of-body experience.

According to the IAC, the out-of-body experience is completely safe, with no dangers of injury, possession, or getting lost or locked out of your body. In fact, the evidence shows the opposite, that the OBE is beneficial in numerous ways.

From Secret Schools of Knowledge

The seminar was a basic introduction to the subject of astral travel. Afterwards, Minero talked about the actual courses offered by the IAC. He first pointed out that much of the information presented in the courses is hundreds of years old, and during the Middle Ages was only available in esoteric secret schools of knowledge taught only to a select few people. Today, however, the information is available to the public. No special qualifications are needed, only the interest, desire, and discipline.

The main IAC courses are comprised of four ten-hour workshops titled the "Consciousness Development Program." As the brochure says, "CDP is designed to provide participants with the groundwork and techniques to master their out-of-body experiences and bioenergies. Every class has practical exercises, which allow the instructor to closely monitor the development of the participant. The program also addresses subjects related to the understanding of nonphysical reality and strives to enable the participant to achieve a greater awareness and consciential (spiritual) maturity through his own experience, without any kind of dependence. The CDP covers a vast amount of information, which given gradually, allows the learner to enhance self-control. It also has purely practical classes in OBE techniques."

Information...Given Gradually

CDP 1 covers the basics of projection, including the benefits of the OBE, theories, laboratory experiments, an introduction to bioenergetics, the abilities of the astral bodies, preparations, and sensations prior to exiting the body, and an analysis of the astral dimensions.

CDP 2 gives five methods to achieve the OBE, presents an introduction to paranormal and psychic phenomena, non-ordinary states of consciousness, telepathy, spirit-guides, and the various astral bodies.

CDP 3 gives eight more OBE methods and describes more advanced astral dimensions, spiritual evolution, out-of-body awareness, karma, ethics, and more.

CDP 4 gives six more OBE methods and discusses advanced topics such as the "multi-existential cycle...life-task planning" and other highly esoteric concepts.

The IAC offers two other extension courses for the advanced student. Both are three-day workshops which involve classes, real-time OBE and bioenergetic exercises, group discussions, and more. To take this course, students must have already taken CDP 4 as a prerequisite.

While I attended only the introductory seminar, I have read the materials provided by the IAC, including the autobiography of and several books by the founder, Waldo Viera.

Objective and Scientific

The IAC approaches the subject objectively and scientifically, with an emphasis on facts gained from first-hand experience. For those who are interested in learning the ability of conscious astral projection, I can confidently say that the IAC provides the information one needs to perfect this ability.

See for Yourself

Again, the IAC has offices worldwide. In the United States, it has offices in New York, Miami, and Los Angeles. The introductory seminar is free. The CDP courses start at a minimum of $95.00 for one course and a maximum of $335.00 for all four courses, which can be repeated at no extra cost.

Location: International Association of Consciousness. 3961 Sepulveda Blvd #207, Culver City, CA 90039. Phone: 310-482-0000 (toll free:877-IAC-4OBE). Fax: 310-482-0001. Email: California@iacworld.org.

Psychic Resources Abound

As can be seen, for those interested in psychic phenomena, California is the perfect place to be. The *Yellow Pages* devotes several pages to various psychics, channelers, healers, palm readers, and other spiritual consultants. But be warned, this particular field is well known for attracting hoaxers and swindlers. However, with a few guidelines, you should have a safe and enjoyable experience.

Useful Tips

First, reveal as little information as possible to the psychic. Make sure that you are not feeding them information through a game of twenty questions, or that they are obtaining their details from your body language.

Second, look for specific details. A bad psychic talks in vague generalities, giving you information that could fit just about anyone. A good psychic will provide highly personal and specific details that nobody else could know, and applies directly to you.

Third, beware of the "hard sell" technique. Some psychics will try to use fear or flattery to part you from your money, or they may try to make you dependent on them for further information. Also, some people can become addicted to psychic readings. While a psychic can provide meaningful insights into your life and profound glimpses of the future, nobody knows more about you than you. Never allow a psychic to run your life. The true answers always come from within.

Otherwise, keep an open mind and have fun. Your future is waiting!

Part Seven
California UFO Hotspots

One of the most persistent mysteries of modern times is the UFO phenomenon. The evidence for extraterrestrial visitation is, by standard classification of evidence, totally conclusive. The evidence comes in many forms, including eyewitness testimonies supported by lie detectors, photographs and moving films, audiotapes, physiological effects (including injuries and healings), electromagnetic effects, metal fragments, animal reactions, implant removal cases, landing trace cases, crash-retrieval reports, and thousands of pages of official United States Government documents declassified through the Freedom of Information Act (FOIA) detailing case after case.

Most skeptics vastly underestimate the amount and quality of UFO evidence. As it turns out, California produces more UFO reports than any other state in the nation. There are currently more than 5,000 recorded encounters, with more reports coming in on a daily basis.

Why California is such a UFO hotspot remains a mystery. Writes prominent California ufologist Bill Hamilton, "Some say it is the Santa Ana winds that created the weird culture of the West Coast. The inhabitants think differently. Westerners are open to new ideas. Visitors from another planet are welcome in California."

In 2003 and 2004, I conducted a comprehensive study of all California UFO encounters, the results of which were published in my book *UFOS Over California* (Schiffer, 2005). To my amazement, I found that UFO activity was occurring in every corner of California. It seemed that the state itself was one gigantic hotspot.

For this book, however, I will focus only on those particular California locations that have consistently produced a disproportionately large number UFO reports for a long period of time. California has several well-known active UFO hotspots, also known as flap areas, and we will examine each in detail.

1. The California Deserts

The vast desert areas outside of Los Angeles produce a high number of UFO reports, especially in the Antelope Valley area.

Welcome to
"Aerospace Valley"

North of Los Angeles lies the Antelope Valley and the surrounding cities of Palmdale, Lancaster, Mojave, Tehachapi, and other nearby desert communities. This area encompasses several hundred square miles. It is not only the location of much of our aviation research, it has also been a hotbed of incredible UFO activity for decades.

Writes Bill Hamilton, "Aerospace Valley would be a good nickname for the Antelope Valley of Southern California. On the north side of the valley is the sprawling Edwards AFB, site of many interesting UFO encounters. On the south side of the valley is Air Force Plant 42 in Palmdale where they rolled out the B2 Stealth Bomber. Northrop has a plant nearby and Lockheed-Martin 'skunkworks' occupies a large imposing building just east of Sierra Highway. On the extreme east end of the valley is a secret Douglas electromagnetic research facility, and on the west side of the valley is the secret Northrop electromagnetic research facility, the Anthill in the Tehachapi Mountains." (Hamilton, 90)

As any UFO researcher will tell you, extraterrestrials are attracted to military and technological installations. What's most surprising about the Antelope Valley and surrounding areas is that the sightings are not better known.

Of Astronauts
and UFOs

The first wave of sightings began in July of 1947 and was centered around Muroc AFB (which would later be renamed Edwards AFB.) The sightings continued regularly through the 1950s. Astronaut Gordon Cooper was at Edwards AFB in 1958 when a metallic disk landed on the dry lakebed and was observed and filmed by several crewmen. Cooper developed and watched the film of the object, which he forwarded to officials in Washington D.C. Says Cooper, "It was a typical circular-shaped UFO. Not too many people saw it, because it took off at quite a sharp angle and just climbed out of sight…I think it was definitely a UFO." (Greer, 76-77)

Fast Jets, Faster Disks

On October 7, 1965, another wave of sightings occurred over Edwards. Numerous jets were scrambled after several unidentified craft that were maneuvering over the base. They were unable to catch the disks.

Sightings continued to occur. In 1967, a pilot flying over Edwards AFB was chased by six UFOs. In 1978, a construction worker next to the base in Mojave observed a small transparent sphere that hovered overhead and then sped towards Edwards.

Keeping Tabs

On October 5, 1987, a family of three observed a large, spinning, disk-shaped object with lights around the perimeter pass at a low altitude over their home located in Palmdale, next to Edwards AFB.

On July 6, 1988, a resident of Lancaster saw two dark ice-cream cone-shaped objects fly low over her backyard and then take off.

On October 26, 1988, numerous residents in west Antelope Valley observed a fleet of saucer-shaped objects surrounding a large boomerang-shaped object flying north towards Tehachapi.

On July 9, 1989, a security guard at Air Force Plant 52 observed a silvery disk hovering nearby the base. One week later, the object returned and was followed by three round spheres. The security officer reported the sighting to his superiors. A helicopter was sent to intercept the objects, which promptly flew away.

The sightings continue. November 18, 1989, Robert Puskus reported his sighting of a 900-foot black boomerang-shaped object pass silently over the valley.

March 3, 1991, Pearl Schultz and Aric Leavitt observed five or six objects moving and darting over the Techachapi mountains.

February 23, 1991, several witnesses, including one pilot, observed four white glowing objects hovering over the Tehachapi mountains.

February 26, 1991, Betty Murray was in downtown Lancaster when she observed a thirty-five-foot dark gray metallic disk hover low over a traffic signal.

Zigzagging and Darting

On May 28, 1991, Bill Hamilton and three others observed three anomalous lighted objects hovering over the west end of Lancaster. They returned the next evening with ten additional witnesses. Together, they observed no less than thirty objects! Writes Hamilton, "Several of these zigzagged at all points of the compass. Two of these also disappeared when in full view." (Hamilton, 148-149)

Hamilton reports that the sightings continued strong throughout the summer, with reports coming in from Lancaster, Victorville, and the surrounding communities. The year 1992 brought a new flood of reports, many of which involved a "dark, triangular, silent object" moving over the San Gabriel mountains. On April 15, 1992, researcher Richard Boylan staked out an area east of Edwards AFB at the Tejon Ranch in the Tehachapi mountains where he observed several highly unusual craft that appear to be ET craft being flown by human beings. Boylan calls the location, "California's Black Budget Palmdale-Lancaster region."

On June 8, 1993, a local sheriff's deputy from Rosamond observed a bright white object hovering motionless in the sky. He then observed the object from his work in Palmdale. This began a series of sightings lasting several months. He was able to bring in numerous witnesses who also observed multiple UFOs, including darting lights, silent boomerang-shaped objects, and more. During one event, the witness was able to snap several photographs of the object. The sightings continued strong through October.

In April 1994, more reports came in of darting objects in the night sky. In 1995, an anonymous civilian witness driving by Edwards observed a large, silver, disk-shaped object moving quickly at a low altitude at a distance of 100 feet.

In December 1998, a Victorville resident observed a "silvery disk" surrounded by several smaller "orbs." As the witness says, "Often we see strange craft coming out of Edwards AFB nearby."

Two Kinds of Sightings

As can be seen, this area is a major hotspot of activity. Apparently there are two kinds of sightings occurring in this area. One involves genuine extraterrestrials who are keeping tabs on our technology. The second involves human test-flights of reverse-engineered ET craft. In either case, the area is well-known for regularly producing UFO reports.

See for Yourself

The Antelope Valley is located north of Los Angeles. Take Highway 5 to Highway 14, also called the Antelope Valley Freeway. The valley opens up to the cities of Lancaster, Palmdale, Rosamond, Victorville, Tehachapi, and Mojave.

2. Tujunga Canyon

Deep in the heart of Tujunga Canyon. It's not hard to believe that UFOs and Bigfoot are attracted to this remote mountain area north of Los Angeles.

Of Missing Time and Flap Areas

Located north of Los Angeles, along the southern edge of the Angeles National Forest in the Angeles Crest Mountains, is Tujunga Canyon. This area first came to the attention of ufologists in 1975 when a resident of the area reported a UFO encounter involving missing time. Prominent southern California investigator Ann Druffel began an investigation. She quickly discovered that many people in the area were having dramatic encounters. Further research revealed a long history of encounters.

Writes Druffel, "The Tujunga Canyons are themselves a hotbed of UFO activity and were so even back in the early 1950s.... Even before Southland research-ers began taking an active interest in the area, however, Tujunga had contributed its share of reports to the Southern California catchall, though it was definitely not recognized as a flap area at that time....We decided to research the canyons' ufological history, basing our study on old newspaper accounts, to determine whether it was, indeed, a flap area as far back as 1953. Our search was positive; in fact, the volume of sightings from this area as far back as 1949 proved astonishing. Although no organized, scientifically oriented research groups were gathering information of UFOs at that time, many citizens reported their sightings to their local papers." (Druffel, 148-149)

The sightings cover not only Tujunga, but the surrounding communities of Glendale, Sunland, San Fernando, and La Crescenta.

Sightings in the 1940s and 1950s

On May 2, 1949, two Glendale residents observed a classic silver disk fly low overhead in the noonday sky.

On May 20, 1949 eighteen witnesses in Glendale observed a large, transparent, oval-shaped object which hovered at a low altitude overhead, emitting a low buzzing noise before disappearing.

On the morning of March 10, 1950, multiple residents in La Crescenta observed a triangular-shaped object move silently overhead. Later that evening, more witnesses reported their sighting of an object over nearby Burbank, coming from the direction of Tujunga.

On October 7, 1950, a pilot and copilot were flying at 4500 feet when they observed an unknown object covered with strange lights turn sharply below them and move off.

On August 25, 1952, numerous Glendale residents observed a golden sphere with a reddish tail zip across the sky.

Bedroom Visitations... Among Other Things

On March 22, 1953, two young ladies experienced a missing time encounter while staying in their cabin in a remote location of Tujunga Canyon. Over the next twenty-five years, the two ladies and four additional friends would experience a series of sightings, bedroom visitations, and onboard encounters. At the time, they had no idea that they were living in the middle of a UFO hotspot.

On January 25, 1954, Rose Sockett of Glendale reported her sighting of two unidentified objects hovering and spinning in the sky above her home for a period of fifteen minutes.

Multiple Witnesses

On May 19, 1955, more than a thousand residents of Tujunga and the surrounding communities observed three silver-colored objects hovering for a period of at least fifteen minutes. Some witnesses were able to use binoculars but were still unable to identify the craft.

On August 28, 1957, two Glendale residents used binoculars to observe an unknown object that hovered completely motionless in the sky above Tujunga.

On September 27, 1957, Glendale residents reported their sighting of a glowing object following two military jets.

Sightings of the 1960s and 1970s

In 1967, three friends followed a UFO from their home in North Hollywood deep into Tujunga Canyon, where they experienced a close-up sighting and possible missing time.

Of Helicopters and UFOs

On September 3, 1975, three Tujunga residents were drawn outside by the sound of a helicopter. Looking up, they saw the helicopter, and above the helicopter was an unidentified glowing object. The helicopter circled around the object in a surveillance pattern. When more helicopters showed up, the unknown object quickly darted away.

In 1977, two Tujunga law enforcement officers were on routine helicopter patrol over La Crescenta when they observed a glowing metallic cylinder dart by their helicopter in excess of 100 miles per hour.

More sightings could be listed, but by now the pattern should be clear. For whatever reason, Tujunga Canyon and the surrounding area is a major UFO hotspot. And as every UFO researcher will tell you, the vast majority of people do not report their sightings. Therefore, when a location like Tujunga produces a flood of reports, the chances are good that the reported sightings represent only the tip of the iceberg.

See for Yourself

Tujunga Canyon can be reached by taking the 210 Freeway (also called the Foothill Freeway), which travels along the southern edge of Tujunga, Sunland, and La Crescenta. Tujunga Canyon itself is bisected by two main roads, Big Tujunga Road and Little Tujunga Road. Both of these steep and winding roads climb through rural sections of the canyons, with plenty of remote turn-offs for UFO watching.

On May 19, 1955, more than a thousand residents of Tujunga and the surrounding communities observed three silver-colored objects hovering for a period of at least fifteen minutes. Some witnesses were able to use binoculars but were still unable to identify the craft.

3. Topanga Canyon

The north edge Topanga Canyon. Dozens of witnesses have observed UFOs scooting low between the canyon walls of this coastal community.

The center of Topanga Canyon and the location of many dramatic UFO encounters.

Topanga State Park. UFOs have been seen landing in this field on several occasions.

Located in the Santa Monica mountains, northwest of Los Angeles along the coast of southern California, this area may be California's most active hotspot. Literally hundreds of encounters have occurred over this mountain range, which includes Topanga Canyon, Santa Monica, and Malibu.

The full story of Topanga Canyon is told in my book, *UFOs Over Topanga Canyon* (Llewellyn, 1999), which presents a comprehensive history of the encounters. Here we shall examine some of the better-known encounters and try to determine the patterns of activity over the area.

Forty Years of Sightings

Encounters in this area stretch back to at least February 25, 1942, when thousands of people observed a large glowing object move over the Santa Monica Mountains and hover over Los Angeles.

In 1950, Freida X. observed a "silver bar" hanging motionless in the sky above her Topanga Canyon home.

Missing Time

In the summer of 1962, a mother and her two daughters experienced a missing time encounter while driving back to their home from the local Topanga market.

Star-like, Egg-shaped, and Anomalous

The 1970s brought a flood of reports. In 1972, an anonymous Malibu resident observed a star-like object darting across the night sky.

The year 1974 brought three more reports, one involving a star-like object, another involving a large, hovering egg-shaped object, and a third involving a four-foot amber-colored disk hovering one hundred feet away from the witnesses.

In 1975, three reports were made of anomalous lights at night. In each case, the objects were observed by multiple witnesses.

On January 21, 1976, Gary Humecke was driving along a canyon road in Malibu when he observed an oval-shaped object with colored lights hovering over a nearby gully. Later that year, three witnesses were walking along Henry Ridge along the west edge of Topanga Canyon when they observed a star-like object darting at right angles.

More Recent Reports

The sightings continued with about two cases per year, all the way up to the 1990s. Then in 1992, Topanga Canyon and the surrounding areas experienced a huge wave of activity.

On June 14, 1992, more than fifteen independent witnesses observed UFO activity over Topanga Canyon. Four witnesses actually called the local police, saying that they were chased down the road by UFOs or were woken up out of a sound sleep by an object hovering over their home, flooding it with light.

Other witnesses called the local Topanga newspaper, *The Messenger*, reporting their sightings of darting star-like lights and unusual beams of light coming from above.

The sightings continued at a feverish pace for more than two years, generating more than forty reported cases! I myself have seen UFOs in Topanga on several occasions. Each case occurred during the 1992-1994 wave and involved anomalous lights in the night sky.

First-Hand Observations

I myself have seen UFOs in Topanga on a half-dozen occasions. In 1992, while driving through the canyon at around 9:00 p.m., I observed a bright, white sphere of light hovering over the Topanga State Park area.

In July of 1994, the television program "Encounters" conducted a live investigation in Topanga and actually observed a large orange-white object bobbing up and down a nearby ridge. The crew was able to capture a few feet of film, clearly showing the bright sphere of light. I was able to observe the object through a powerful pair of binoculars. I still couldn't identify the light.

A few weeks later, I led another group up into the Topanga State Park area and I observed another anomalous light. While nobody else in the group saw it, other witnesses to the event surfaced a few weeks later.

Gigantic Sphere

In the fall of 2004 I received a call from another Topanga resident who told me that she was recently woken up in the middle of the night to find her house flooded with light. She ran outside and observed a gigantic sphere of white light hovering near her home, sending off huge beams or arcs of light. After a few moments, it disappeared or moved quickly away.

One day, in the fall of 1994, I was visiting a friend who lived on Saddle Peak, one of the highest points in Topanga, when we both observed an extremely bright flash of light over the canyon ridge. It was way too bright to be anything conventional. It was gone as fast as it had appeared.

In 2001, "The Learning Channel" contacted me, interested in trying to make contact. I organized a small group and we traveled with the crew to an undisclosed and remote spot in the canyon. As soon as the crew attempted to switch the film in their cameras, a bright white object swooped forward, hovered over a nearby hillside, and quickly darted away.

> I myself have seen UFOs in Topanga on several occasions. Each case occurred during the 1992-1994 wave and involved anomalous lights in the night sky.

See for Yourself

As can be seen, if you want to see a UFO, Topanga Canyon has more than its share of activity. The entire Santa Monica Mountain Range seems to attract the activity, including the cities of Agoura, Camarillo, Ventura, Malibu, Topanga Canyon, Santa Monica, and Woodland Hills. The adjacent San Fernando Valley has also had its share of encounters.

It's difficult to pinpoint the best viewing spots to see a UFO simply because the area is so active. Some choice spots include: Saddle Peak, a road which winds along the peaks of Topanga Canyon; Santa Susanna Pass at the extreme north end of Topanga Canyon Boulevard has produced a number of reports; and the Top O' Topanga Outlook, which overlooks the San Fernando Valley to the north and Topanga Canyon to the south, is another good spot. Reports come regularly from Old Topanga Canyon Road and all along Highway 21 or Topanga Canyon Boulevard, which stretches from the coast north through Woodland Hills, Canoga Park, and Chatsworth. Trippett Ranch in Topanga State Park up Entrada Road has also produced literally dozens of reports.

4. An Underwater UFO Base

Photo by Young Chyren of a metallic saucer hovering over Santa Monica Bay in 2004. *Photo credit: Young Chyren, courtesy of ufoevidence.org.*

While many underwater encounters up and down the California coast are presented in my book, *UFOs Over California*, I have since uncovered more reports and further confirming information regarding one particular area of California coastline which has produced an abnormally large concentration of encounters. This section of coastline, which stretches from at least as far south as Palos Verdes Peninsula and as far north as Santa Barbara, has been and continues to be an incredible hotbed of UFO activity.

Five Decades of Offshore Activity

For more than fifty years, UFOs have been seen not only above this body of water, but coming *in and out of it.* All the evidence points towards the existence of an un-

Numerous underwater UFO reports point to the strong possibility of an underwater UFO base somewhere in the Santa Catalina Channel.

derwater UFO base somewhere deep along or around the Santa Catalina Channel.

Experts Agree

While underwater UFOs have been seen in California as far back as 1947, it wasn't until the mid-1950s that this particular stretch of southern California coastline became the focus of extraterrestrial visitations. Writes southern California researcher Ann Druffel, "This body of water lies between the coastlines of southern California and Santa Catalina Island, twenty miles offshore to the southwest. The area has for at least thirty years been the scene of UFO reports of all kinds – surface sightings of hazy craft which cruise leisurely in full view of military installations, aerial spheres bobbing in oscillating flight, gigantic cloud-cigars, and at least one report of an underwater UFO with uniformed occupants." (Rogo, 160)

Most southern California UFO investigators can only nod their heads in agreement. Writes Bill Hamilton, "For years witnesses have seen many types of UFO cruising off the Palos Verdes Peninsula in southern California. UFOs have actually been seen to come out of the water in the San Pedro Channel." (Hamilton, 107-112)

Family Night at the Beach

Another investigator is Robert Stanley, editor of the now-defunct magazine, *Unicus.* Writes Stanley, "Well, even in the 'sixties, families were going down to the beach and waiting for a UFO to pass by…By the 1970s, whole families were going down to the beach at Point Dume at night to watch the multi-colored UFOs [that] would sink under the water at times." (Stanley, 16-17, 31)

Formation Flight

In 1953, engineer Frederick Hehr observed a "squadron of saucers" performing maneuvers over the Santa Monica Bay. He and several others observed the objects on two separate occasions on the same day, lasting about ten minutes each.

UFO Rising

On August 8, 1954, the crew of the steamship Aliki were outside Long Beach when they had a dramatic sighting of a glowing object that moved in and out of the ocean and then flew away.

UFO Tracks Boat

On July 10, 1955, a family of three named Washington was boating thirteen miles off the coast of Newport Beach on their way to Catalina Island when they observed a "perfectly round, gray-white" craft about 2500 feet above their boat. When the object maintained its position over their boat, the Washingtons radioed the Coast Guard. The Coast Guard sent out a plane to investigate, but the object darted away.

Submersible UFOs

On January 15, 1956, in Redondo Beach, dozens of witnesses including security officers and policemen observed a large, glowing object glide down out of the sky and float on the surface of the ocean about seventy-five yards offshore. The object then sank beneath the waves, although its glow could still be seen. Divers were called in to investigate, but by then the object was gone.

Less than one month later, on February 9, military personnel observed a fireball-like object which struck the water and submerged.

Encounter with the S.S. *Ramsey*

The sightings continued on a regular basis. In December 1957, a crewman on the British Steamship S.S. *Ramsey*, off the coast of San Pedro, sighted and photographed a large metallic-gray disk with antennae-like projections which hovered over the ship only a few hundred feet away.

Not a Submarine?

On July 28, 1962, the skipper of a chartered fishing boat in the Santa Catalina Channel observed what he thought was a Russian submarine with five men on top, dressed in strange clothing. Says the anonymous captain, "I was certain it was a submarine low in the water, steel gray, no markings, deck almost awash, with only its tail and odd aft-structure showing."

While the captain assumed it was a Russian submarine, it seemed unusual for it to be so close to the shore and remain in view. Then suddenly it performed a maneuver which left the captain amazed. The mystery sub moved towards the boat as if to ram it. The captain made an emergency turn to avoid the sub, which moved past them at high speed, emitting no noise and leaving no wake except for a "good-sized swell."

Concerned, the captain contacted the Navy, but after reviewing photographs of various submarines, the captain was still unable to identify it. The case was investigated by famed UFO investigators Jim and Coral Lorenzen, who write, "This high surface speed, lack of wake and sound, and the huge swell makes this object suspect." One might also mention the odd shape of the submarine itself, and its lack of fear of observation. (Lorenzen & Lorenzen 1968, 52)

Of Actors, Therapists, and UFOs

Sometime in 1960, actor Chad Everett was on the rooftop of his home in Beverly Hills when he and two friends observed a bright object darting back and forth at high speeds over the nearby ocean. He is certain that the object was not a helicopter because it moved too quickly and turned at right angles.

In 1980, therapist Linda Susan Young was driving along the Pacific Coast Highway in Santa Monica when she observed a large glowing object floating on the surface of the Santa Monica Bay. Puzzled by its brightness, she was shocked when it suddenly "shot straight up in the air and blinked out."

Hotdogging and Other Malibu Encounters

On May 4, 1990, two Malibu surfers observed a "brushed aluminum saucer with a bump in the middle [which] approached the shoreline from out of the fog bank sitting about a mile offshore." They watched the strange craft dart back and forth and then move back out to sea.

Late one evening in early 1991, Malibu resident Tony X. was admiring the ocean view from his home directly on the coast when he saw a brilliantly lit object that appeared to be floating on the surface of the water several miles out to sea. "It looked like a big prism, kind of various colors out there. I got a telescope out there...when I looked at it, it even seemed more like a prism, just different colors."

Tony was puzzled by its strange appearance as he had lived in the location for many years and never seen anything like it. After a few hours, it winked out. Two years later, in January of 1993, the glowing prism-like object returned. The vivid colors made Tony speculate that a boat might be on fire. He contacted the Coast Guard who suggested that the lights might be from a fishing boat. Tony, however, says again that he had never seen anything like it before.

On May 5, 1992, two friends were on Malibu Beach when they saw a "sort of light/fireball" descend from the sky and into the ocean. Says one of the witnesses, "It was going at an incredible speed and it was less than a mile away. It looked like it hit the ocean...my guess is it went underwater." (Dennett 1999, 159-162)

Close Pass

According to Bill Hamilton, in the early 1970s, an anonymous gentleman was sailing from Catalina Island to San Pedro Harbor when he saw a metallic flying saucer move silently overhead. The craft was so close, the witness was able to clearly observe four "hemispherical pods" on the underside of the craft.

Barnstorming UFOs

Robert Stanley has uncovered other cases. As he says, "In 1973, a swirling patterned crop circle appeared overnight in a field of wheat overlooking Zuma Beach...one particular family that lived in the neighborhood swore that a UFO landed in their yard as they watched in amazement ... then there was the man who lived on Point Dume, who woke up late one night to go to the bathroom, and witnessed a UFO flying sideways between [his house] and his neighbor's house." (Stanley, 16-17)

On Easter week in 1975, George Gray (pseudonym) was driving along the coast in Santa Monica when he observed a bright light zooming at super-high speeds up and down the coast. He pulled over to watch, and the object zoomed towards him and sent down a beam of light. Says Gray, "The UFO was over where the beach was, where the wet sand would be, hovering I would say maybe a hundred, two hundred feet in the air. It was silver. It was your basic UFO, like two saucer shapes…it was definitely completely metallic with a silver dome on top and a silver dome on the bottom of it, like two plates put together. And they had little lights around it." (Dennett 1999, 147-150)

In 1980, private pilot Toshi Inouye was flying with a student over the Santa Monica Bay when they observed a large, red, glowing, cigar-shaped object hovering near their plane. Says Inouye, "It was standing still in the air, glowing red. We were kind of stunned. We didn't know what to do…it was glowing red in the shape of a cigar." (Dennett 1999, 144-146) Inouye was considering calling the nearby airport control tower when the object suddenly darted away.

In 1981, a group of teenagers at Leo Carrillo Beach observed two red lights moving in zigzagging patterns.

One summer evening in 1988, professional photographer Kim Carlsberg was relaxing on the porch of her beachfront home when she noticed a strange looking star low on the horizon. As she watched, the star-like object darted across the horizon, from Palos Verdes Peninsula north to Point Dume. Carlsberg stared in amazement as the object suddenly darted towards her! Writes Carlsberg, "As though it responded to my thoughts, the brilliant point of light advanced until it became a luminous sphere some fifty feet in diameter. It ominously hung in the air a hundred feet from my window…the apparent standoff lasted no more than a minute before the sphere departed as quickly as it appeared. It tore away diagonally through the night sky and vanished." Carlsberg has since had numerous other experiences, including apparent onboard encounters. (Carlsberg, 31-42)

Beneath the Waves

Hamilton has uncovered several other cases in the area. As he writes, "Strange blue-green lights have been seen in the water since 1989. In 1989, and again in 1990, witnesses have seen as many as twenty events an hour. One large light appeared to be as much as 100 feet in diameter. This large light spawned babies no larger than ten to twelve feet in length. These lights were seen to move swiftly under the ocean's surface some 500 to 1000 feet from the coastline in Abalone Cove…. One of the lights was reported to have emerged from the water." (Hamilton, 107-112)

Adam, Mario, and the Black Diamonds

In 1998, two gentlemen, Adam and Mario, were driving along the Pacific Coast Highway in Malibu when they saw six black, diamond-shaped objects hovering off the coast. As they watched, the objects darted up and down the coast at high speeds. The two men were so impressed by the sighting that after the objects left they continued driving up and down the coast, hoping for another appearance. While the UFOs didn't return that day, they did see other UFO watchers. Says Adam, "We did come across a couple of people who were just sitting there in their lawn chairs along the road. I don't know if this has anything to do with it, but they were just sitting there along the side of the road, parked, just looking up." (Dennett 1999, 168-170)

Of Government Agents and Underwater Bases

Hamilton also investigated a series of 1994 sightings off the coast of Rancho Palos Verdes, off Abalone Cove, near Sea Cove Drive, the former location of *Marineland*. The sightings were reported by at least two witnesses who observed glowing disks floating in the water.

One of the witnesses observed black helicopters surrounding the objects. This witness was then confronted by unnamed individuals (government agents, men in black?) who told him in no uncertain terms that the area was off-limits.

Caught on Film

On the afternoon of January 3, 2004, Young Chyren observed a silver saucer-shaped craft that appeared to be hovering directly above a small boat out at sea. Chyren grabbed his camera and snapped a photograph.

So Many Cases, So Few Reported

Many other cases could be cited. And again, only about one person in a hundred reports their sightings in any official capacity. The fact that this area has earned a public reputation for such high levels of UFO activity, and has dozens of recorded encounters, means that actual number of sightings is probably in the *thousands*! This activity is also directly adjacent to Topanga Canyon and the Santa Monica Mountains, which is a leading California hotspot.

Underwater Base

For whatever reason, UFOs are obviously very active along this small stretch of coast. Two abductees have told me that they have strong intuitive feelings that there is an underwater base in the area. Two others have actually reported being taken to an underground base.

See for Yourself

Today this area remains a prime viewing spot for UFOs. The activity can be viewed from anywhere along the southern California coast, but particularly from Palos Verdes north to the Channel Islands, including the cities of Palos Verdes, Hermosa Beach, Redondo Beach, Manhattan Beach, Marina Del Rey, Venice, Santa Monica, Topanga Canyon, Malibu, Ventura, and Santa Barbara. All of these beaches are prime tourist locations with camping, boating, surfing, fishing, and other recreational activities. The more adventurous can head out to sea to Catalina Island or any one of the many Channel Islands.

5. Mount Shasta

We have already examined numerous strange facets of Mount Shasta, from Bigfoot on the slopes to ancient civilizations beneath the mountain. Not surprisingly, the area is also a major UFO hotspot.

Early Reports

The first UFO reports came in the early 1930s, around the same time as the Lemurian accounts began to surface. According to author Wishar Cerve, numerous witnesses came upon areas in the foothills that glowed with "powerful illuminations."

Temporary Paralysis

Some people who ventured into the area would find themselves temporarily paralyzed. Some of the first electromagnetic effects from UFOs were reported at Mount Shasta. Writes Cerve, "At an unexpected point where a light flashed before them the automobile refused to function properly for the electric circuit seemed to lose its power and not until the passenger emerged from the car and backed it on the road for a hundred feet and turned it in the opposite direction, would the electric power give any manifestation and the engine function properly." (Cerve, 249-250)

Peculiarly Shaped Boats

Although the modern age of UFOs wouldn't begin for another decade, Cerve uncovered many accounts. Writes Cerve, "There are hundreds of others who have testified to having seen peculiarly shaped boats which have flown out of this region high in the air over the hills and valleys of California and have been seen by others to come on to the waters of the Pacific Ocean at the shore and then continue out on the seas as vessels…and others have seen these boats rise again in the air and go upon the land of some of the islands of the Pacific…Only recently a group of persons playing golf on one of the golf-links of California near the foothills of the Sierra Nevada Range saw a peculiar silver-like vessel rise in the air and float over the mountaintops and disappear. It was unlike any airship that has ever been seen and there was absolutely no noise emanating from it to indicate that it was moved by a motor of any kind." (Cerve, 249-250

Sightings in the Modern Age

On the evening of October 24, 1955, Mount Shasta resident W.A. Barr, his wife, and their housekeeper observed an unusual object moving in small circles just above the mountain. Says Barr, "It had every color and glittered like a diamond."

Also in October 1955, J.O. McKinney was making his rounds as a night watchman for the McCloud River Lumber Company in Mount Shasta when he had an incredible encounter. "Eight or ten 'lights' came swooping toward the tower in formation, very rapidly, with no sound

> An anonymous Mount Shasta police officer told reporter Garth Sanders that in 1963 he and another officer were patrolling the area during the night when they saw what they first thought was a jeep on a logging road in the local foothills. However, when they observed the object with binoculars they saw a fifty-foot wide "saucer" with green, red and silver lights around its perimeter.

at all. They were white and brilliant and looked as though they were flying 300 to 400 feet above the ground."

Mistaken for a Jeep

An anonymous Mount Shasta police officer told reporter Garth Sanders that in 1963 he and another officer were patrolling the area during the night when they saw what they first thought was a jeep on a logging road in the local foothills. However, when they observed the object with binoculars they saw a fifty-foot wide "saucer" with green, red and silver lights around its perimeter. As they watched, the saucer darted away at super high speed.

The officers reported their sighting to the Air Force who sent them questionnaires. A few years later, one of the officers had another sightings. He was alone in his patrol car north of Mount Shasta when he observed a forty-foot-wide saucer hovering above his car. The object gave off a bright blue light. The officer radioed his station and another dispatcher also observed the object. As both officers watched, the object darted over the St. Germain Foundation amphitheater on McCloud Avenue in Mount Shasta City before it hovered and darted towards Mount Shasta.

Strange Cloud

In 1973, an anonymous resident of Mount Shasta City told researcher Emilie Frank that she observed a "disk-shaped spaceship" covered with "iridescent-colored lights" which hovered about 400 feet above the valley floor. The witness first noticed the craft because it was directly beneath a strange plume-shaped cloud.

Happy Camp Saucer

In November 1975, several residents of Happy Camp noticed bright lights hovering in the nearby hills. One evening, five people went to investigate. They not only saw the lights close-up, they also saw a metallic saucer emitting strange sounds. They fired at the object, at which point they all reported a difficulty in breathing.

Two of them returned to the site on November 23 and said that a large object landed near their car and took off. After the object left, the witnesses observed "tripod-like impressions" in the ground. The witnesses returned later with more people. On this occasion, they saw bright lights, heard strange tones, and saw figures moving in the nearby bushes. They took off in their vehicle. They reported that the light chased their car down the road.

In February 1976, California investigator Paul Cerny heard about the hotspot and decided to investigate first-hand. To his amazement, he had his own encounters. He and another resident observed a rectangular-shaped object glowing an intense bright orange light. Cerny also talked to numerous other people who confirmed that there were continuous sightings in the area.

Abduction

In November 1976, Helen White was on nearby Cade Mountain when she and two men were abducted while driving. White reports that they were taken inside a craft and examined. They were returned to the car unhurt. In the years following, White reported several other encounters. In 1978, she and her grandson had a face-to-face encounter with gray-type ETs that landed in a UFO while they were cutting wood in the wilderness. In 1979, she had another identical encounter in the Mill Creek area. On this occasion, she had missing time and was unable to recall the details of her encounter.

Paced from Above and Other Aerial Acrobatics

Meanwhile, the sightings continued. On July 14, 1979, an anonymous couple was driving their camper along Highway 139 late at night when a large torpedo-shaped object appeared directly above them and cast down a bright beam of white light. The object paced their vehicle along the highway, then raced ahead and disappeared.

In October 1979, residents from Yreka, Crescent City, and neighboring counties observed a bright glowing object darting at high speeds and low elevations.

On January 6, 1980, a Dorris resident was driving outside of town when he was paced by a thirty-five-foot-wide saucer-shaped craft that was so bright it lit up the entire surrounding area. The craft paced his car for several miles through thick fog before suddenly darting away.

The year of 1980 turned out to be particularly active. In September, houseboaters on Trinity Lake observed several star-like objects darting over the skies of Lewiston. One month later, the Weed Police Station received several calls from residents reporting a star-like light over the southern shoulder of Mount Shasta. An officer was sent to investigate, and he also observed the UFO.

Mass Sighting

One month after that, a mass sighting hit the area, covering the cities of Redding, Red Bluff, Shasta, McCloud, Beaver Creek, and other areas. Several officers and residents observed UFOs close-up.

Personal Communication

In the summer of 1992, I went on a camping trip with my extended family. As part of the trip, we went to several spots in northern California, including a campground near Mount Shasta.

It was around 11:00 p.m., and everyone had gone to sleep except for me, my brother Marco, and his wife Christy. We three stood around the campfire, looking at the bright stars. Redwoods towered more than a hundred feet around us so only a small portion of the sky was visible. Suddenly Marco cried out, "I just saw a bright light!" He pointed straight up. "It just flashed on and off!"

Christy and I looked at him in disbelief, though he was clearly serious. At the same time, we knew we were in a UFO hotspot. In fact, we had a powerful flashlight ready, hoping to communicate with any UFOs that might show up. Marco said, "Get the flashlight and flash it!"

Christy grabbed it, pointed it to the sky, and flicked the switch on and off. Suddenly, and apparently in response, the light flashed back. We all three saw it flash brightly on and off. My first thought was it was a satellite.

"Flash again!"

Christy flashed the flashlight twice. The light flashed twice back in response from a slightly different position. Christy flashed once more and it flashed once more in response. After that, it disappeared.

We looked at each other in amazement. Did we just see *and communicate with* a UFO? It clearly wasn't a plane, helicopter, satellite, blimp or shooting star. We could only shake our head in wonder. It seemed the stories about the area were true.

As recently as 2002, reporter Jeff Sens traveled to Mount Shasta. While he didn't see anything, he did find a local UFO witness who observed strange lights hovering over the mountain.

See for Yourself

Mount Shasta is located at the extreme north end of California.

6. Other Possible Hotspots

A significant portion of California's UFO activity seems to center around the defense and aviation industries, much of which is located in southern California. However, many other areas throughout the state have produced reports on a fairly regular basis.

Aliens Favor Deserts

The Inland Empire east of Los Angeles has produced a number of encounters over the years. Much of the activity is again in the largely desert regions of Twentynine Palms, Yucca Valley, Joshua Tree, Palm Springs, and the surrounding areas.

Rural Reports

The rural counties above San Diego have also produced a fairly steady stream of reports as investigated by the Mutual UFO Network (MUFON) and the private UFO group *Orion*.

Northern California is also very active. Prominent northern California researchers Edith Fiore Ph.D., Jacques Vallee, Richard Boylan Ph.D., and others have uncovered literally *hundreds* of people in the rural northern California areas who have had extensive UFO experiences, including onboard and face-to-face encounters. Some of the cities that seem particularly active include San Francisco, Santa Rosa, Santa Clara, Santa Cruz, Clearlake, and the areas surrounding these cities. Northern California has also experienced regular and very intense UFO waves involving hundreds of witnesses.

Alien Exhibitionists

The waves of activity seem to flare up sporadically and unpredictably, including during the years of 1947, 1960, 1978, 1981, and 1999. Each of these waves involves scores of witnesses, including police officers and other officials. It appears that during these waves, the UFO occupants *want* to be seen and are putting on public displays for the witnesses, chasing them down roads, hovering near homes, and moving at low altitudes over densely-populated areas.

Every Airbase!

Some other areas that have gained a reputation for UFO encounters are California Air Force Bases, the three top producing ones being Edwards AFB, Hamilton Field, and George AFB; however, *any military base or technological installation* will attract UFOs. Incredibly, Los Angeles International Airport has also provoked UFO encounters on more than a dozen occasions.

7. California UFO Groups

For those who would like to learn more about the UFO presence in California, the Mutual UFO Network (MUFON) is a national non-profit organization with chapters in every state. California has several chapters, including in San Diego, Orange County, Ventura, Los Angeles, and one in northern California. The groups meet monthly and feature leading researchers in the field as well as providing current updates on local UFO activity. If you would like to meet UFO witnesses firsthand and learn about the latest encounters, a visit to one of these groups is strongly encouraged. You can not only learn about local encounters, you can talk firsthand with UFO witnesses and abductees. Information: www.mufon.com. 1-800-836-2166. MUFON ORANGE COUNTY: 5267 Warner Ave, PMB 275, Huntington Beach, CA 92649. 714-520-4UFO. www.mufonoc.org.

MUFON LA. PO Box 94, El Segundo CA 90245. 818-663-8360. www.mufonla.com.

Members of another, perhaps more extreme, group call themselves the *Unarians* or the *Unarius Academy of Science*. The Unarius Academy of Science is one of those places you'd really have to see to believe. Located in the El Cajon, just east of San Diego, this "academy" is actually a group of individuals who have come together to follow the teachings of the late contactee Ruth Norman. The group's activities include meditations and lectures on various cosmic principals, with a strong focus on reincarnation. Each of the members eventually go through reincarnation therapy in an attempt to recover the memories of their past lives. Part of this therapy involves actually dressing up in old-style costumes and physically acting out the role you played in a past life.

Intertwined through the philosophy is the prophecy that friendly ETs are going to land in a specific area of the California desert to prepare for the evacuation of humanity. Norman's visions are bizarre, even by UFO standards, and when the predicted 2001 landing failed to appear, many Academy members remained steadfast in their support. The landing didn't take place, explained members, because the human race is not yet ready.

One thing that makes the Academy really stand out is their abundant use of flashing colored lights, shining silver and gold surfaces, and rainbow bright colors. The inside may remind you of a 1950s science fiction movie set.

Ruth Norman herself often wore an elaborate lacey gown that was thickly coated with gaudy costume jewelry. She wore a crown and carried a scepter as she channeled her wisdom from the space brothers. She is still revered by her followers and the Unarius Academy will likely provide its unique spiritual wisdom to visitors for years to come. For those wanting more info, visit: www.unarius.com. The Academy is located at 145 South Magnolia Avenue in downtown El Cajon. The nearest cross street is Douglas Avenue.

Conclusions

As we have seen, California is definitely a strange place. Ghosts haunt the roads, parks, and buildings. UFOs roam the skies above. Bigfoot lurks in the forests and gigantic sea monsters slither through the deep waters below. Rocks in the desert are moving by themselves. People are communicating with the dead. Jesus is appearing on bathroom windows. Ancient civilizations thrive beneath the mountains. And cars are rolling mysteriously uphill. This is *definitely* weird!

What is most amazing is just how many of these locations and events there are. One or two hundred UFO reports might not be very convincing, but more than 5,000 are hard to ignore. And hundreds of Bigfoot reports have come from so many people for so many years, making a very convincing case for an active Bigfoot population inhabiting the California countryside. California is also the only state in the United States with three prominent lake monsters, not to mention the various coastal sea serpents.

Why is California the center of so much weirdness? Could it be too much smog? Maybe it's the hot sun. Maybe it's the earthquakes. Maybe it's the people. Who knows? The answer itself remains a mystery. As author Janet Hearne says, California is America's most "altered state."

Epilogue

There you have it. If you want to experience an unexplained event of virtually any kind, it can be found in California. I was skeptical until I visited many of these locations for myself. Needless to say, after encountering a wide range of so-called "paranormal" events, including UFO encounters, a Bigfoot encounter, ghost encounters, psychic readings, and more, I am no longer so skeptical. There is nothing quite like personal experience. For that reason, I encourage any interested parties to visit these locations for themselves and experience firsthand the many supernatural mysteries of California.

Sources

Adams, Jason. "Ridge Light." *Obiwan's UFO-Free Paranormal Page.* www.ghosts.org/ghostlights/ridgelight.html.

American Automobile Association (AAA). *California-Nevada Tourbook.* Heathrow, FL: American Automobile Association, 1995.

Asp, Andy. "Enigma Unsolved: California's East Bay Walls." *Fortean Times.* www.forteantimes.com/exclusive/caliwalls.shtml.

Bartholemew, Steve. *Ancient Ogam in California.* www.chargedbarticle.com.

_____. *Baby Rock.* www.chargedbarticle.com.

_____. *The Standing Stones of Point Reyes.* www.charged barticle.com.

_____. *Two California Ogam Stones.* www.chargedbarticle.com.

_____. *A Wall Unseen.* www.chargedbarticle.com.

Bord, Janet and Colin. *The Bigfoot Casebook.* New York: Granada Publishing, 1982.

Brown, Greg. "La Jolla Gravity Hill." *Roadsideamerica.com: Your Online Guide to Offbeat Attractions.* www.roadsideamerica.com.

Campbell, Doug. "Confusion Hill." www.confusionhill.com.

Carlsberg, Kim. *Beyond My Wildest Dreams: Diary of a UFO Abductee.* Santa Fe, NM: Bear & Company, Inc., 1995.

Cerve, Wishar. *Lemuria: The Lost Continent of the Pacific.* San Jose, CA: The Rosicrucian Press, 1931, 1980.

Coleman, Loren. *Bigfoot: The True Story of Apes in America.* New York: Paraview Pocket Books, 2003.

Coleman, Loren and Patrick Huyghe. *The Field Guide To Lake Monsters, Sea Serpents, and Other Mystery Denizens of the Deep.* New York: Jeremy Tarcher/Penguin, 2003.

Coleman, Loren. *Mysterious America.* Winchester, MA: Faber & Faber, Inc., 1983.

Corrales, Scott. *Chupacabras and Other Mysteries.* Murfreesboro, TN: Greenleaf Publications, 1997.

Costello, Peter. *In Search of Lake Monsters.* New York: Berkley Publishing Corp., 1974.

Dennett, Preston. *California Ghosts: True Accounts of Hauntings in the Golden State.* Atglen, PA: Schiffer Publishing, 2004.

_____. *One In Forty – The UFO Epidemic: True Accounts of Close Encounters with UFOs.* Commack, NY: Kroshka Books, 1997.

_____. *Out-of-Body Exploring: A Beginner's Approach.* Charlottesville, VA: Hampton Roads Publishing Co., 2004.

_____. *UFOs Over California: A True History of Extraterrestrial Encounters in the Golden State.* Atglen, PA: Schiffer Publishing, 2005.

_____. *UFOs Over Topanga Canyon.* St. Paul, MN: Llewellyn Publications, 1999.

Druffel, Ann and D. Scott Rogo. *The Tujunga Canyon Contacts.* New York: New American Library, 1980, 1988.

Frank, Emilie A. *Mount Shasta: California's Mystic Mountain.* Hilt, CA: Photografix Publishing, 2001.

Goodman, Rachel Anne. "Hitting the Mystery Spot." *The Savvy Traveler.* www.savvytraveler.publicradio.org/show/features/2000/20000415/spot.

Grant, John. *Monsters and Mysteries.* Secaucus, New Jersey: Chartwell Books, Inc., 1992.

Greer MD, Steven. *Disclosure: Military and Government Witnesses Reveal the Greatest Secrets in History.* Crozet, VA: Crossing Point Inc., 2001.

Hamilton III, William F. *Alien Magic: UFO Crashes, Abductions, Underground Bases.* New Brunswick, NJ: Global Communications, 1996.

Hauck, Dennis William. *Haunted Places: The National Directory to Ghostly Abodes, Sacred Sites, UFO Landings and Other Supernatural Locations.* New York: Penguin Books, 1994, 2002.

Hearne, Janet. *Only In California: Fabulous Facts, Weird Happenings and Eccentric Ephemera from America's Most Altered State.* New York: Penguin Books, 1993.

Heuvelmans, Bernard. *In the Wake of the Sea-Serpents.* New York: Hill and Wang, 1958, 1968.

Holzer, Hans. *Hollywood Ghosts.* New York: Bobbs-Merrill Company, Inc., 1974.

Jameson, W. C. *Buried Treasure in California: Legends From California's Mountains, Deserts, Beaches and Cities.* Little Rock, AR: August House, Inc., 1995.

King, Joseph J. *Winter of Entrapment: A New Look at the Donner Party.* (Revised Edition.) Lafayette, CA: K & K Publications, 1992, 1994.

Lorenzen & Lorenzen. *UFOs Over The Americas.* New York: New American Library, 1968.

Louise, Cherie. "Who Is Tahoe Tessie?: The Lake Tahoe Water Monster, Fact or Fiction – An Expert and Locals Weigh In." *Reno News and Review Arts & Culture*. Jan 22, 2004. (www.newsreview.com/issues/Reno/2004-01-22/arts.asp.html.)

Marinacci, Mike. *Mysterious California: Strange Places and Eerie Phenomena in the Golden State*. Los Angeles, CA: Panpipes Press, 1988.

May, Antoinette. *Haunted Houses of California: A Ghostly Guide to Haunted Houses and Wandering Spirits*. San Carlos, CA: Wide World Publishing/Tetra, 1990, 1993.

McCormick, Bob. *The Story of Tahoe Tessie: The Original Lake Tahoe Monster*. Kings Beach, CA: Tahoe Tourist Promotions, 2000.

Murphy, Joyce. "Chupacabras and UFO Activity in Southern California: Coyotes and Rabbits Said Disappearing." *Beyond Boundaries UFO Research Organization*. www.rampages.on.ramp.net/~jmurphy. (see also: www.rense.com/ufo/chupanew.)

Myers, Arthur. *A Ghost Hunter's Guide To Haunted Landmarks, Parks, Churches and Other Public Places*. Chicago, IL: Contemporary Books, 1993.

Olsen, Brad. *Sacred Places North America: 108 Destinations*. Santa Cruz, CA: Consortium of Collective Consciousness, 2003.

Reinstedt, Randall. *Mysterious Sea Monsters of California's Central Coast*. Carmel, CA: Ghost Town, 1977.

Rogo, D. Scott (editor). *Alien Abduction: True Cases of UFO Kidnappings*. New York: New American Library, 1980.

Russell, David Allen. "The Monster in the Lake." *Elsinore Daily News*. (www.geocities.com/elsinoredailynews/interest. html.)

Senate, Richard. *Ghost Stalker's Guide to Haunted California*. Ventura, CA: Charon Press, 1998.

Sens, Josh. "The Truth is Out Here...Somewhere." *AAA Travel: VIA – Mystery Spots in the West*. www.viamagazine.com. May 2002.

Sheffield, Keith. "Tessie Pops Up for an Afternoon Appearance." *Tahoe World* News; Tahoe City. April 29, 2005.

Smith, Barbara. *Ghost Stories of California*. Renton, WA: Lone Pine Publishing, 2000.

St. Clair, David. *The Psychic World of California: An Informal Look at Great Mediums, Astrologers, Clairvoyants, Tarot Readers, Flying Saucer Buffs, Healers, Witches and Other Members of the Occult in California*. Garden City, NY: Doubleday and Company, 1972.

Stanley, Robert. "UFOs Over Malibu." *Unicus Magazine*. Manhattan Beach, CA, Vol 4, No 1, 1995.

Steiger, Brad. *Alien Meetings*. New York: Ace Books, 1978.

Tyson, Peter. "A Tree's Secret to Living Long." *Nova Online*. www.pbs.org/wgbh/nova/methuselah.

Valenya. "Besides Bigfoot." *Fate*. Lakeville, MN: *Fate Magazine*, November 2004, 62-67.

Van Duzer, Chet. "The Dragon's Pearl." *101 Fun Things to Do at Lake Tahoe*. (www.tahoesbest.com/101/dragons pearl.htm.)

Young, James. "My Trip to the Mystery Spot." www.jimy.org/mspot4/html. July 4, 1995.

Websites

www.americanmonsters.com
www.angelfire.com
www.bigfootencounters.com
www.calicotown.com
www.chargedbarticle.org
www.cmdrmark.com
www.confusionhill.com
www.cryptozoology.com
www.csaa.com
www.desertusa.com
www.elchupacabra.com
www.eureka4you.com
www.forteantimes.com
www.forums.ghosttowns.com
www.ghosts.org
www.highbeam.com
www.hodgee.com
www.home.nycap.rr.com

www.iacworld.org
www.indolink.com
www.io.com
www.jimy.org
www.losangelesalmanac.com
www.mcn.org
www.midnightsociety.com
www.monsterhindig.com
www.mysteryspot.com
www.newsreviews.com
www.nuforc.com
www.n2.net
www.paranetinfo.com
www.pbs.org
www.pierceclemmer.us
www.prestondennett.com
www.rampages.onramp.net

www.rense.com
www.roadsideamerica.com
www.sacredsonoma.com
www.savvytraveler.publicradio.org
www.sniff.org
www.sonic.net
www.sunnyvaletemple.org
www.tahoesbest.com
www.themiraclespage.org
www.theseason.org
www.toosquare.com
www.treesofmystery.net
www.tripee.com
www.ufomind.com
www.visionslaketahoe.com
www.visionsofjesuschrist.com
www.vortexmaps.com

Contact

To contact the author, please email him at prestone@pacbell.net, or write c/o the publisher.